BEHOLD
YOUR
GOD

A Daily Encounter with God

Mary R. Bolton

WINEPRESS WP PUBLISHING

ISBN 1-57921-184-4
Library of Congress Catalog Card Number: 99-62939

This book is dedicated to my husband, John, who has been a constant source of encouragement and support. I want to express my deepest love and appreciation to him for seeing something within me of which I was not aware and encouraging me to fulfill God's call on my life.

Acknowledgments

I wish to express my deepest gratitude to Beth Arnurius and Beth Bowman for spending hours editing this book. Their friendship and belief in this work have been a tremendous blessing to me.

My love and appreciation go to my husband and family who were supportive and understanding about the time required for writing this devotional. I also want to thank my prayer partners, Maxine Raines, Pastor Sharon Welch, and Paula Travis, whose continued prayer support and friendship have greatly enriched my life.

Most important, I want to express my heartfelt love and gratitude to the Lord who sat with me at the computer and guided me continually, giving inspiration for this devotional about entering into a face to face relationship with Him!

Contents

Introduction

"O Zion, you who bring good tidings, get up into the high mountain; O Jerusalem, you who bring good tidings, lift up your voice with strength, lift it up, be not afraid; say to the cities of Judah, 'Behold your God!'" (Isa. 40:9).

The people of Zion are instructed to go up on the mountain and lift up their voices, proclaiming with strength to the cities of Judah, "Behold your God!" This daily devotional is intended to help us pull away from the busyness of our everyday world and go up on the mountain to commune with our God where we will truly behold Him in all His majesty and splendor. As we behold Him, we will come to know Him in all His glory. His attributes and character will become so real to us and so much a part of our lives that we will be able to go forth, as the people of Zion, and lift up our voices with great strength and shout to the world, "Behold your God!"

When we share the good news of Jesus Christ with the world, we can rest assured that others will come to know God as we have come to know Him.

We can see the purpose of God for our lives unfold as we draw close to Him. Our lives will be refreshed with His living water, and we will enter into a place of rest that comes from trusting Him. His life and light will shine forth from us as we bask in His glory, and we will be a reflection of His love as we share His truth powerfully with others. Join me in a daily journey of entering into the presence of God Almighty and watch your life being transformed from glory to glory into His image!

Come Away, My Beloved

"My beloved spoke, and said to me: 'Rise up, my love, my fair one, and come away'" (Song of Sol. 2:10).

*O*ur Father calls us to come away and spend wonderful, precious time with Him. He expresses His longing for our company when He uses the term "My beloved." Just as we make the time to spend with our loved ones, our Lord is asking us to make that time to spend with Him. Nothing else that we could do during that time will benefit us more! What can we expect from that time with Him? To know Him! To know Him in all His fullness, in all His glory, and in all His majesty.

As we draw close to Him, He will reveal His very nature to us so that we can begin to become as He is. Second Corinthians 3:18 says, "But we all, with unveiled face, beholding as in a mirror the glory of the Lord, are being transformed into the same image from glory to glory, just as by the Spirit of the Lord." How precious that time with Him can be, how life changing for us that time can be if we will only choose to spend time drawing close to Him! Can you imagine the joy of being transformed into the image of God Almighty!

He is waiting for us right now with open arms. Seek Him with your whole heart today and listen to Him as He speaks to you the wonders of His truth. Receive His life-changing words and presence into your life!

The Voice of My Beloved

"The voice of my beloved! Behold, he comes leaping upon the mountains, skipping upon the hills" (Song of Sol. 2:8).

What does it mean that our beloved is leaping on mountains and skipping on hills? It means that our Lord is jubilant about spending time with us. This scripture says, "Behold, he comes," which means He is seeking us. In other words He waits on us to come into His presence and spend time with Him. He is never too busy, and He never puts us off while He finishes something. He never says, "I do not have time for you right now." Our Lord is eager, ready, and waiting for us, and all we have to do is simply give Him our time and ourselves. If He is never too busy for us, how can we be too busy for Him? But more often than not, we are.

How must that make Him feel, when He is leaping on mountains and skipping on hills at the thought of spending time with us, and we are too busy for Him? What in this world can be more important than spending time with our Lord and Savior?

Give Him all the time He wants from you today. Walk with Him, talk with Him, share your heart with Him, and listen as He shares His heart with you. Listen for the voice of your beloved!

My Beloved Is Mine

"My beloved is mine, and I am his. He feeds his flock among the lilies" (Song of Sol. 2:16).

The Lord is reassuring us that, even though He belongs to all of the billions of people on the earth who have received Jesus as their Lord, the relationship that He has with us individually is so intimate that "He is mine and I am His." His love is so great and so large that it encompasses the world, and yet so intimate that it can be very real to each one of us personally.

When we draw close to Him, He responds with the glory of His presence. While we are in His presence, He feeds us (His flock) with His truth, His Word, and His light. As we come before Him, hungry for more of Him, He shares with us that which satisfies—the truth of His Word.

Matthew 5:6 says, "Blessed are those who hunger and thirst for righteousness, for they shall be filled." Let us come into His presence hungering for more of Him, and we shall be filled with His righteousness and all His fullness. What is His fullness? All that He is—His goodness, His mercy, His grace, His lovingkindness, His power, His glory, His love, His light, and all that is told of Him in His Word.

Simply respond to Him today and say, "Yes, Lord, I am hungry. Fill me with Your righteousness. Fill me with Your fullness." Receive from Him now as He holds out to you all of His fullness!

His Banner Over Me Was Love

"He brought me to the banqueting house, and his banner over me was love" (Song of Sol. 2:4).

The love of Jesus for us is so deep and so wide that it took Him to the cross for us. He said, "I am the bread of life. He who comes to Me shall never hunger, and he who believes in Me shall never thirst" (John 6:35). He wants to fill us to overflowing with Himself, His love, His power, His goodness, His purity, His righteousness—all that He is. As we come to Him, He opens the door to His banqueting house and invites us in to fellowship with Him and to partake of the Bread of Life. The Bread of Life will always sustain us, nurture us, and provide all that we need. Jesus says, "Take, eat, this is My body which is broken for you; do this in remembrance of Me" (1 Cor. 11:24).

As we partake of Jesus in His banqueting house, His love is poured out on us, and we become filled and empowered to take His truth to those who are hurting and desperately in need of that which only Jesus can supply. His love can become so great within us that we see others as He sees them, and we love them as He loves them. Then we become His hands and feet extended on this earth to fulfill His love to others.

Enter into His banqueting house today and partake of all that He holds out to you! Eat of the Bread of Life and see what He will do in and through you to express the love of Jesus upon this earth!

Beloved of God—David

"That Your beloved may be delivered, save with Your right hand, and hear me" (Ps. 108:6).

David, who wrote this psalm, was a man after God's heart. We also know that David was not perfect as we are not perfect. Although he loved God greatly, David sinned against Him, and yet he was still greatly loved by God. This gives us hope, and it also can give us some insight into how we can be a person after God's heart.

God's love is always present—His love never changes, and He never leaves nor forsakes us. The actions and choices that we make, however, can separate us from God. Even though David sinned, he had such a heart for God that he could not continue to live in sin. He confessed his sin before God with great sorrow and repentance.

God is a God of righteousness and justice, and He cannot accept sin. We need to search our lives and repent of any sin that creeps into our lives. We need to know that the blood of Jesus on the cross paid the price for all sin, and we need to apply that to our lives on a daily basis in order to walk in a manner that is pleasing to our Father.

Draw close to your Father in heaven today, repent of any sin that He brings to your mind, receive His wonderful forgiveness, and bask in His glorious presence!

Beloved of God—Daniel

"O Daniel, man greatly beloved, understand the words that I speak to you, and stand upright, for I have now been sent to you . . ." (Dan. 10:11).

Daniel was also a man who loved God. He lived in exile in Babylon under the pagan rule of Nebuchadnezzar, and yet his total dedication to the one, true, living God was unshakable. He was a prophet who heard from God and was faithful to speak God's truth, even when he had no idea how he might be received or what would be the outcome of his faithfulness. Daniel was used to interpret Nebuchadnezzar's dream and also to interpret the handwriting on the wall. These actions caused others in the kingdom to become so frightened and angry that they began to plot his death. This is what eventually led to Daniel being thrown into the lion's den where his faith was greatly tested and where the Lord miraculously expressed His great love for Daniel.

Daniel is a great example for us of standing firm in the face of life-threatening adversity and remaining completely obedient to the will of our Father. The Lord is calling us to a place of obedience and trust, and we need to build ourselves up by reading His Word and seeking His presence with all that is within us. Only then will we have the strength that comes from Him to overcome and be victorious in the face of great difficulties.

Wherever you are and whatever your circumstance today, put your trust and your faith in the Lord Jesus Christ. As you put your faith in Him and expect to receive from Him, He will shower His love upon you.

Beloved of God—Solomon

"Did not Solomon king of Israel sin by these things? Yet among many nations there was no king like him, who was beloved of his God; and God made him king over all Israel. Nevertheless pagan women caused even him to sin" (Neh. 13:26).

*E*ven though Solomon had sinned by taking a pagan wife (marrying an unbeliever), he was greatly loved by God. Even though there may be things in our lives that are displeasing to God, He still loves us. The closer we draw unto Him, the more we will want to be pleasing to Him. We will begin to see the things that are sin in our lives from His standpoint, and they will no longer be so appealing to us. God gives us the grace and the ability to turn our backs on sin when we are seeking Him with our whole heart and longing to be in His presence. There is no greater joy than being in the presence of our Father. The more we experience that joy, the more often we will desire to have that time with Him. The things of this world will lose their luster in the light of His glory and splendor.

Know that you are His beloved, and He is reaching out His hand to you today. He is asking you to come into His presence and bask in the knowledge of His everlasting love. Will you respond to Him today, seeking Him with your whole heart, and receive His wondrous love that is unlike anything you have ever experienced before?

Moses Went Up to God

"And Moses went up to God, and the Lord called to him from the mountain, saying, 'Thus you shall say to the house of Jacob, and tell the children of Israel'" (Exod. 19:3).

The phrase "And Moses went up to God" shows us that Moses separated himself from the people and went aside to seek God. When he did, God spoke to him and told him things to share with the people. When we take the time to separate ourselves from the busyness of everyday life and from the things of this world to spend time with God, we are not disappointed. Instead we are greatly encouraged, lifted up, and strengthened. Entering into the presence of God is a powerful experience. Once we have experienced His presence, we want to enter in again and again. Nothing on this earth can compare with an encounter with the one, true, living God.

His love is so great for us that He is waiting for us to make that step and seek Him. Can you imagine that the God of the whole universe, the one, true, living God, the great I Am, Jehovah God, is actually waiting to spend time with you, with me, with us? How can we say, "No, I am too busy to spend time with You right now. Can You come back tomorrow, next week, next month?"

The Creator of the Universe, Jesus Christ, Lord, Savior, Master is right here now.

Will you say, "Here am I, Lord"?

The Lord Showed Him

"Then Moses went up from the plains of Moab to Mount Nebo, to the top of Pisgah, which is across from Jericho. And the Lord showed him all the land of Gilead as far as Dan" (Deut. 34:1).

When Moses went up on the mountain to be with God, God showed him wondrous things. When we pull aside to spend time with our Lord, He will do the same for us. There may be questions about your future. You may need some direction in your life, or you may need some answers concerning your family, your job, or some difficult relationship. You may be in a place that seems totally desperate to you, and you feel you have no place to turn.

Rest assured that the Lord has answers for you. When you take time to be alone with Him and seek Him, He is always there with you and will show you the way. Nothing is too difficult for Him. Place your need, your problem, your question with Him and sit in His presence. Wait upon Him and listen for His direction. There may be a knowing that comes from within. A scripture may come to your mind, or a great peace may simply come over you.

Whatever you need, our Lord has the answer, and He knows how to communicate to you what you need. Enter into His presence today. Listen to Him with a heart and mind that are ready to receive the answers that you need!

Safety in His Presence

"They departed and went to the mountain, and stayed there three days until the pursuers returned. The pursuers sought them all along the way, but did not find them" (Josh. 2:22).

There is safety in the presence of the Lord. When we seek Him and enter into His presence, He truly becomes a place of refuge for us. Psalm 17:8 says, "Keep me as the apple of Your eye; hide me under the shadow of Your wings." When we are fearful or in some kind of danger, we should always turn to the Lord and enter into His presence. Whenever we enter into His presence, we find the solace, comfort, and safety that we need. He is always there for us.

When I am afraid or feel that there is some kind of danger, I read and meditate on Psalm 91. As the reassuring words of Life begin to enter into my spirit, I begin to be encompassed with peace. God's peace, which passes all understanding, is truly supernatural. We cannot make it happen—it comes only as we put our trust in God Almighty who is greater than anything we face.

If you are fearful today, look into the face of Almighty God and receive the peace that comes from only Him. "Now may the Lord of peace Himself give you peace always in every way" (2 Thess. 3:16).

To the Mountain to Pray

"And when He had sent them away, He departed to the mountain to pray" (Mark 6:46).

Jesus had been with a multitude (five thousand to be exact), and a miracle had occurred! The multitude had been listening to Jesus teach when the hour grew late, and the disciples were concerned about the crowd growing hungry. Jesus, with great compassion, multiplied five loaves and two fish so that all were fed, and there was even an abundance left over. Jesus had been giving of Himself all day in ministry to the needs of many, but what did He do once the people were fed? He went to the mountain to pray.

If Jesus needed to go to the mountain and pray, how much more do you and I need to go aside and spend time with our Father and pray? Not only did Jesus feel the need to pray, I believe He longed for that special time with His Father. I believe He knew how precious that time would always be. Prayer was something Jesus did, not out of obligation or in resignation, but out of great love, anticipation, and longing for the presence of His Father. He knew that His Father could supply everything He needed to live on this earth perfectly. How much more we need to spend that time with our Father and receive strength, peace, and joy from Him.

To Pray by Himself

"And when He had sent the multitudes away, He went up on the mountain by Himself to pray. Now when evening came, He was alone there" (Matt. 14:23).

*M*atthew tells us that when Jesus went up on the mountain to pray after feeding the five thousand, He went alone. At times it is very important to pray with others, but there are also times it is important to pray alone. That very special time alone with our Father God is unlike any other time. It is a time of fellowship with Him on a very personal and intimate level. It is a time that He can reveal Himself to us, and we will not be easily distracted by others. We will not be tempted to attribute the "realness" of His presence to the prayers of those around us. He becomes real to us individually because we are the only one present at that time.

Individual prayer helps us to know how very much God loves each one of us. Nothing is quite like experiencing the love of God on such a personal basis. It is also a time when He can reveal things to us about ourselves. It is a time when we can repent and become free of sin that can so easily become a part of our lives. Being alone with our Father is an important need in all of our lives.

Choose to take that time alone with Him today and enter into that intimate presence with your heavenly Father. See what glorious things He reveals to you!

Prayed All Night

"Now it came to pass in those days that He went out to the mountain to pray, and continued all night in prayer to God" (Luke 6:12).

How many times do we go to pray and become distracted, spending only five, ten, or twenty minutes in prayer? Jesus continued all night in prayer. He needed prayer with His Father, and He was diligent in setting aside time to fill this need. We also need to be diligent in our time of prayer with our Father in order to grow in our relationship with Him and to become more like Him. The more time we spend in prayer with Him, the more we see Him as He is. The holy nature of the one true living God is revealed to us. As His nature is revealed more fully to us, we will begin to see the things in our lives that are displeasing to Him. When we see these displeasing things and repent, we will begin to be profoundly changed. We will truly become more like Him.

All of this takes time, and we need to dedicate ourselves to spend the time with our Father that it takes to see real changes occur in our lives. We will find that as we spend more time with Him and come to know Him better, we will want to spend even more time with Him. We will find that time with Him is a glorious taste of heaven on earth!

The Transfiguration

"As He prayed, the appearance of His face was altered, and His robe became white and glistening" (Luke 9:29).

Transfiguration means to be changed into another form physically, and it can also mean a spiritual transformation. When Jesus went up on the mountain to pray and entered into the presence of His Father, He was transfigured and the glory of the Lord came upon Him. When we spend time with our Father and seek to know Him and be in His presence, we are transformed spiritually. We cannot be in His presence without change occurring in our lives.

The question is, how do we enter into the presence of God the Father? It is simply by taking time to be alone with Him, seeking Him with all of our hearts and diligently continuing with Him, even if at first it seems difficult, and we do not seem to be making much progress. As we persevere and continue to seek Him and pray, we will find that there comes a time of breakthrough. It is at this breakthrough that all heaven opens up, and we are truly in the presence of the Lord. It is truly worth the time and perseverance.

Choose to persevere and be strong in the Lord today. Enter into His wondrous presence and see what kind of transformation will begin to take place in your life!

Draw Near to God

"Draw near to God and He will draw near to you. Cleanse your hands, you sinners; and purify your hearts, you double-minded" (James 4:8).

James' statement sounds strong, but it is definitely true. He admonishes us to draw near to God and promises that God will draw near to us. The first step is in our ball court. When we move toward God, He responds by immediately drawing near to us. And what happens when God draws near to us? We begin to see ourselves as God sees us, and all the ugly things that have been a part of our lives suddenly are revealed for what they are. When we are in the presence of the Lord, we no longer want to be involved in sin because we are transformed! We find that we really want to walk in purity, cleanness, and holiness. We become repentant, and we are filled with sorrow because of our sins.

James 1:8 speaks of the double-minded. That is someone who attempts to hold on to God and the world at the same time. When we are in the presence of the Lord, we no longer want to hold onto the world. The things of the world become unimportant.

If you are having trouble letting go of the things of the world, simply enter into the presence of the Lord. He will become so real to you that you will no longer want to hold onto the things of the world.

They Shall Know

"I will dwell among the children of Israel and will be their God. And they shall know that I am the Lord their God . . ." (Exod. 29:45–46a).

*T*he Lord was dwelling in the midst of the children of Israel and revealing Himself to them. He was a cloud by day to protect them from the sun and to direct them. He was fire by night to warm them, and He rained down manna from heaven for them to eat. He also provided quail for them when they wanted meat to eat. He was most definitely in their midst. He wanted them to know Him and to love Him.

He is there for us today also, reaching out to us in the center of our need. Just as the people of Israel, who were constantly murmuring and complaining, did not always recognize Him, we often do not see His work in our lives today. When we are murmuring and complaining, we need to take inventory to see what is in our heart. God is here waiting and ready for us to turn to Him, and we need to seek Him with all our hearts.

He wants to spend time with us and reveal Himself to us in ways that would relate to our everyday life. We are not wandering in a wilderness in the Middle East, but sometimes it seems that we are definitely in a wilderness and need direction.

He is just as real for us today as He was for the Israelites back then. All we have to do is reach out to Him and give Him some of our time. Will you make that decision to enter into His presence and let Him reveal Himself to you in all His goodness and glory!

Consider in Your Heart

"Therefore know this day, and consider it in your heart, that the Lord Himself is God in heaven above and on the earth beneath; there is no other" (Deut. 4:39).

The scripture for today instructs us to consider in our hearts that the Lord is God. What does it mean to consider in our hearts? Scripture often uses the terms heart and mind interchangeably. Therefore we can come to really know that the Lord is God by dwelling in our minds about Him and His truth. Proverbs 4:20–21 says, "My son, give attention to my words; incline your ear to my sayings. Do not let them depart from your eyes; keep them in the midst of your heart." If we study God's Word, keeping it before our eyes (or reading it), listening to sermons and teachings on His Word (or inclining our ears to His sayings), then we are keeping His truth in the midst of our heart. We consider Him and get to know Him by studying His Word and spending time in His presence. His Word leads us to know Him through the work of the Holy Spirit who brings us into His presence and gives us understanding.

If you have not already made the choice to spend time in God's Word each day, make that choice today and enjoy the riches and treasures that come from the pages of the only book on earth that truly brings life to us.

25

Behold the Faithful God

"Therefore know that the Lord your God, He is God, the faithful God who keeps covenant and mercy for a thousand generations with those who love Him and keep His commandments" (Deut. 7:9).

One of the things we can come to know about our God as we spend time with Him is that He is faithful. He never leaves us nor forsakes us. Even when everyone else has turned their backs on us, He is always there.

When we accept Jesus Christ as our Lord and Savior, we enter into covenant with our Father. We might go against our word or break a covenant, but our Father never breaks covenant. He is full of mercy and compassion, and He is always there for us. Whenever we fail by sinning, He is there holding out His everlasting arms showing us the way to restoration. In this day that we live in, keeping one's word or being faithful is not the norm. In fact, we may be so unfamiliar with the concept that its real meaning has become vague and hazy in our minds.

But if we study God's Word, we will learn the meaning of faithfulness. Faithfulness is exhibited in the life of Jesus Christ and throughout Scripture.

Let us draw near to the Father, get into His Word, and learn about His faithfulness to us today. Let us receive the joy and wonder of knowing about His wondrous perfect love!

Know Our God Is Among Us

"So Joshua said to the children of Israel, 'Come here, and hear the words of the Lord your God.' And Joshua said, 'By this you shall know that the living God is among you . . .'" (Josh. 3:9–10a).

Do you want to know that the living God is among you, and that He is with you? You can know without a doubt that He is with you. Pick up your Bible and begin to read about His love for you and His plan for His people. Read in the Book of John about how He sent His Son Jesus, God in the flesh, to this earth to reveal the Father to us and make a way for us to be a part of His family. Read about the life of Jesus and how He went about teaching, healing, and bringing deliverance to the captives. Read about His great sacrifice of going to the cross to pay for my sins and your sins. And then read about His glorious resurrection from the dead and ascension into heaven. Read about the Holy Spirit whom Jesus sent to be with us, guide us, comfort us, and teach us.

Yes, God is with us. He never leaves us nor forsakes us, and He has a plan for you and for me. The way to know Him better and to know His plan for our lives is to draw close to Him through His Word and through prayer and communion with Him. Draw close to Him today and experience knowing that He is with you. Let Him shower you with His love!

Solomon's Prayer

"That all the peoples of the earth may know that the Lord is God; there is no other. Let your heart therefore be loyal to the Lord our God, to walk in His statutes and keep His commandments, as at this day" (1 Kings 8:60–61).

The scripture reference for today is a part of King Solomon's prayer for the people as he was dedicating the temple that had been built to bring glory to God. His prayer was that all the people of the earth would come to know our God. That should be our prayer today also.

How can we be a part of revealing God to all the people of the earth? The more we know our Father, the more our lives will be an example of His love and grace. The more we know our Father, the more we will want to reach out to others and share the good news that is so much a part of our lives. So many people in the world today are hurting and in desperate need. So many people need to know the mercy and love of our Father, and yet it is impossible for you as one person to reach everyone. But if we all will take the love of Jesus to those around us, the people our Father puts on our hearts, then His love will begin to be spread to many. If each person does his part and walks in obedience to the leading of the Holy Spirit, then the whole earth can be reached with His love. The task does not seem so large when we all do our part.

Draw close to Him today and ask Him whom He would have you reach out to with His good news.

Be Still and Know

"Be still, and know that I am God; I will be exalted among the nations, I will be exalted in the earth!" (Ps. 46:10).

There are times to rejoice greatly before the Lord with exuberance and enthusiasm, but there are also times to be still before Him. It is during these still times that we can hear God and sense His presence so strongly that we can come to know Him better. Our time with Him is very precious when we cease from chatter, busyness, and all the confusion of this world and begin to be very still before Him. The reality of His presence comes over us as His peace begins to permeate our very being. The stillness and quietness enable us to rest in the presence of our Lord in ways that other settings cannot provide for us.

Some of the most special times that I have spent in the presence of the Lord have been when I have stopped my petitioning to the Lord and have simply been very quiet in order to listen to Him. In that quietness I have been surprised at how the Lord has responded to me. I have not always heard Him guide or direct me or "speak" to me, but His presence has been so real that I did not want to leave that time of quiet and stillness. Be still before Him today and let Him share His glorious presence with you!

Come Before His Presence with Singing

"Serve the Lord with gladness; come before His presence with singing. Know that the Lord, He is God; it is He who has made us, and not we ourselves; we are His people and the sheep of His pasture" (Ps. 100:2–3).

*W*e can enter into the presence of our Lord through being still before Him, and we can also enter into His presence by worshiping Him through praise. Singing praises to Him is a wonderful way to express the love that is in our hearts for our Father.

When we speak words, it is powerful. But when we sing words, they seem to take on a much greater power. I believe this is because singing touches the heart and soul so beautifully.

You may not have a wonderful voice, but when you begin to lift up your voice in singing praises, it brings a wonderful feeling into the very depths of your spirit. I believe that is the reason we are admonished so often in Scripture to sing before the Lord, and to sing a new song unto Him. Ephesians 5:19 says, "speaking to one another in psalms and hymns and spiritual songs, singing and making melody in your heart to the Lord." What a wonderful way to express our love for our God. What a wonderful way for us to be built up in the Lord. When we sing praises to Him, we acknowledge that He is greater than any of our circumstances and truly worthy of our praises!

Lift up your voice in praise to your Lord and Savior now and continue praising Him in song as you go about your day.

To Know and Believe

"You are My witnesses, says the Lord, and My servant whom I have chosen, that you may know and believe Me, and understand that I am He. Before Me there was no God formed, nor shall there be after Me" (Isa. 43:10).

God has chosen us to be His witnesses, we who know and believe Him and understand that He is God. The more we draw close to our Lord, the more we will know Him in all His glory and majesty, and the more we will understand the character of God. When we see His glory and know His character, we become more like Him. We are given the strength and knowledge to be the witnesses for Him that He has called us to be.

Have you ever felt that your light was hidden under a bushel? You can lift that bushel and let the light shine forth from your life by drawing close to the Lord. The way to accomplish this is through reading and studying His Word and spending time in His presence. When we draw close to Him, our lives are changed. His light shines so brightly in us that there is nothing that can keep it from reflecting to others.

Do you want to be a witness who reflects the light of Jesus to others brightly? Simply determine to spend the time it takes to know Him better through studying His Word; entering into His presence with prayer, praise, and singing; and being still before Him. You will find that your life will be changed as you give your time to Him on a regular basis. You will also find that your time with Him will become your greatest priority because it is so wonderful basking in His presence!

A Heart to Know God

"Then I will give them a heart to know Me, that I am the Lord; and they shall be My people, and I will be their God" (Jer. 24:7).

Getting to know God is not really hard for He has given us a heart to know Him. It simply requires a choice on our part to seek Him and spend time with Him. He not only has given us a heart to know Him, but He also calls us His people and says that He is our God. What does it mean to have a heart to know God? It means that we have within us a knowing that there is a God. Romans 1:21 tells us that all people know in their hearts that God exists.

However, all do not glorify Him or thank Him for all that He has done for them. He has placed within us the knowledge that He is God, and, if we make the choice to seek Him, He is definitely waiting with open arms to receive us.

How are you responding to the knowledge of God today? Are you seeking Him, listening to Him, and getting to know Him better? There is no greater joy on this earth than spending time with our Father. He is in heaven, waiting with open arms to receive us and reveal more of Himself to us, waiting to show us His great love for us, and waiting to share His truth and His wonders. The presence of the Lord is a gift that is surpassed only by the gift of the sacrifice of Jesus on the cross. Make that choice today to spend time with the Creator of the heavens and earth and rejoice in His presence!

Great Exploits!

". . . the people who know their God shall be strong, and carry out great exploits" (Dan. 11:32b).

Do you want to be strong in the Lord? You will be if you draw close to Him where you can come to know Him better. Then you will find yourself growing stronger and stronger in your walk with Him. You cannot be in the presence of the Lord without seeing Him as He really is. When you see Him as He really is, your life is changed. We begin to see ourselves as we really are, repentance occurs, and we begin to be transformed into the image of God.

Jesus said in John 14:12, "Most assuredly, I say to you, he who believes in Me, the works that I do he will do also; and greater works than these he will do, because I go to My Father." When we are told in Daniel that we will do great exploits, we can believe it because Jesus has told us the same thing. The more we know God for who He truly is, the stronger we become. It is hard to believe that we will do the works of Jesus and even greater things, but we will!

Do you really believe that it is possible for you to do what Jesus did? Determine today to seek Him with all that is within you, enter into His presence, and ask Him what great exploits He would have you do to further His kingdom on this earth. We do not seek to do exploits, but we seek Him who is able to do all things and reveal Himself to us and those around us. We yield ourselves to Him to be used as He chooses. Seek Him today!

Knowing the Only True God

"And this is eternal life, that they may know You, the only true God, and Jesus Christ whom You have sent" (John 17:3).

Knowing God results in eternal life. What is eternal life? Eternal life is a gift from God that comes from accepting Jesus Christ as Lord and Savior. It is a treasure that is without measure. Sometimes when we think of eternal life, we think of endless life, but eternal life is more than endless life. It is spiritual life that goes on abundantly with our Father in Heaven. It is time spent in praising our glorious Lord in a way that we have only begun to touch on this earth. There is such joy in heaven, and heaven will be the greatest part of eternal life.

Eternal life, however, encompasses more than heaven. It starts on this earth when we become one with God the Father through our relationship with Jesus Christ as Lord and Savior. We can begin to know the joy and peace that comes from Him on this earth. We can begin to experience His presence in our lives now and come to realize that Christ in us is truly the hope of glory (Col. 1:27). We have the hope of life that goes on eternally with God. Although our physical body dies, our spiritual life goes on and on. We truly do not understand the significance of what that means or the expanse of joy that awaits us throughout eternity.

Choose today to become closer to the Lord and begin to receive the joy of eternal life that begins now with Jesus and goes on in heaven forever and forever.

The Power of His Resurrection

"That I may know Him and the power of His resurrection, and the fellowship of His sufferings, being conformed to His death" (Phil. 3:10).

When we think about actually being able to experience the power of His resurrection, it is overwhelming. The same power that raised Jesus from the dead is available to us when we know Him. Now that is power! Do you know of someone who came back to life after being dead? We know Lazarus was raised from the dead by Jesus, and we may have heard of someone in today's time that has experienced death and come back to life. These people have a tremendous testimony! Only God can do something that powerful, and He tells us in His Word that when we know Him, we may know the power that raised Jesus from the dead. This same scripture also tells us that we can know the fellowship of His sufferings. That is not something we get as excited about. We do not usually want to experience suffering, and yet so often that is what draws us closer to God. It would be wonderful if we would draw closer to God in the good times (and I believe God wants us to), but usually it is during the time of suffering that we call on God and begin to seek Him with all our heart and mind.

Whatever you are going through today, call upon Him and draw close to Him. You may be going through a very difficult time. Call on Him and He will hear and answer. Your life today may be very smooth, and everything seems great. Do not let that stop you from calling on Him and drawing close to Him. The more we draw close to Him in the good times, the stronger we will be in the difficult times. Let Him reveal His resurrection power to you today!

Understanding of Him

"And we know that the Son of God has come and has given us an understanding, that we may know Him who is true; and we are in Him who is true, in His Son Jesus Christ. This is the true God and eternal life" (1 John 5:20).

Yes, God has given us an understanding of Himself, and there is really no excuse for not knowing Him. He sent His Son Jesus Christ to reveal His nature to us, and then He recorded the life of Jesus in Scripture so that there would be a record passed down through the ages. He placed within us the knowledge of Himself, and during our lives, He draws us through the power of the Holy Spirit. We have the choice of whether or not we will respond to all He has made available to us that will enable us to know Him. Once we make the decision to accept Jesus as our Lord and Savior, then we must determine how much of our life we will make available to Him. We can spend time with Him daily, or we can go on our busy way. In the day and age that we live, everyone seems extremely busy. That is an excuse we all can use, and sometimes it is very difficult not to let our busyness overcome us. If we spend that precious time with Him each day, however, we will find that our daily routine will run much smoother, and He will redeem our time. Give Him that time today and enter into His presence. Then watch how He creates peace in your life today instead of confusion!

Filled with the Fullness of God

"That Christ may dwell in your hearts through faith; that you, being rooted and grounded in love, may be able to comprehend with all the saints what is the width and length and depth and height—to know the love of Christ which passes knowledge; that you may be filled with all the fullness of God" (Eph. 3:17–19).

This prayer by Paul was for the church at Ephesus, but it is also for all believers today. It is for you and for me. Do you want to be filled with all the fullness of God?

The best way I know to be filled with His fullness is to have daily quiet time with the Lord where we soak up His truth through reading the Bible. As we read His Word, we let Him reveal greater understanding to us as He communicates His love and His presence to us. This combination is powerful in changing our lives into the image of God. His glory transforms our lives!

When the children of Israel were in the wilderness, they complained so often and got off track because they were afraid of the presence of God. Because of their fear, they told Moses to go and talk to Him. The life of Moses was transformed through being in the presence of God and listening and responding to His Word, but the children of Israel continued to complain because they had to rely on Moses' relationship with God instead of having that relationship themselves. We cannot rely on someone else's relationship with God. We must have that personal, close relationship ourselves. Enter into His presence today and know Him better!

Revelation of the Knowledge of God

"That the God of our Lord Jesus Christ, the Father of glory, may give to you the spirit of wisdom and revelation in the knowledge of Him, the eyes of your understanding being enlightened; that you may know what is the hope of His calling, what are the riches of the glory of His inheritance in the saints, and what is the exceeding greatness of His power toward us who believe, according to the working of His mighty power" (Eph. 1:17–19).

Paul prayed some very powerful prayers, and if we try to understand them, our lives can be changed. Again, Paul is praying just as much for you and me as he was for the church at Ephesus. He is praying that we would understand Jesus, what He has done for us, what He makes available to us, and the power that He wants to work through us. God's power is not available to us to misuse. It is available to us when we truly understand our inheritance through Jesus Christ. We are being changed into His image. When our will, purposes, and desires line up with Jesus' will, purpose, and desire, we respond to situations and to others as He would. At these times His power is available to us.

Draw close and yield yourself to Him today so that you may be changed into His image and respond to those around you as He would. Watch Him trust you with His power as you come to understand Colossians 1:27, "Christ in you, the hope of glory!"

Imitators of God

"Therefore be imitators of God as dear children. And walk in love, as Christ also has loved us . . ." (Eph. 5:1–2a).

This scripture is reassuring us that we are dear children of God. We do not have to doubt His love because His love is not conditional on how we act, what we do or do not do, how well we perform, or our success or lack of success. His love is unconditional and everlasting. His love is held out to everyone. He, therefore, wants us to become imitators of Himself and hold out His love to others.

That is something we cannot do on our own. It does not come naturally with us. We have to rely on Him, know Him better, enter into His presence, and let His love envelop us in such a way that we become transformed into His image and actually begin to act like Him. To become imitators of Him is not natural. It is supernatural and comes only through the power of the Holy Spirit. Acts 1:8 tells us that the Holy Spirit comes into our lives to empower us to become witnesses of Jesus in Jerusalem, and in all Judea and Samaria, and to the end of the earth.

Yield yourself to the Spirit of God today and let Him use you to be a witness in the world in which you live! Step out in your workplace, at school, at home, or as you are going about your daily routine. Let the love and light of Jesus Christ shine forth from you to those who need that special touch that comes from the One who knows us best!

Seek Him with Your Whole Heart

"But from there you will seek the Lord your God, and you will find Him if you seek Him with all your heart and with all your soul" (Deut. 4:29).

We find an important key to entering into the presence of God in this scripture for today. We will find Him if we seek Him with all our heart and with all our soul. What does it mean to seek God with all our heart and with all our soul? It means to seek Him earnestly with every ounce of our being and to want to spend time with Him over and above other priorities. It means putting Him first in our lives. There are things that we need to do. There are things that we are required to do, but none of this should keep us from sincerely seeking God.

We can get up a little earlier in the morning to read our Bible and pray and spend time in the presence of the Lord. We might turn off the radio when we are driving to work and use that time to pray and listen to Him. We could turn off that television program in the evening and read the Bible or an inspirational book that helps us grow in our knowledge of our Lord and gives us further instruction about how to walk a victorious and obedient Christian life.

Choose today to make Jesus the number one priority in your life and know the joy of spending time with Him who gives you life abundantly!

Rejoice!

"Glory in His holy name; let the hearts of those rejoice who seek the Lord!" (1 Chron. 16:10).

When we seek the Lord and make Him our number one priority, we truly do have reason to rejoice. When we seek Him, we enter into His presence. When we enter into His presence, we see Him for who He is, the Creator of the whole universe. He is omnipotent, all powerful, loving, and merciful. When we begin to see Him in all His glory, we cannot help but rejoice in the presence of Him who is full of majesty, splendor, and power.

Like those before the throne of God who cried out, "You are worthy, O Lord, to receive glory and honor and power; for you created all things, and by Your will they exist and were created" (Rev. 4:11), we also will cry out praises to our King as we rejoice before His throne in that special time that we spend with Him. Entering into His presence brings praises to our lips, and we become so very thankful to Him for all His goodness. We become overwhelmed with the knowledge that even in all His majesty, He allows us (and even longs for us) to be a part of His life.

Rejoice in His presence today and sing praises to Him. Lift up your voice on high and tell Him how glorious He is!

Arise and Build

"Now set your heart and your soul to seek the Lord your God. Therefore arise and build the sanctuary of the Lord God . . ." (1 Chron. 22:19).

David instructed his son Solomon about building the temple for God. Notice his directions. He told Solomon to set his heart and soul to seek the Lord, and then he told him to arise and build the sanctuary. When we seek the Lord with all our heart and soul, we are in His presence. We are pulled away from the world, from things that bring busyness into our lives, and we are communing with our heavenly Father.

When we are in His presence, He is showing us things, giving us direction, changing us into His image, preparing us to do His will and to be His hands and feet extended upon this earth. After we have had that time in His presence, then we will arise, and we will go forth, and we will do that which He has instructed us to do while we were in His presence. We will do what He has purposed for us, that which is our part, in helping to build His kingdom on this earth.

Enter into His presence today and let Him share with you what His will is for you in helping to further His kingdom. Then arise and go forth and begin to build!

Loyal Heart and Willing Mind

"As for you, my son Solomon, know the God of your father, and serve Him with a loyal heart and with a willing mind; for the Lord searches all hearts and understands all the intent of the thoughts. If you seek Him, He will be found by you . . ." (1 Chron. 28:9).

David had a loyal heart toward God, and he advised his son Solomon to follow in his footsteps and have a loyal heart and a willing mind toward God. We, as human beings, like to do things our way. We do not really like to be told by others how to handle situations, and we do not usually like to ask for advice. It takes significant effort on our part to submit our wills to the Lord in order to have a "willing mind."

We need to realize that the Lord knows all things, and regardless of how competent or smart we think we are, His knowledge and understanding of any situation is far greater than ours. We need to learn to trust Him completely in all things, and then we will find that our lives will be filled with the peace and contentment of knowing that He is in control.

Again we are promised that if we seek Him, He will be found by us. When we seek Him with a loyal heart and a willing mind, He is waiting right there for us. He is waiting to share Himself with us, to guide and direct us, and to save us from the frustrations and confusions that so often fill our lives when we do things our way instead of His way.

Seek and Obey

"He commanded Judah to seek the Lord God of their fathers, and to observe the law and the commandment" (2 Chron. 14:4).

When we seek after the Lord with our whole heart, entering into His presence, we become so one with Him that our desire is to do His will and to be obedient to His Word.

Mary, the mother of Jesus, had a visitation from an angel named Gabriel who announced God's plan that she was to become the mother of the Messiah. She was a young woman who was humble and deeply loved and worshiped God. When she was told about what was to come, she simply said, "Be it done unto me according to your word." If she had allowed herself to dwell on the possible consequences, she might have become too frightened or would have been tempted to say, "No, not me." She was, however, one who sought her Lord, loved Him, and was totally committed to Him.

We are told in Luke 1:46–55 about the song of worship that Mary sang to her Lord because He had chosen her to be the mother of the Messiah. She began her song with praises to God, saying, "My soul magnifies the Lord, and my spirit has rejoiced in God my Savior." She expressed her love and worship of God not only through song and words but also by deed and action. She is a beautiful example to us today of obedience to our Father.

Seek Him with such commitment that you would be willing to say to Him, "Be it done unto me according to your word," even if He asks something of you that would be very difficult for you to do. Let us learn from our beautiful example, Mary, the mother of Jesus!

Covenant to Seek Him

"Then they entered into a covenant to seek the Lord God of their fathers with all their heart and with all their soul" (2 Chron. 15:12).

When we covenant to seek God, that means that we are so determined to seek Him that we will not allow anything to hinder us from spending time with Him. Covenant means to enter into an agreement, contract, or promise. God does not break covenant. He always does what He says He will do. His promises are true, and we can be assured that He will fulfill His Word. When we enter into a covenant as the people of Judah did in the scripture reference above, it means that we intend to keep it.

This scripture should encourage us to understand the importance of seeking God with all our heart and with all our soul. It is something we should be committed to do on a daily basis, realizing that this time is so special and so important that other things must not be allowed to interfere.

Would you be willing to make a commitment to your Father in heaven today to spend time with Him on a daily basis? You will grow closer to Him and develop into the child of God that He created you to be, and you will fulfill His purposes for you on this earth. If your answer is yes, go before Him now and say, "Here am I, Lord. Reveal yourself to me today, and help me grow into that person You know I can be through Your strength and power."

Prepared Heart to Seek Him

"And [you] have prepared your heart to seek God" (2 Chron. 19:3b).

It is important that we prepare our hearts to seek God. This daily devotional is meant to help us to prepare our hearts to seek God on a regular basis. How do we do this? We can prepare our hearts by reading His Word, studying His Word, and meditating on His Word. We can also prepare our hearts by making choices to set aside time to praise Him and spend time in prayer.

I believe an important way to prepare our hearts to seek Him is to surround ourselves with people who love God and spend time with Him, reaping the rewards of a deep, close relationship with Him. When we are in the presence of others who have a deep and yielded relationship with the Lord, they inspire us to follow in their footsteps. We see the fruit in their lives, and we are drawn to the Spirit of God who is so clearly at work in them.

Who do you know who vividly exhibits the fruit of the Spirit? Choose today to spend time with that person. Join a Bible study or a prayer group and surround yourself with people who love God and know Him well. Spend time alone with Him, but also spend time with His people, learning and growing in your knowledge of Him.

Set Yourself to Seek the Lord

"And Jehoshaphat feared, and set himself to seek the Lord, and proclaimed a fast throughout all Judah" (2 Chron. 20:3).

Armies were coming against the people of Judah, and King Jehoshaphat was afraid. Do not wait until you are afraid to seek God. When we seek Him daily and develop a close relationship with Him, we will be prepared to face the battles and crises that come up in life, drawing on the strength and courage that flow from Him. We must determine to seek Him regularly when life is going smoothly and our circumstances are good. It can be very hard to seek God in these times because we think we can handle life ourselves when everything is on an even keel. We must remember that even though God gives us all the gift of faith, the amount we use our faith determines how strong it will be when we need it.

Faith is like a muscle. It grows stronger and more powerful with exercise. If we are faithful to use weights and workout on a regular basis, our physical muscles will grow over a period of time. If we do not exercise, however, our muscles will be very weak and flabby. If someone breaks into our house when we have not been on a regular exercise program, we will not be strong enough to fight him off. If we have been strengthening our muscles through exercise, however, we will be able to face him and protect ourselves.

The same principle is true with faith. If we exercise our faith by spending time with the Lord on a regular basis, when trouble comes our way, we will have the resources to fight the good fight of faith. Set yourself to spend time with the Lord today and let your faith grow!

Coming to Seek the Lord

"So Judah gathered together to ask help from the Lord; and from all the cities of Judah they came to seek the Lord" (2 Chron. 20:4).

It is important to seek the Lord alone, but there are times when we should seek Him with others. The nation of Judah realized that they were in trouble when they heard that vast armies from other nations were marching against them. In response, King Jehoshaphat sought the Lord himself, and then he called the entire nation of Judah to come together in fasting before the Lord.

In Deuteronomy the Bible speaks of one man putting a thousand to flight and two men putting ten thousand to flight. There is strength in coming together with other believers to pray, fast, and seek the Lord for answers in time of trouble. Regardless of how we seek the Lord, we know we will see results! We can seek Him with several others in a Bible study or prayer group, or we can join with just a single prayer partner. We can and should seek the Lord alone often.

Let your circumstances be your guide as to whether you come alone or with others, but determine to spend time with the Lord each day renewing your faith and growing stronger in His presence.

Seek and Prosper

"And in every work that he began in the service of the house of God, in the law and in the commandment, to seek his God, he did it with all his heart. So he prospered" (2 Chron. 31:21).

This scripture refers to Hezekiah, king of Judah. Hezekiah was one of the kings of Judah who had a heart for God and sought Him throughout his life. He not only sought the Lord, but he sought Him with all his heart. Hezekiah was a king who brought reform through purging, repairing, and opening the temple. He rooted out pagan cults and contaminations. He was also a warrior of great strength, and he used this gift to bring about moral and spiritual changes in his country. The name Hezekiah means "Jehovah is strength," and his life exemplified the meaning of his name. He knew that strength to rule the nation of Judah could only come from Jehovah God, so he determined to do whatever he could to encounter the one true living God. Because Hezekiah sought the Lord and followed the Lord's direction for ruling the nation of Judah, Judah prospered under his reign.

Seeking after the Lord with your whole heart will cause you to prosper in your walk with the Lord. Let Hezekiah be an example for you today.

Decide to seek after the Lord with your whole heart and see how He will choose to prosper you!

Separated from Uncleanness

"Then the children of Israel . . . separated themselves from the uncleanness . . . in order to seek the Lord God of Israel. And they kept the Feast of Unleavened Bread seven days with joy; for the Lord made them joyful . . ." (Ezra 6:21–22a).

What does being separated from uncleanness mean to us today? It means that we separate ourselves from those things that are not of God. We steer clear of sin and anything that could lead to sin in our lives. The more time we spend in the presence of our Lord, the more we will find ourselves turning away from sin and separating ourselves from anything that could lead to sin in our lives. The greatest deterrent to sin is knowing our God in all His love, goodness, forgiveness, comfort, and mercy. When we draw close to Him and enter into His presence, we begin to see Him for who He is. The result is that we want to leave the old things behind. The things that once seemed so important, so much fun, and so inviting no longer have the drawing or attraction they once had. Compared to the glory of God Almighty, they are nothing.

When we seek God and come to know Him in all His fullness, overwhelming joy rises up within us. Our priorities change, and we become sold out to God. We want to be pleasing to Him, and we want to allow Him first place in our lives. Seek Him today and learn of His grace and His love for you. Rejoice in His presence!

Trust and Be Not Forsaken

"And those who know Your name will put their trust in You; for You, Lord, have not forsaken those who seek You" (Ps. 9:10).

*W*hat does it mean to know the name of God? It means to know His nature and His character. It does not mean to simply know how to pronounce or spell His name.

When we know the nature of God, there is no way that we can keep from trusting Him.

If there is no other person on the face of the earth that you can trust, you can trust God with all your heart because "there is no guile in Him" (1 Pet. 2:22). "He is not a man that He should lie" (Num. 23:19). Place your trust in Him today, seek Him with all your heart, and know that you are not forsaken. He will never forsake anyone who seeks after Him. His Word tells us, "I will never leave you nor forsake you" (Heb. 13:5). His mercy endures forever, and His love is everlasting to the ends of the earth. He is the one you can always trust with everything. Look to Him with complete confidence and know He will be waiting and listening, ready to respond to your every need. He has the answer to every question you could ask Him. Do not delay, but approach Him now with that need that weighs heavily upon you.

Let His great strength take over and receive the release that comes from only Him!

Let Your Heart Live Forever

". . . those who seek Him will praise the Lord. Let your heart live forever!" (Ps. 22:26b).

There is no doubt that when we seek the Lord, we will praise Him. When we come to know Him as we seek after Him, our hearts are so filled with joy that it just seems to spill over through our lips. We find ourselves praising God with all that we are. Those things that seemed so heavy on us before, lose their importance in the presence of the everlasting King of kings! Praises come naturally in the presence of Jehovah God for He truly is worthy of our praises.

When we read Psalms, we find that they are filled with praise to God. Many psalms were written by David, who had a heart for God and whose heart, mind, and mouth were filled with praises to His Lord. He knew God, and he entered into His presence in such a way that he became one of the strongest and most respected men of God in all of Israel's history. We can learn much from David about "letting our hearts live forever." I believe that in the scripture above this means that through truly seeking and praising God, our hearts become so filled with joy and life from our Father that we cannot contain it.

It is praise and joy that spills out to all those around us. We become witnesses of the glory of God!

Behold the Beauty of the Lord

"One thing I have desired of the Lord, that will I seek: that I may dwell in the house of the Lord all the days of my life, to behold the beauty of the Lord . . ." (Ps. 27:4).

In this passage penned by David we find again why he was a man after God's heart. He had such a love and passion for God that his desire, his one desire, was to be in the house or the dwelling of God. In other words, he wanted more than anything to be in the presence of the Lord forever, beholding His glorious beauty.

Have you ever experienced the presence of the Lord in such a way that you could behold His beauty? If you have not, now is the time. Simply determine with all your heart and with all your soul that you want to seek after God until you behold Him in all His glory and beauty. Can you feel with David what he was experiencing when he wrote these words? Read this passage over several times and let David's yearning for more of God fill your heart and mind. Then begin to seek after God with deep passion, just as David did. God's Word is alive. When you read, meditate, and study His Word, it changes you. It inspires and brings life to you.

An old term that we do not hear very often today is "quicken." It is hard to improve on this word. It means that sometimes God's Word may actually seem to jump out at you. As you repeatedly read the passage above, and other psalms of praise by David, they will be "quickened" to you and take on greater meaning. Read with new enthusiasm and receive from God's Word the life you need to behold the beauty of God!

Shall Not Lack Any Good Thing

". . . those who seek the Lord shall not lack any good thing" (Ps. 34:10b).

David told us in this psalm that if we seek the Lord, we will not lack any good thing. Does that mean that we have instant gratification? Does that mean that we will instantly have anything and everything we want? No, it means that when we seek after the Lord with all our heart, we will begin to move into a place of receiving those things that are beneficial for us to have.

By "those who seek the Lord," this scripture refers to ones who continue in the presence of the Lord, going before Him on a regular basis so that their relationship with Him is always growing. As our relationship with Him grows, we are continually being transformed from our former selves into His image. Our desires become more aligned with His desires, and our wills become submitted to Him so that we begin to want what He wants and no longer think as selfishly as before. As our desires change and as our wills are submitted to Him, we may find that what we consider "good things" may change. We can be assured that He will give us the good things that He knows we need and that He wants us to have.

Seek Him with all your heart today and let Him change your desires. Submit your will to Him so that you will know the peace and joy of being in the center of His will.

Seek and Rejoice

"Let all those who seek You rejoice and be glad in You; let such as love Your salvation say continually, 'the Lord be magnified!'" (Ps. 40:16).

When we seek the Lord, we cannot help but rejoice and be glad in Him. Seeking Him leads to entering into His presence, which brings great joy into our lives. Being in the glorious presence of the Lord is such a powerful, overwhelming experience because we begin to see Him for who He is: a loving God whose mercy encompasses us and lasts forever. We see Him in all His majesty and glory, and we find it difficult to believe that He would allow us to come into His presence to experience such closeness with Him. Our hearts overflow with love and joy for a God who would reveal Himself to us and allow us to experience Him in all His fullness. When our hearts are full, we find ourselves along with David saying, "The Lord be magnified!" Our mouths are filled with praise and thanksgiving to our Lord who can compare with none other. Sometimes we are so filled with praise and worship of Him that we simply cannot express all that we are feeling.

Seek Him and experience His love and mercy as you enter into His presence today. Let your mouth be filled with praises as you rejoice in the one true living God!

Sing and Rejoice

"Sing to Him, sing psalms to Him; talk of all His wondrous works! Glory in His holy name; let the hearts of those rejoice who seek the Lord!" (Ps. 105:2–3).

Something about singing touches the heart and also expresses what is in the heart. We are admonished in Psalm 105 to sing unto the Lord. When we seek the Lord and lift our voices in praise and worship to Him, we find that He is very near. Psalm 22:3 says that God inhabits the praises of Israel. This means that God comes to dwell in the praises of His people. Whether we lift our voice in praises to God in speaking or in singing, He draws near to us. He rejoices in our praises as we rejoice in Him and His presence.

The scripture for today also tells us to glory in His holy name. What does that mean? It means to honor and praise His holy name, to exult in great joy and triumph in who He is as exemplified by His name, and to thoroughly enjoy and be ecstatic in His presence.

If you have never been comfortable praising God in song, today in the privacy of your home (or wherever you can find privacy) lift up your voice in a simple song of praise to God. You will be amazed at the joy that will well up within you. He is not interested in the quality of your voice or how well you know the song. He is looking at your heart, and He is rejoicing that you will take the time to express from your heart the praises that are dwelling within you.

Seek and Be Blessed

"Blessed are those who keep His testimonies, who seek Him with the whole heart!" (Ps. 119:2).

We are blessed when we seek Him by keeping His testimonies. This lengthy psalm tells us the importance of studying, believing, and acting upon the Word of God. How important it is to seek God through His Word! His Word points us to God, reveals Him to us, gives us wisdom, and brings the very life of God to us.

When we seek to enter into the presence of God, we can come to Him in many ways. We can praise Him, we can be quiet and still, we can be alone, or we can be with others, but one thing we always need to do is to refer to His Word. His Word confirms to us what is truly from Him and what is not. Sometimes we can become sidetracked with something that is not from God, but when we verify everything with God's Word, we know that it will bring His light into every question or situation.

In your quiet time with Him today, let Him speak to you through His Word. Read, believe, and then move out and begin to act on what He brings alive to you from Scripture. Receive from Him through the gift of His inspired Word!

Diligently Seek

"I love those who love me, and those who seek me diligently will find me" (Prov. 8:17).

Do you seek the Lord diligently? Diligence means to be attentive with perseverance. In the world that we live in today, we are used to instant results rather than persevering. We are surrounded by instant potatoes, instant coffee, fast food, and microwave ovens. When it comes to diligence, we are not as accomplished as our forefathers. If we want a close relationship with the Lord, we must be diligent in seeking Him. Being diligent in seeking the Lord expresses our love for Him.

If you have an ambition to be the very best you can be in your vocation, you strive to do your job with excellence. You persevere in accomplishing your goals and excelling at your work. If your goal is to be an exceptional student, you work hard, study a great deal, and do everything you can to learn and to make good grades. You are diligent in these efforts. We need to apply this same diligence to our relationship with our Father in heaven in order to express our love for Him and to allow Him to mold us into the child of God He created us to be. Then we are enabled to fulfill His purpose in our lives and bring glory to His name!

Understand All!

". . . those who seek the Lord understand all" (Prov. 28:5b).

Do you want to have greater understanding in your life? There is a simple way to accomplish this: Seek the Lord! We are finding day by day, as we seek the Lord through this devotional, the importance of seeking Him and entering into His presence. Nothing else, except reading and studying His Word, is so vitally important in our lives. Seeking Him brings comfort, strength, growth, changes toward holiness, a greater understanding of who we are and of God's purpose for our lives, and stronger relationships. In other words, seeking the Lord brings greater understanding in every aspect of our lives.

I have been amazed at the things that the Lord has revealed to me as I have sought Him more and more over the years. He has given me greater understanding of how to pray in certain situations, and then I have seen those prayers answered. He has guided me in difficult decisions when I simply did not know what to do, and then I have marveled at how well these situations have turned out as a result.

If you are in need of greater understanding in any area of your life today, seek the Lord and let Him give you the wisdom and understanding you need to make the very best decision possible for you and everyone concerned. He is faithful to make known to you everything you need to know. Notice I said everything you need to know, not everything you want to know. Trust Him to do what is best for you, and He will not fail you!

Seek and Be Righteous

"Listen to Me, you who follow after righteousness, you who seek the Lord . . ." (Isa. 51:1).

We will walk in righteousness more and more as we seek the Lord continually. We are called righteous by God when we receive Jesus Christ as our Lord and Savior. When we accept the sacrifice that Jesus paid for us on the cross by shedding His blood for us, our Father sees us through the blood of Jesus, complete and righteous as Jesus is complete and righteous. Second Corinthians 5:21 says, "For He made Him who knew no sin to be sin for us, that we might become the righteousness of God in Him." Therefore we are righteous in God's eyes, but in our own eyes we know that we do not always walk in righteousness. We begin to walk more and more in righteousness as we seek Him more and more. What happens to us when we enter the presence of God, our Father? We are changed from glory to glory into His image! In other words, we begin to walk more and more like Him, which is righteousness!

Begin to seek Him with diligence today, enter into His presence, be changed from glory to glory into His image, and begin to walk more like Him. Walk in the righteousness that has already been purchased for you.

Seek While He May Be Found

"Seek the Lord while He may be found, call upon Him while He is near" (Isa. 55:6).

When is the Lord near? He has told us, "I will never leave you nor forsake you" (Heb. 13:5). That must mean that He is always near to us. Second Corinthians 6:2 says, "Behold, now is the accepted time; behold, now is the day of salvation." I believe those two scriptures show us that the Lord is always near, and today is the day we should seek Him. Today, tomorrow, the next day, and every day of our lives is the day that He is near. Each day He may be found, and each day we should seek Him with all our heart, diligently thirsting after more of Him until we see Him face to face. He has so much for us in His presence if we would only give Him the time to offer us His precious gifts. If we continually put off seeking Him, the day may come when it is too late. We do not know what is ahead. We do not know how many days, months, or years we have left on this earth.

Seek Him today and get to know Him better. Let Him pour out His love on you today. No person on this earth can show you the love that your heavenly Father can show you. Put aside all those things that seem so pressing and crawl up on His lap. Let Him be the Father to you that He wants to be, and you will find that your day will go better. Those pressing things will fall into place, and you will be so blessed that you will wonder why you did not crawl up on His lap sooner!

Seek Him Daily

"Yet they seek Me daily, and delight to know My ways, . . . they take delight in approaching God" (Isa. 58:2).

When we seek God daily, it truly does become a delight to approach Him. Sometimes we have to make ourselves approach God because we are busy, we have so much on our minds, and there seems to be so much pressing in on us. We may feel that it's simply impossible to take the time to get quiet before God. But as we make that decision to let the things of this world go and approach the throne of God to spend precious time with Him, communing in holy fellowship, we will find such joy and such peace that we will wonder why we have not spent more time with Him.

When things press in on us from all sides and our needs are greatest, that is the very time we most need to approach the throne of God and spend time with Him. He has every answer to every need. He not only has solutions, but peace, joy, love, comfort, strength, and absolutely everything that we could possibly need. He has more than we need because in Ephesians 3:20 it says, "Now to Him who is able to do exceedingly abundantly above all that we ask or think . . ." When we are stressed to our limits or seem to be too busy to breathe, we need to turn to Him and let Him refresh and renew us in the way that only He can!

Search with All Your Heart

"And you will seek Me and find Me, when you search for Me with all your heart" (Jer. 29:13).

To search for God with all your heart means that He is your number one priority. Nothing else in this world can take precedence over Him. Sometimes we say to ourselves or even to others that God is number one in our lives. But does our life reflect that? What do we spend the most time doing? What do we spend the most time thinking about? If we pray a short prayer in the morning and then go all day without giving our Father another thought, that is not giving Him number one priority in our lives. If we briefly acknowledge Him a couple of times a day, that is not reflecting the idea that we love God with all our hearts. When we search for God with all our hearts, we are thinking about Him, talking to Him, or fellowshiping with Him in some way a good part of the day.

If you are not used to having the Lord on your mind a good part of the day, try an experiment today and see how the Lord will meet you and create a sense of excitement and joy in your life. Ask Him to help you to practice His presence. Ask Him to help you to begin to talk things over with Him throughout the day, things at work, things at home, important things, small things, and especially those things that are confusing or frustrating. Do not get discouraged if you do not spend much time in His presence at first, but try again tomorrow, the next day, and so on. Before long you will find yourself communing with the Lord on a much closer basis, and your life will reflect the glory that comes from making Him first in your life!

Seek Until He Rains Righteousness

"Sow for yourselves righteousness; reap in mercy; break up your fallow ground, for it is time to seek the Lord, till He comes and rains righteousness on you" (Hos. 10:12).

Fallow ground is ground that is not cultivated or prepared for seed. Just as we cannot bring forth good vegetables from a garden unless we plant in rich, cultivated ground that has been properly prepared, we must also prepare our hearts to bring forth righteousness. One way we can prepare our hearts, or "break up the fallow ground," is to seek the Lord and keep on seeking Him until He comes and rains righteousness on us. The more we spend time in His presence, the more our hearts will be softened and changed to bring forth good fruit for His kingdom.

The term "fallow ground" indicates hard ground. Sometimes when we allow sin in our lives over a period of time, our hearts can become hardened. We can break up the fallow ground by coming into the presence of God where He begins to show us the things that are in need of repentance. Through repentance we find our hearts will become softened and pliable in God's hand, and He can then begin to change us and mold us into the people that He created us to be. Enter into His presence today and let your heart be softened and changed as He reveals His goodness and His glory to you!

All Things Shall Be Added to You

"But seek first the kingdom of God and His righteousness, and all these things shall be added to you" (Matt. 6:33).

When we seek the kingdom of God first, all other things that are necessary or beneficial in our lives are added unto us. In other words, God takes care of every need when we put Him first in our lives. The scripture verses that precede the one for today talk about basic needs such as food and clothing. We are instructed not to worry about tomorrow. God assures us that when we put our trust in God and place Him first in our lives, we will find that tomorrow takes care of itself. Our Lord is able to take care of our every need, and He knows far better than we do what our needs are and what will be best for us.

When we are used to being self-sufficient, it is difficult to turn our lives over to the Lord and put our complete trust in Him, but that is what Scripture instructs us to do. As we trust Him more and more in each situation, our faith will grow stronger. Ever-increasing trust in the Lord will become easier regardless of what we face. He is always faithful, and His compassion is everlasting. Sometimes His response to our "need" is not what we thought we wanted, but we find out later that He has our best interest at heart. His response is always the right response: the response that is best for us and everyone concerned.

Seek and Be Rewarded

"But without faith it is impossible to please Him, for he who comes to God must believe that He is, and that He is a rewarder of those who diligently seek Him" (Heb. 11:6).

Faith is a vitally important component of our walk with the Lord. Without faith we cannot please the Lord. Do you want to please the Lord? Decide to exercise the gift of faith that the Lord has given you and watch it grow in your life. Faith is like a muscle: as you exercise it, it will grow stronger. Faith is believing the Lord means what He says and then acting on that belief. Faith is diligently seeking the Lord and never giving up. When we seek Him diligently, believing Him and living our belief, He rewards us.

What are our rewards? Our rewards are the fruit of the Spirit and the joy of being in His presence, the joy of knowing Him better, the joy of being considered and treated as His child, and the joy of drawing closer and closer to the God of the whole universe.

Just imagine, the great Creator of all that is good and wonderful loves you and wants to spend time with you. Not only does He want to spend time with you, expressing His love to you, He wants to reward you as well. What is taking you so long? Begin to seek Him diligently today, enter into His presence, hear from Him, believe Him, act on what He shows you, and have the joy of pleasing Him!

Seek the Things Above

"If then you were raised with Christ, seek those things which are above, where Christ is, sitting at the right hand of God" (Col. 3:1).

Paul told us in this verse and those that follow that when we accept Jesus Christ as our Lord and Savior and begin to walk this Christian walk, we become dead to the things of this earth and alive to the things above. Our home is not here but in heaven. When we seek the things above, we place our trust in God to take care of the things on this earth. That does not mean that we bury our heads in the sand and ignore issues that need to be addressed, but it does mean that as we set our minds on things above, we have a clearer understanding of how the Lord would have us respond to the issues that are so difficult for us as Christians to accept.

So much in this world today is full of darkness and despair. If we continually dwell on the problems, we will become surrounded by darkness and despair. We need to dwell on the Lord and His solution to the problems that are all around us. God will give us hope and faith that He is in control. He will show us His plan for each one of us in overcoming the darkness that is very much a part of this world in which we live.

Seek the things above today and begin to become a part of God's solution to the problems that are so overwhelming in this world. Be a part of God's plan and fulfill His purpose for you!

My Soul Pants for You

"As the deer pants for the water brooks, so pants my soul for You, O God" (Ps. 42:1).

When I used to read this scripture, I thought that the deer panted for the water because he was thirsty. That is true, but there is more to the story. Hunters have told me that deer run toward the water when they are in danger. They immerse themselves completely until only their noses are above the water, and the wild animal or hunting dog that is chasing them will lose their scent. They find safety and refuge in the water as well as quenching their thirst. That can be true for us as well. When we need safety and refuge, we need to go to the one who gives us living water. We need to seek Him with all the yearning that the deer does when he is thirsty or when he is in danger.

When we find great distresses in our lives, there is really only one answer. Jesus! How do we find Him? We find Him by simply seeking Him—calling out to Him, praying, praising, and entering into worship. Scripture tells us that God inhabits the praises of His people. Another verse in Hebrews tells us to offer up a sacrifice of praise. When we are going through a very difficult time, a time of adversity or even of danger, we need to cry out to the Lord and offer up praises to Him. You may be saying, "Why should we praise God when things are so bad?" Because He is able to deliver us from adversity and help us to become overcomers in distressing situations. When we praise Him, we acknowledge that He is greater than our difficulties, and we put our complete trust in Him. Praise Him today as you seek Him with your whole heart in the midst of adversity.

Appear Before God

"My soul thirsts for God, for the living God. When shall I come and appear before God?" (Ps. 42:2).

The Hebrew word for appear is raah, which means to see or look upon. This word gives the idea of asking, "When shall I come and see or look upon the face of God?" The psalmist compares his yearning for God to how a deer longs for water. He paints a picture of deep longing and yearning in the midst of adversity. He uses the term "thirsts" to show the deepness and eagerness of his longing. When we are thirsty, we cannot wait to get something to drink to quench the thirst we feel. That cool water tastes wonderfully refreshing. As we drink, the terrible dryness just melts away. When we are thirsty spiritually, nothing will satisfy us other than coming into the presence of God and seeing Him face to face.

We must seek His face to grow closer and more intimate with Him. He wants us to seek His face and to have a "face to face" relationship with Him. We can learn from the experiences of men such as Moses and Jacob about the vital significance of meeting God face to face. When we see Him face to face, our lives are transformed. The time spent in His presence face to face will have such an impact on our lives that we will want to spend more and more time with Him. He will become the number one priority in our lives, and all other things will pale in the sight of our Lord and Master.

Enter into His presence today and seek His face. Let Him share with you, talk with you, and let Him show you how much He loves you. Seek Him today! Seek Him now!

Jacob Sees God

"So Jacob called the name of the place Peniel. 'For I have seen God face to face, and my life is preserved'" (Gen. 32:30).

Jacob sees God face to face. And what is his experience? What happens to Jacob because he saw God face to face? Jacob's name means "deceiver," and the record we have in Scripture of his life reveals that he had character weaknesses. When he got to a very low point in his life (he thought he would be facing an angry brother who might kill him and his family), he began to seek God. He wrestled with God all night long and would not give up until God blessed him. He is a beautiful example of perseverance in spite of the fact that his character was weak in some areas.

Are you perfect? Of course not! None of us is perfect. Just like Jacob, we have some weaknesses in our lives. Because we are not perfect does not mean we cannot seek God, persevere, and have a "face to face" encounter with Him just as Jacob did. Jacob's life was transformed by his encounter with God, and our lives can be changed also as we seek to have a "face to face" encounter with Him. Jacob left behind the old ways of deception, and he became a man who loved God, believed God, and was strong in faith. Jacob is the father of the twelve tribes of Israel. He is one of the fathers of the Jewish faith, and he is one of the fathers of the Christian faith. Jacob's life was turned around, and your life and my life can be turned around more and more each time we encounter God face to face.

Face to Face—Moses

"So the Lord spoke to Moses face to face, as a man speaks to his friend" (Exod. 33:11).

Moses had a very intimate relationship with the Lord. He was actually a friend with the Lord. Have you ever wondered if you could have the same type of relationship with the Lord that Moses had? You can and I can! Moses was a man who had a deep commitment to the Lord. His first reaction when God told him the overwhelming purpose He had for him was to say, "Not me, Lord. I am slow of speech." Moses did not think that he was adequate to fulfill God's purpose for him.

Have you ever felt that way? I know I have, but I also have learned that God is able to provide whatever is needed for me to accomplish His will for my life. It is not my ability, but it is my availability. And that is precisely what Moses learned. Once he realized that God's purpose would be accomplished through God's strength and not through the ability of Moses, his commitment was strong. Both his commitment and relationship with the Lord were so strong that he actually knew God face to face.

Make a commitment today to follow after God, seek Him with everything that is within you, make Him the number one priority in your life, and see how He draws you unto Himself to become that close, intimate friend with Him.

The Lord Knew Moses Face to Face

"But since then there has not arisen in Israel a prophet like Moses, whom the Lord knew face to face" (Deut. 34:10).

In the Old Testament days only a few who were committed and faithful were chosen to be filled with the Spirit of God and to accomplish the works of God on this earth. Moses was one of those dedicated people, and he was acclaimed among the Israelites. When Jesus died upon the cross and ascended into heaven to sit at the right hand of God the Father, He sent the Holy Spirit to dwell within His people. We today, who are born again into the kingdom of God, receive the gift of the Holy Spirit into our lives. With this precious gift, we can enter into a relationship with the Father that is just as close and intimate a relationship as Moses had with the Father. We simply need to spend time in communication with our Lord.

Communication is a two way street—it requires sharing and talking on our part, and it also requires listening on our part so that we can hear what our Lord is saying to us. He will give us clear direction, and He will give us the information that we need to function in this world. He certainly provided everything that Moses needed. He showed him what was required to lead a very large group of disgruntled people out of Egypt. Whatever your situation today may be, look up; look into the face of your Lord, and receive the direction and strength you need for your life today!

Your Face, Lord, I Will Seek

"When You said, 'Seek My face,' my heart said to You, 'Your face, Lord, I will seek'" (Ps. 27:8).

King David wrote this psalm in which he said that the Lord told him to seek the Lord's face. Do you think the Lord may be expressing His desire to meet with you face to face? I believe He is saying that to you, to me, and to all His children.

What was David's response when the Lord asked him to seek His face? He said that his heart responded by saying, "Your face, Lord, I will seek." Your heart may be responding today as you read this devotional.

Your heart may be crying out to God, wanting to draw closer to Him and wanting to enter into such an intimate relationship that you could actually see Him face to face. Some of you may be thinking, "I could never see God face to face. That is impossible!" Regardless of where you are or what your thoughts are concerning the possibility of seeing God face to face, I challenge you to give it a try. God will never fail you or let you down. If you are willing to meet Him, He is certainly more than willing and waiting with open arms to meet you.

Draw aside to a quiet place where you will be alone, read some Scripture (a psalm or a passage from the book of John), and begin to offer praises to Him. If that seems totally unfamiliar to you, begin to read Psalms 145–150, which are filled with praise. As you offer up praises to Him, think about His goodness, His mercy, His grace, and His love. Close your eyes, worship Him, and let Him reveal Himself to you. No experience on earth can compare with the glorious experience of knowing our Father face to face. Enter into the presence of our heavenly Father today, and you will never be the same again!

Seek His Face Evermore!

"Seek the Lord and His strength; seek His face evermore!" (Ps. 105:4).

We learn through this psalm that we are not to seek God's face just one time, but we are to seek His face evermore. We continually need to deepen our relationship with our Lord. We need desperately to draw closer to Him on a regular basis. He has all the correct answers for every problem, need, and concern in our lives today. He not only has the answers for everything that we face in the future, but He knows already what we will face. We can rest in the assurance that He can prepare us for whatever the future holds for us. We need to put our complete trust in Him today and rely on His great strength, His knowledge, and most of all on His everlasting love.

Sometimes we as human beings feel so low and so weak. But we can know that God is our strength! As we draw closer to Him and as we spend more time face to face with Him, then we are being built up with His strength. He enables us to be strong children of God: not strong in our own strength but strong in His strength. As we draw close to Him and are infused with His strength, He will show us how He can use us in ways we never dreamed. He is able to provide everything we need to be the people of God that He has created us to be. Our part is simply to draw close to Him and let Him fill us with His strength!

Humble Yourselves

"If My people who are called by My name will humble themselves, and pray and seek My face, and turn from their wicked ways, then I will hear from heaven, and will forgive their sin and heal their land" (2 Chron. 7:14).

There is a great deal of information in this scripture for us to understand about seeking the face of God. The first instruction is for us to humble ourselves. Humility is vital to the Christian's life. I have often said, "If pride is the basis of all sin (and I believe it is), then humility is the basis of holiness." So many scriptures point to the importance of walking in humility before God and before others. Matthew 23:12 says, "And whoever exalts himself will be humbled, and he who humbles himself will be exalted."

How do we humble ourselves? Humility comes through putting God first and also by putting others first. We need to consider what the Lord says to us through His Word, through spending time with Him, by listening to Him, and then by being obedient to what He is telling us to do. We also need to consider others' needs and what is important to them. Instead of the "me first" attitude that is so prevalent today, we should care for others in a way that they know that we love them and respect them. When we humble ourselves and seek the face of God, we can expect to be heard and to receive answers to our prayers. Let us seek Him today in humility and receive from Him!

Pray and Seek My Face

"If My people who are called by My name will humble themselves, and pray and seek My face, and turn from their wicked ways, then I will hear from heaven, and will forgive their sin and heal their land" (2 Chron. 7:14).

When we humble ourselves, pray, and seek the face of God, we can know that God hears our prayers. It is imperative in our Christian life that we spend time praying. Jesus spent many hours on the mountain praying to His Father. If He needed to pray in order to complete His purpose on this earth, we certainly need to pray even more to fulfill God's calling upon our lives. We need to pray in such a manner that we grow so close to the Lord that we actually know Him face to face. Sometimes, when I think about the magnitude of an intimate relationship with the God of all the universe, I become overwhelmed that He would actually allow me to know Him face to face. But I have come to know and to experience that truth in my life.

He loves each one of us with such an everlasting love that He not only allows us to know Him face to face, He wants us to know Him face to face. As we spend time in prayer with Him, talking with Him and opening up to Him from our hearts, making requests for our loved ones, friends, and country, listening and hearing from His heart, we will grow so close to Him that we will find that He is our Friend. We will also find that He is our Comforter, Counselor, Strength, and that He is all that we need.

Will you take the time today to humble yourself, pray (opening up from your heart), and seek His face? What joy awaits you as you enter into the throne room to fellowship with God Almighty!

Turn from Your Wicked Ways

"If My people who are called by My name will humble themselves, and pray and seek My face, and turn from their wicked ways, then I will hear from heaven, and will forgive their sin and heal their land" (2 Chron. 7:14).

Now we finally get to the last condition that the Lord gives in this scripture in order that He hear from heaven and heal our land. We must turn from our wicked ways! You may be saying as you read this devotional that you do not have any wicked ways. But we all have some sin that creeps into our lives. One of the sins found most often in Christians' lives is that of omission: the sin of complacency or of not responding to need.

When we look about us today and see the sin and darkness that prevails in the world, we need to be praying for the overcoming light of Jesus to come forth. We also need to put feet to our prayers and begin to seek the Lord about how He would have us as individuals respond to the issues that are so devastating in so many parts of the world. We need to be on our knees, asking the Lord's forgiveness for the sins that are so much a part of our nation. Yes, there is wickedness in our lives, and we need to turn from that wickedness.

As we humble ourselves, pray, and seek the face of God, and turn from our wicked ways, then the Lord will forgive our sin and heal our land. Join with me today and pray, expecting to be heard, asking for forgiveness. Let us be a part of seeing our nation be healed by the hand of Almighty God who is the only one with the answer for what our nation faces today!

Lift Up Your Face to God

"For then you will have your delight in the Almighty, and lift up your face to God" (Job 22:26).

When we seek the face of God, we need to come to Him, delighting ourselves in Him and lifting up our face to Him. What does it mean to lift up your face to the Lord? Have you ever had a small child lift up his face to you, hold out his arms to you, and expect you to pick him up? What a precious moment it is in all of our lives when our child, our grandchild, or a small friend looks at us with that delight and anticipation of being picked up! Picture yourself as that small child, with your face lifted up to God, delightfully anticipating being in His presence face to face. What a joy that is for us, but what is hard to understand is that it is also a joy for Almighty God! He wants to lift you up into His glorious presence! He wants to shower His love and blessings upon you!

Delight in Him today and let Him reveal the greatness of His mercy and the greatness of His love toward you. Receive all that He has to give you today, and your cup will truly overflow. Think of what brings the greatest delight to your heart; and then see if the delight of being in the presence of your Lord, of receiving His love and mercy, and of basking in the glory of His goodness is not greater than anything you have ever experienced before!

Before Your Face Forever

"As for me, You uphold me in my integrity, and set me before Your face forever" (Ps. 41:12).

Do you believe it is possible to be set before the face of God forever? That is what this scripture tells us. Seeking the face of God is not just a one time thing. It is something that we can expect to happen in our lives on a regular basis. When we seek to be face to face with God, our integrity will certainly be upheld. We cannot know God personally, face to face, without walking in integrity. Our whole life will be transformed as we seek Him face to face on a regular basis. We will find habits that have been hard to overcome will begin to diminish. We will find that the tendency to tell a "little" white lie occasionally will suddenly be gone. We will find that we have no desire to gossip as we used to do. We will find that the resentful thoughts that used to be such a part of our everyday lives are no longer plaguing us.

Are you frustrated because you cannot seem to live the Christian life, as you believe you should? Begin to spend more time seeking the face of God, and you will see differences within your life. You cannot be in His presence without being aware of the sin that is in your life, and you cannot be in His presence without transformation happening within your life. Seek Him today with all your heart and see what glorious changes begin to come about within you!

His Face to Shine Upon Us

"God be merciful to us and bless us, and cause His face to shine upon us" (Ps. 67:1).

When Moses had been in the presence of the Lord, his face shone so that he eventually wore a veil. When we seek the Lord face to face, He will cause His face to shine upon us. What does it mean to have the face of God shine upon us? It means that His countenance will be upon us, and when we are in His presence, His very nature becomes a part of us. Transformation takes place in our lives, and the glory of God comes upon us.

When we have been in the presence of the Lord, seeing Him face to face, receiving His glory that shines upon us, we will reflect that glory to others around us. People will begin to notice a difference about us, and they may say something to us such as, "You have a glow about you." They may also remark about us seeming to be different or changed. Being in the presence of the Lord brings about obvious change that others cannot help but notice. When this happens, it is a wonderful opportunity to be a witness of the truth of the gospel. The good news of Jesus Christ is happening in our lives, and we are being changed from glory to glory into His image. Seek Him today and let Him shine His face upon you. Receive His glory!

The Lord Make His Face to Shine Upon You

"The Lord bless you and keep you; the Lord make His face shine upon you, and be gracious to you; the Lord lift up His countenance upon you, and give you peace" (Num. 6:24–26).

*I*f you have been in church most of your life, this scripture is very familiar to you. Sometimes things that we have heard often lose some of their meaning in our lives because of familiarity. I have heard this scripture quoted as a benediction in church most of my life, but it has only been in the past few years that this scripture has taken on real meaning and impacted my life. Because I had been entering into the presence of the Lord, seeking His face, and experiencing Him face to face, suddenly I understood how powerful this scripture could be in my life and yours as well.

If we truly believe that this word from God literally means what it says, we can experience Him shining His face upon us. We can experience Him lifting up His countenance upon us and our lives will be greatly changed. We will become more like Him. We will love as He loves, we will have mercy as He has mercy, and we will exhibit His goodness more and more in our lives. Will you enter into His presence today and let Him shine His face upon you? Let Him lift up His countenance upon you and see the changes that begin to occur in your life!

Then They Will Seek My Face

"I will return again to My place till they acknowledge their offense. Then they will seek My face; in their affliction they will earnestly seek Me" (Hos. 5:15).

When it seems that there is a brick wall between us and God, it could be that there is some offense or some sin in our life that is separating us from Him. There have been times in my life that I have prayed and prayed and seemed to get nowhere. When that happens, I have learned to ask the Lord to reveal any sin in my life so that I can repent. When repentance occurs, then there is restoration of that close communion and fellowship with my Lord.

No sin is worth the separation that occurs in our lives as a result of living a selfish and self-centered life. God is a God of love and mercy, but He is also a God of justice and righteousness. He cannot and will not condone sin, and therefore we need to daily seek forgiveness from sin that may creep into our lives. First John 1:8–9 says, "If we say that we have no sin, we deceive ourselves, and the truth is not in us. If we confess our sins, He is faithful and just to forgive us our sins and to cleanse us from all unrighteousness." All we have to do when we sin is to ask God's forgiveness, then receive His forgiveness, and walk in fellowship with Him once again.

If you are having trouble entering into His presence today, ask Him to reveal any sin in your life. As He shows you, ask His forgiveness and then walk in the sweet fellowship of His presence once again.

Come Boldly to the Throne

"Let us therefore come boldly to the throne of grace, that we may obtain mercy and find grace to help in time of need" (Heb. 4:16).

When we are in need (and really any time), we are told in this verse that we can come boldly to His throne. Does that amaze you that we are told in Scripture that we can come boldly to the throne of God? It amazes me, and yet I know it is true. Scripture is true—it does not lie! This is one of those verses that, although it is definitely true, it is still very difficult to believe. Do you come boldly to the throne of God? We need to let this scripture become real and alive to us so that we will practice what it tells us to do. How do we let this scripture become real to us? We need to read and meditate on this scripture over and over until it is so alive to us that we actually begin to come to the throne of God boldly.

Coming boldly means to come with confidence and assurance. We can come boldly because the Lord has given us assurance and confidence in what He has done for us. He died on the cross to pay for our sins that we might have a close and confident relationship with Father God. We can come confidently because God's throne is a throne of grace rather than judgment. Come boldly to His throne today and fellowship with Him, receiving His grace and His mercy into your life.

Shine Upon Me and Save Me

"Make Your face shine upon Your servant; save me for Your mercies' sake" (Ps. 31:16).

The greatest and most important decision that we can make in this lifetime is to accept Jesus as our Lord and Savior. When we accept Him as our Lord and Savior, He makes His face to shine upon us. Do you remember the joy that you experienced when you were first saved? Salvation brings about a joy and peace that nothing else can equal. When I was born again into the kingdom of God, it was as if light came into the room. It was not a literal light, but it was as if a light came on within me. I experienced the presence of God in such a way that there could be no doubt that Jesus had entered my life.

Every person's experience is unique and different, and your experience will not be like mine. But regardless of any feeling that you may or may not have had at the time of your salvation, His face was shining upon you. There was a change in your countenance because one cannot turn his life over to the Lord without a change coming within and also without. One's expression actually changes as the peace of God begins to permeate his being. More than likely, if you are reading this book, you are a Christian. If you have, however, never accepted Jesus into your life or if you do not have an assurance of salvation in your life, I would like for you to take the opportunity to make that decision today. Ask the Lord of lords and King of kings to come into your heart today and be Lord of your life. Receive His forgiveness, His grace, and begin to walk joyously with Him day by day!

Gladness in My Heart

"Lord, lift up the light of Your countenance upon us. You have put gladness in my heart" (Ps. 4:6b–7a).

When the Lord shines His face upon us, He puts gladness in our hearts. Entering into the presence of God face to face brings such joy into our lives that it is almost impossible to describe it. Joy is overwhelming, and it just seems to bubble up within us. So many scriptures tell us what joy can mean in our lives. Nehemiah 8:10 says, "For the joy of the Lord is your strength." When we have gladness or joy in our hearts, then we become stronger in the Lord. When we go through difficult times and God's joy is in our hearts, it shows that we are trusting in Him. During times of adversity I have often said and I have heard many of my friends say, "I do not see how anyone could go through this without the Lord." Knowing Him intimately and living for Him continuously makes all the difference in our lives.

Having the joy of the Lord during adversity does not seem possible from the world's standards, but as Christians we can certainly experience His joy and share His joy with others. Proverbs 17:22 tells us that "a merry heart doeth good like medicine." In other words, the joy of the Lord brings about such peace and healing in our lives that we are actually physically improved. Today we are hearing reports from doctors about how important a good outlook is in recovering from disease. There are reports of actually seeing the difference prayer and faith in God make in the recovery of those suffering from illness. Prayer, faith, and the joy of the Lord can make a tremendous difference in your life today if you will seek Him with your whole heart.

Teach Me Your Statutes

"Make Your face shine upon Your servant, and teach me Your statutes" (Ps. 119:135).

As we enter into God's presence and He shines His face upon us, we can learn so much from Him. During these times with Him, He can bring enlightenment to us from His Word. Psalm 119:105 says, "Your word is a lamp to my feet and a light to my path."

We receive greater realization of God's direction for our lives when we have more knowledge of God's Word.

Spending time reading and studying His Word on a daily basis is a good discipline for us to have as Christians. I have found in my own experience that there will be days when I enjoy reading and have enlightened understanding of what I am reading. There will be other days when I do not seem to understand anything I am reading, and I really do not want to read. I know, however, the importance of spending time in God's Word, so I keep on reading, expecting God to bring enlightenment. Even if there seems to be no enlightenment that day, I believe His Word is going down in my spirit, and it is being reserved for another day when I will need that particular scripture to help me in my daily life. When I put His Word down in my spirit by reading and meditating on it, it will be there when I need it!

Choose to read and study His Word today in His presence, and let Him teach you. What better teacher could you or anyone else have?

Do Not Fear the Face of God

"The Lord talked with you face to face on the mountain from the midst of the fire. I stood between the Lord and you at that time, to declare to you the word of the Lord; for you were afraid because of the fire, and you did not go up the mountain" (Deut. 5:4–5).

In the passage for today Moses speaks to the Israelites. The Israelites were afraid to face God. God is powerful—more powerful than any of us can possibly imagine! But even in all His power, He is a gentle, loving, and merciful God. He longs to have fellowship with us—the same kind of fellowship that we enjoy having with our children. We should not let fear of God keep us from seeking Him, entering into His presence, and spending time with Him face to face.

Let us be strong and of good courage as Joshua 1:6–9 instruct us. Let us walk with our Lord day by day, face to face, learning from Him and loving Him with our whole heart. Let us look to Moses and David as our examples rather than the Israelite people. A reverent fear of the Lord draws us to Him—it does not keep us away from Him. We should recognize fear that keeps us away from our Lord for what it is and resist it. What we find in the presence of the Lord is good! God is a good God! Draw close to Him today, expecting to receive that which is good and excellent from Him!

Israelites Afraid of God's Presence

"If we hear the voice of the Lord our God anymore, then we shall die . . . You go near and hear all that the Lord our God may say'" (Deut. 5:25b, 27a).

The Israelites wanted Moses to go up on the mountain to hear what God had to say to them because they were afraid of God. We do not have to fear God today—we can go into His presence as a friend just as Moses did. He wants to spend quality time with us and develop a relationship with us so that He can call us friend also.

Is it hard for you to imagine that Almighty God wants you to be His friend? You were created to praise God, to fellowship with Him, and to love Him. He created you for that purpose so that He could fellowship with you, build a relationship with you, and call you His friend.

Look to Him today and let Him know that you want to be His friend. Take the time with Him that you would take if you were developing a friendship with someone that you work with or with one of your neighbors. Spend the time with Him that you would with a golf buddy, a tennis partner, or that very special friend whom you call on the phone every time something important happens or because you are feeling a little lonely. He is a friend who is always there waiting to talk with you. He is never out of town, gone shopping, too busy, or whatever else you might experience with your human friends. He has greater knowledge, is a better counselor, is more loving, and is more than enough to provide all that you need in a friend.

See His Face with Joy

"He shall pray to God, and He will delight in him, he shall see His face with joy, for He restores to man His righteousness" (Job 33:26).

We have seen scriptures that tell us to delight in seeking God face to face, but the verse for today tells us that God delights in us when we pray. When we pray, not only does God delight in us, but He also allows us to see His face. When we see His face, we are filled with immense joy. It can be no other way—there is indescribable joy in the presence of the Lord! Psalm 40:16 says, "Let all those who seek You rejoice and be glad in You; let such as love Your salvation say continually, 'The Lord be magnified!'" The natural response to being in the presence of the Lord is to rejoice and to begin to offer up praises to the King of kings and Lord of lords.

What does it mean to you that the Lord would delight in you? It thrills me to know that He could delight in me. It makes me want to lay down everything else, to seek Him, to spend time with Him, to praise Him, to worship Him, and to fellowship with Him. If we can begin to grasp what it can mean in our lives to develop a closer relationship with our Father God, we would have a much different attitude toward setting aside time to be with Him.

Set aside that time with Him today, and tell Him of your love for Him. Let Him delight in your presence and in your desire to be with Him!

Always Before My Face

"I foresaw the Lord always before my face, for He is at my right hand, that I may not be shaken" (Acts 2:25).

*P*eter quotes David in the scripture for today, and David says that he always saw the Lord before his face. David had such a close and intimate relationship with the Lord that it would seem that he continually walked with the Lord and sought after the Lord. We know that David sinned, so he had times that he did not walk closely with the Lord. But on the whole, he had a very close relationship with the Lord, and we can gain great insight from his experiences.

Even when David sinned, he had no peace until he confessed his sin and began to walk in a right relationship with the Lord again. He says in the scripture for today that the Lord was at his right hand keeping him from being shaken. In other words, he says he can do anything that God wants him to do because the Lord is right there strengthening him, giving him wisdom, providing everything he needs to be successful in accomplishing the will of God. David knew God so well that he knew that if God were not there with him, there was no reason to expect any good thing to happen. He knew his source of strength, and he knew whom to trust in all things. Let David be your example today and seek the Lord with all your heart, knowing that He is the one to look to and to trust in all things.

Fullness of Joy

"You have made known to me the ways of life; You will make me full of joy in Your presence" (Acts 2:28).

*A*fter talking about the Lord always being before his face, David says that the Lord makes him full of joy in His presence. Have you experienced fullness of joy in the presence of the Lord? Fullness of joy brings such a glorious contentment within, knowing that all is well with your soul. Fullness of joy brings such happiness within that you feel as if you cannot keep still or quiet about the goodness and glory of the Lord who has been so gracious to you as to allow you to experience His glorious presence. You feel as if you are being overwhelmed with the grace of God. You begin to identify with David and his psalms that express praises to God over and over. David expresses praises in many ways—exalting the name of the Lord, magnifying Him, and exulting in the glory of being His child.

If you have trouble expressing what you feel in your relationship with the Lord, begin to read some of the psalms that are filled with praise. You will find that David expresses well what you can feel today as you enter into the presence of the Mighty King! Today read Psalm 100 and let that be a beginning of your praise to the Lord. Then as you begin to sense His presence with you, just begin to lift up praises to Him from your heart. Enjoy His presence in your life today!

Do Not Hide Your Face from Me

"Do not hide Your face from me in the day of my trouble; incline Your ear to me; in the day that I call, answer me speedily" (Ps. 102:2).

The psalmist cries out to the Lord as a man who knows that God is his only hope. When we are in trouble, there is nothing on this earth that can come to our aid that can compare to our precious Lord. The psalmist had such a close relationship with the Lord, having experienced His presence and having experienced being face to face with Him, he knew that God and God alone could be his refuge and his strength. The psalmist was a man of prayer—he called out to God. He not only called out to God, but he cried out to God also. He was a man in trouble, and he needed help!

Where do you go when you need help? I have learned over the years that the only place to go is to the Lord. He is the one who listens, He is the one who cares, He is the one who comforts, and He is the only one who has all the answers. He is my rock and my refuge. He is a very present help in time of need.

If you are in trouble today, if you are going through some kind of difficulty, or if you need someone who cares, call upon the One who is always there. Call upon the Lord and give Him the opportunity to provide all that you need.

He Will Not Turn His Face from You

"For if you return to the Lord, your brethren and your children will be treated with compassion by those who lead them captive, so that they may come back to this land; for the Lord your God is gracious and merciful, and will not turn His face from you if you return to Him" (2 Chron. 30:9).

Hezekiah was a godly ruler of Judah. When he began to rule, he brought about important changes that would turn the people back to the Lord. He cleansed the temple and restored worship of the one true God in the temple. He also restored the celebration of Passover with great emphasis on the festivity. In the passage of scripture for today, he encourages the people to return to the Lord. He tells them that, if they return, God will not turn His face from them.

The Lord is always holding out restoration and forgiveness to us. When we are going our own way, involved in our own things, and ignoring the things of God, He is always there waiting for us to return. He wants us to recognize that there is nothing in or on this earth that should be of more importance in our lives than He. He is great and mighty! He is the Rock of all ages! He is King of kings and Lord of lords! If we find that there are things in our lives that have greater priority than He does, then we need to repent, ask His forgiveness, and give Him the place that He deserves in our lives.

Seek Him today, let Him reveal those things that are displeasing to Him, and then turn back to Him. He is waiting to restore you to full relationship with Him, shine His face upon you, and be gracious to you.

Pure in Heart Shall See God

"Blessed are the pure in heart, for they shall see God" (Matt. 5:8).

*H*ave you ever read the scripture for today and thought, "I guess that means I will never see God because my heart certainly is not pure"? "Pure in heart" does not mean that you never do anything wrong or that you never have a wrong thought. It means that you have a heart that desires God. Like David you have a heart that deeply longs for God and continually seeks Him. You and I sin sometimes, but all we have to do is to repent and ask God's forgiveness. He is quick to forgive us when we are sincere.

The pure in heart love God with all their heart and long to be obedient to Him. They yearn for a close relationship with Him. They want to spend quality time with Him, sharing their heart with Him, and letting Him share His heart with them. The pure in heart long to be in the wonderful presence of God and to see Him face to face. They want to grow daily in their walk with Him.

If this sounds like a description of you, then begin praising Him and worshiping Him today. If this does not sound like a description of you, do not despair. You can have a pure heart. Ask God to place within you a hungering and thirsting for more of Him in your life. And then watch for the changes that will begin to occur in your life as you become on fire with a new and fresh love for your Lord!

Stephen Saw Jesus Standing in Heaven

"But he, being full of the Holy Spirit, gazed into heaven and saw the glory of God, and Jesus standing at the right hand of God, and said, 'Look! I see the heavens opened and the Son of Man standing at the right hand of God!' . . . Then he knelt down and cried out with a loud voice, 'Lord, do not charge them with this sin'" (Acts 7:55, 56, 60a).

*W*hen Stephen was being accused, he literally saw Jesus standing at the right hand of Father God. He was so overcome by seeing them in heaven that when the crowd began to stone him, he asked the Lord to forgive them. He was so full of the Spirit of God as he looked into heaven that he had no anger or resentment toward his accusers who were determined to kill him.

When we have an encounter with the Lord where we enter into His presence and see Him, we will find that the resentments, the anger, and all those things that have been within us that are not godly will melt away. We cannot encounter our Lord without a transformation occurring within us. When Stephen told about seeing Jesus standing at the right hand of God, the crowd became enraged with him. Sometimes when we experience intimacy with our Lord and changes occur in our lives, there will be people around us who will not like the changes. That is all right—we must move ahead with God. We cannot sacrifice our relationship with the Lord in order to please others.

Look up into heaven today and see your Lord. Let Him draw you into a place of sweet communion with Him where you will meet Him face to face. Then watch as transformation begins to occur within your life!

My Eyes Have Seen the King

"Woe is me, for I am undone! Because I am a man of unclean lips, and I dwell in the midst of a people of unclean lips; for my eyes have seen the King, the Lord of hosts" (Isa. 6:5).

Isaiah had an overwhelming vision and saw the wondrous glory of the Lord. When he came into the presence of the Lord, his first response was repentance for anything that was ungodly in his life. He not only repented for his own sin, but he repented for the sins of his people.

I encourage you to read the entirety of Isaiah 6. You will find that as soon as Isaiah began to repent, cleansing from the Lord occurred. When we repent of our sins, the Lord is faithful and just—He immediately forgives. After the cleansing occurred, the Lord said, "Whom shall I send, and who will go for Us?" The result of being in the presence of the Lord is for us to move out and fulfill His purpose in our lives. Isaiah immediately responded, "Here am I! Send me."

First we seek the Lord with all our heart, and we enter into His presence. When we see Him, we repent of our sins and receive His forgiveness. Our lives are changed! Once we receive His cleansing, we are ready and willing to fulfill His purpose for us. We want to be obedient to Him!

Seek Him today and begin to experience the wonder of being in His presence. See what changes will be brought about in your heart, and then be ready to walk in the joy of fulfilling His purpose in your life!

I Will See Your Face

"As for me, I will see Your face in righteousness; I shall be satisfied when I awake in Your likeness" (Ps. 17:15).

In the psalm for today David prays to the Lord. We have learned, as we have looked at other psalms and also as he is quoted in Acts, that David continually sought the Lord and sought being in His presence.

He knew the indescribable joy and peace that came from seeking the Lord. In this particular psalm David seems to say that no matter what happens on this earth and no matter what situation he finds himself in, when he awakes (or when he comes face to face with Him after death), He will see the Lord in righteousness.

David knew that he was righteous—not because he lived a perfect life because he did not! He knew he was righteous because he trusted in his Savior—the Messiah who was to come.

We can come into the presence of the Lord often, and that is what He wants for us. But even if we never experience seeing Him face to face while we live on this earth, we have assurance that when our life is over we will meet Him face to face. That is the joy and promise of salvation—spending eternity with our Father in heaven.

If you have never accepted Jesus Christ as your Lord and Savior, make that decision today. Accept Him into your heart and have the assurance of spending eternity with Him. Life with Him is pure joy! Do not wait another day or another minute, but let Him show you the joy of belonging to Him!

But Then Face to Face

"For now we see in a mirror, dimly, but then face to face. Now I know in part, but then I shall know just as I also am known" (1 Cor. 13:12).

As often as we enter into the presence of the Lord and actually see Him face to face, we will never come to the place that we have full understanding. Each time we have an encounter with Him, we will grow in our walk with Him. We will become more like Him. We will grow in our love for others and our outreach to them. Each time we are with Him, we are being transformed, and our lives will never be the same. And yet, there is always more of Him to experience and more of Him to be revealed to us. The only time that our understanding will be full is when we meet Him face to face in heaven. Then we will see clearly and understand fully. Until then we can look forward to continually growing and learning and experiencing more and more of Him each day.

There is such excitement in this Christian walk! There are new things to learn each day, and there are new things to experience each day. We never know, when we wake up each day, what great joys and what opportunities to learn and grow await us. We need to wake up with a prayer on our lips that says, "Lord, I give You this day. I look forward to what You will reveal to me and teach me during this day. Help me to be sensitive to Your Holy Spirit at work in my life, and may I bring glory to You throughout this day." Let that be your prayer today, and watch and see what happens as you allow Him first place in your life!

His Name Shall Be on Their Foreheads

"They shall see His face, and His name shall be on their foreheads" (Rev. 22:4).

When that day comes in heaven, and there is a new Jerusalem, we shall see the Lord face to face. Our fellowship with Him will be perfect, and we will know and understand perfectly. He tells us in Revelation that His name will be on our foreheads. Have you ever wondered what that means? Why would He put His name on our foreheads? I believe that He will put His name on our foreheads to show that we belong to Him. It is a means of identification, and He identifies us as His own. I believe that it also shows that our character and nature have been changed to be a reflection of Him and all that He is and represents.

As we draw closer to Him, study His Word, pray, and spend time in fellowship with Him, we are being changed from glory to glory into His image. When we see Him face to face in heaven, that transformation will be complete, and we will truly reflect His character and nature. We are His own, and His name on our foreheads reveals this to all.

Let me encourage you today to draw closer to the One who can change you from glory to glory. Let me encourage you today to seek the One who will one day write His glorious and wondrous name on your forehead. Let me encourage you today to enter into the presence of the One who can shine His light forth from you now on this earth so that you will be a reflection of Him to those who are hurting and need to know Him.

Abide in Me

"Abide in Me, and I in you. As the branch cannot bear fruit of itself, unless it abides in the vine, neither can you, unless you abide in Me" (John 15:4).

Jesus tells us here that we are to abide in Him, and He will abide in us. What does that mean? How is that possible? When we seek Him through His Word and through spending time in fellowship and communion with Him, we abide in Him. Being obedient to His Word and to His direction for our lives is also abiding in Him. He abides in us through the Holy Spirit. When He ascended into heaven to sit at the right hand of Father God, He sent the Holy Spirit to reside in us. When we accept Jesus as our Lord and Savior, the Holy Spirit comes to dwell within us.

We can open up our hearts to allow the Holy Spirit to rule and reign in our lives, or we can quench the Spirit of God by living as we please and by ignoring His guidance. First Thessalonians 5:19 says, "Do not quench the Spirit." The Holy Spirit was sent to bring comfort, counsel, peace, direction, the power of God, and much more into our lives. He avails Himself to us in order for God's purpose to be fulfilled in our lives. God's purpose is for fruit to come forth and many to be born into the kingdom of God.

Avail yourself to Him today and allow His Spirit to bring forth fruit for the kingdom of God. Seek Him and let Him show you how He chooses to use you to bring forth His light into the world around you today!

Without Me You Can Do Nothing

"I am the vine, you are the branches. He who abides in Me, and I in him, bears much fruit; for without Me you can do nothing" (John 15:5).

One of the ways we can check ourselves to see if we are abiding in Christ is to see if we are bearing fruit for His Kingdom. If we spend time with Him, both in His Word and fellowshiping with Him, then we will see fruit in our lives. You may ask, "What is fruit? How can I recognize fruit in my life?" Galatians 5:22–23 tells us what fruit should be in our lives. It says, "But the fruit of the Spirit is love, joy, peace, longsuffering, kindness, goodness, faithfulness, gentleness, self-control." When the fruit of the Spirit is in evidence in our lives, then we will bear fruit for the kingdom of God. The fruit of the Spirit is not something that we can make happen in our lives. It is not something that we simply will to happen in our lives, but it is something that occurs more and more as we spend that precious time fellowshiping with our Lord and Savior. It happens more and more as we spend time in God's Word reading, studying, and putting into practice what we learn through His Word.

Let me encourage you to go before the Lord of lords and King of kings today and seek Him with all of your heart. Be open to what He may show you through His Word or through simply giving you a desire or inclination that would be in line with His Word. As He shows you direction, make that decision to follow through in obedience to Him. You will see that not only will you bear fruit in your life, but more than likely there will be fruit born for the kingdom of God.

Ask What You Desire

"If you abide in Me, and My words abide in you, you will ask what you desire, and it shall be done for you" (John 15:7).

Do you want to see answers to you prayers? There is a way! All you have to do is to abide in Jesus and let His Words abide in you, and then whatever you ask for will be done for you. Now that is not a "quickie" answer, but that takes a commitment on your part. It means spending time with Jesus day by day, developing a close relationship with Him. Abiding happens over a period of time. Abide means to continue in a place, to stay, or to remain. When you have been in the presence of the Lord, committed to Him, staying in His Word, and putting His Word into practice in your life, then you may ask what you desire and you will receive it.

Applying His Word and being in His presence bring such changes in our lives that we find that our desires change to be like His desires. No longer will we ask for frivolous or selfish things, but we will want only what is pleasing to our Father in heaven.

If abiding in Him is a new idea to you, begin the process today. If you have been walking in the way of abiding in Him, continue in your walk with Him today.

Draw close and let Him show you the glories of knowing Him better, and let Him change your desires to be His desires. Ask of Him and receive the answers for which you have been waiting!

Abide in My Love

"As the Father loved Me, I also have loved you; abide in My love" (John 15:9).

Can you imagine what it means to abide in the love of God? God is love. He is everything that love is! We can abide in the same love with which God loved Jesus! Sometimes it is hard for us to comprehend how much God loves us, but we do not have any problem understanding that the Father loves His Son. We can relate to the love of a father for his son. Jesus tells us that, just as His Father loves Him, He loves us. He also tells us to abide in His love. How do we abide in His love? When we read about the love of God in Scripture, it becomes more real to us. He brings His love alive to our spirits as we read, meditate on, and study His love. When we spend time in His presence, we become more aware of His love. As we draw close to Him and bask in His presence, His love becomes alive to us. As He shines His face upon us, we cannot help but know that Almighty God loves us!

What joy there is in experiencing the love of our Savior! Enter into His presence today, and let Him express to you the great love that comes from the throne of heaven right down to earth to be with you and to abide within you! Let Him shower His love within you, and then you will be a shining example of God's love to those around you.

Keep My Commandments

"If you keep My commandments, you will abide in My love, just as I have kept My Father's commandments and abide in His love" (John 15:10).

An evidence of our love for the Father is keeping His commandments. First John 2:5 says, "But whoever keeps His word, truly the love of God is perfected in him." This means that when we keep His Word, we have reached a place of maturity in living His Word in this world. How difficult is it to keep our Father's commandments? If we are in fellowship with Him, reading His Word, and studying His Word, then walking in obedience to His Word is not as difficult as it would be if we were not doing those things.

It is very difficult to be obedient to something if that something is not kept before you on a regular basis. If you have a daily exercise routine, you will find that it is simply something you plan to do. But, if you have not developed that habit of exercising, then you may think to do it and you may not think to do it. Spending time with the Lord and in His Word on a daily basis is a discipline that you need to develop. It is something that you choose to do. You have to decide daily to sit down with God's Word and read it. You need to choose to be obedient to His Word once you have read it. Life is full of choices, and the choices you make can affect the kind of relationship you have with Almighty God.

If you are wanting to express your love for the Father today, pick up your Bible and read it. Ask the Father to show you what He wants you to know and understand today. Choose to walk in obedience to what He shows you through His Word. Let your life be an expression of love to your heavenly Father!

May Your Joy Be Full

"These things I have spoken to you that My joy may remain in you, and that your joy may be full" (John 15:11).

Do you want joy to be strong in your life? There is a way! Jesus teaches us to abide in Him. He says in the previous verse that we must keep His commandments to abide in His love. He shares with us an enlightening key to experiencing joy in our lives—not only experiencing joy, but joy in abundance! If you truly want joy in your life, all you have to do is to be obedient to God's Word. When you obey His Word, you abide in His love, and that brings joy into your life. Joy is a fruit of the Spirit, which is listed in Galatians 5:22. Words cannot describe the peace that will come into your life when joy is in evidence in your life. This joy that you experience is the same joy that dwells within the heart of God. He gives you His joy, which exceeds the gladness or happiness that the world may know.

As you draw close to your Father, letting His Word dwell richly within you, and walking in obedience to His instructions in the Bible, you will begin to know the joy of the Lord in greater measure. Let Him know today of your desire to be obedient to Him and experience His joy as He floods you with His presence!

Being One in Us

"That they all may be one, as You, Father, are in Me and I in You; that they also may be one in Us, that the world may believe that You sent Me" (John 17:21).

*B*eing one with the Father and Jesus Christ is a hard concept for us to understand. We look at ourselves and our hearts, and we know the kind of people that we are. To think that Almighty God could want us to be one with Him seems impossible; however, He looks at us through the redemptive power of Jesus' sacrifice on the cross. He looks at us through the righteousness of Jesus and His life that He led on this earth. We can never live up to the righteousness of Jesus Christ, and we certainly do not deserve to be one with God; however, because of His great love for us, He has made a way for us to know Him intimately and to be one with Him.

Oneness with the Father means that we are being changed into His likeness and into His character. We take on His nature, and the way we live begins to look like Him. Our decisions, unlike those made in the past, are godly choices.

Look unto Him today, draw close to Him, seek Him with all your heart, meet Him face to face, and know the wonder of being one with Him!

That the World May Know

"I in them, and You in Me; that they may be made perfect in one, and that the world may know that You have
sent Me, and have loved them as You have loved Me"
(John 17:23).

When we are one with God, then the world will see the
change that is in us. Those within the world will know
that there is something different about us. We cannot be one
with God without His nature becoming a part of our nature.
This becomes evident to the people that we encounter daily,
and they will begin to see changes within us. They will notice the way we respond to anger, hurt, and all the things
that happen within this world. Our response will not be as it
used to be but will reflect the nature of God—His grace,
mercy, forgiveness, and love.

The world is hungry for a Savior, and we can be light to
those around us as we express the blessing of receiving the
Savior Jesus Christ into our lives. I believe the world today is
in a very grave place, and there is nothing within this world
that can save it; however, we serve a God of power and might!
He is able to do all things well! Nothing is too difficult for
Him. There is a Savior for this world, and His name is Jesus.

Do you want to be a part of sharing the good news of
salvation for this world? Let the light of Jesus Christ shine
forth from your life. Draw so close to Him that your life will
be changed as you see Him face to face. Let that change radiate from you as you go through your daily life reaching out to
those who are hurting and in need.

Beholding His Glory

"Father, I desire that they also whom You gave Me may be with Me where I am, that they may behold My glory which You have given Me; for You loved Me before the foundation of the world" (John 17:24).

Jesus asked His Father that we may be where He is, beholding His glory. He wants us to dwell with Him or to be one with Him. When we are one with Him, we see Him in all His glory. As we draw close to Him, seeking Him, and entering into His presence face to face, we will truly know Him in all His glory. We will be able to say as Isaiah said, "I saw the Lord sitting on a throne, high and lifted up, and the train of His robe filled the temple."

Our lives will never be the same again after we behold the Lord Jesus Christ face to face in all His glory. We will want to spend as much time with Him as we possibly can. As we spend time with Him, His heart's desire becomes our heart's desire. We begin to see others as He sees them, and we begin to love others as He loves them. We see the need to reach out to others in ways that will bring an answer to many of their needs.

Seeing the Lord in all His glory is not something that just brings "goosebumps" into our lives. It brings love and compassion for others into our lives. It also brings about the wisdom to know how to reach out to others and meet their needs in a way that will be lasting. We will know how to meet their physical and spiritual needs, and we will have new courage and boldness to share the good news of Jesus.

Draw close today and behold the glory of Jesus Christ. Let His glory shine forth upon you and within you in such a way that you become a light to those around you!

His Love May Be in Us

"And I have declared to them Your name, and will declare it, that the love with which You loved Me may be in them, and I in them" (John 17:26).

*H*ave you ever stopped to think about the scope of God's love? When we read about His love in Scripture, it goes beyond anything that we can comprehend and understand. And yet in John 17 we are told that His love may be in us! When Jesus says that He declares the name of the Father to us so that His love will dwell within us, He reveals to us the nature of God—goodness, kindness, love, joy, peace, strength, power, forgiveness, mercy, and grace. God cannot go against what He represents for He is absolutely honest, true, and of the utmost integrity. Jesus came to reveal the nature of Father God to us so that we could begin to understand the magnitude of His love for us.

When we look at Jesus' sacrifice on the cross, we see God's love with a new respect. He allowed His Son to suffer shame, pain, anguish, and death in order to restore man to Himself. But that was only the beginning because Jesus rose from the dead, ascended to heaven, and sits at the right hand of Father God. That unconditional and sacrificial love of God dwells within you and me as believers in Jesus Christ. As we draw close to Him daily, His love will shine brighter and brighter from us. Let Him use you today.

Filled with All the Fullness of God

"That Christ may dwell in your hearts through faith; that you, being rooted and grounded in love, may be able to comprehend with all the saints what is the width and length and depth and height—to know the love of Christ which passes knowledge; that you may be filled with all the fullness of God" (Eph. 3:17–19).

When Christ dwells in our hearts and we are one with Him, we begin to have greater understanding of the love of God. As we look up into the face of our heavenly Father, we see Him in all His glory. He begins to reveal the greatness of His nature to us, and His nature is love! We are told in Scripture that God is love, and we can be assured that He wants us to dwell close to Him and bask in the wonder of His love. As we seek Him in all His fullness and understand the depth of His love, we are filled up with His fullness.

What does it mean to be filled up with the fullness of God? It means that His nature is growing within us. Day by day, as we spend precious time with Him, we see changes in our response to people. We find ourselves showing the love of Jesus in situations where before we would have been angry, resentful, or unforgiving.

Make your way into the dwelling place of Jesus today and seek Him with a heart that is full of gratitude for all that He has done for you. Seek Him, expecting to receive His wondrous love into your life with fullness so that you can share His love with others!

You Are the Temple of the Living God

"For you are the temple of the living God. As God has said: 'I will dwell in them and walk among them. I will be their God, and they shall be My people'" (2 Cor. 6:16).

*I*s it hard for you to think of yourself as the temple of the living God? How can that be? Does He not dwell in the churches, cathedrals, temples, and sanctuaries built by men? No! He dwells in you and me as believers in Jesus Christ!

When Jesus ascended into heaven to sit at the right hand of Father God, He sent the Holy Spirit to dwell within us. When I was born again into the kingdom of God, I realized that the Holy Spirit was the presence of Jesus with me. Have you come to this realization?

When Jesus walked this earth, He was limited to space and time just as we are; but when He ascended into heaven, He sent His Spirit, who is not limited to time and space, to indwell us. His intent is to use us as His hands and feet on this earth to accomplish His will and purpose. In John 14:12, Jesus tells us that whoever believes in Him will do the works that He does and greater works will he do.

He wants to use you and me to fulfill His perfect will on this earth. He wants to use us to do the works that He did. All that we have to do is believe that He wants to use us, and He will use us. His Spirit resides within us and waits for us to allow Him the freedom to work through us and fulfill the will of the Father.

Will you allow Him that place in your life today? Will you acknowledge that you are the temple of the living God, and that He wants to make Himself known to you and through you? Let Him know that you delight to be His dwelling place!

The Spirit of God Dwells in You

"Do you not know that you are the temple of God and that the Spirit of God dwells in you?" (1 Cor. 3:16).

Even though we are not worthy and have done nothing to deserve it, God Almighty has sent His Spirit to dwell within us and calls us His temple. This is a wonderful gift that He holds out to us, and the way that we receive it is to receive Jesus Christ as our Lord and Savior.

What is a temple? It is a holy dwelling place of God. Do you feel as if you qualify to be called a temple of God? Obviously we do not and can not qualify, except through the blood of Jesus; however, God has chosen us to be His dwelling place. This means that He actually resides within us. He knows us, walks with us, talks with us, and calls us His friend.

His Spirit enables us to be what we never thought we could be. He enables us to have strength to overcome difficult situations. He also gives us the encouragement that we need to carry on when we want to give up. He provides the direction that we need to make hard decisions, and He comforts us when we have been greatly hurt. He wants to help us, but He also wants to fellowship with us. He dwells within us because He longs to spend time with and communicate with us.

Will you reach out to Him today and let Him know of your love for Him? He is waiting for you with open arms!

The Temple of God Is Holy

"If anyone defiles the temple of God, God will destroy him. For the temple of God is holy, which temple you are" (1 Cor. 3:17).

When you read this scripture, do you feel as if you need to do something to become more holy so that you can be the temple of God? I believe that is the way we often think, but that is not accurate according to Scripture. We can do nothing to become holy because our holiness comes through the blood of Jesus. Second Corinthians 5:21 says, "For He made Him who knew no sin to be sin for us, that we might become the righteousness of God in Him."

God has chosen to call us His temple and to dwell within us through His Spirit, but we can defile His temple. In what ways can we defile the temple of God? We can defile His temple by allowing sin to be a part of our life. We all sin from time to time and have to repent and ask for forgiveness; however, when sin becomes a habit in our lives, then we defile His temple. Sometimes these sins have a hold on our lives, and even though we want to quit them, it seems that we cannot. We need the power of the Holy Spirit to break through the bondage and be set free.

If you are experiencing an ongoing habit that is sin in your life and want to be free, ask the One who came to set the captives free to come to your rescue so that you will not defile the temple of God. He is willing and able to help you overcome anything in your life that is not of Him. Isaiah 61:1 says, "The Spirit of the Lord God is upon Me, . . . to proclaim liberty to the captives . . ." Trust in the overcoming power of Almighty God today to set you free!

Christ in You

"To them [the saints] God willed to make known what are the riches of the glory of this mystery among the Gentiles: which is Christ in you, the hope of glory" (Col. 1:27).

Paul, in his letter to the Colossians, reveals a mystery, which is the fact that Christ dwells in us. Christ dwells in us through the power and work of the Holy Spirit. If you have ever experienced the work of the Holy Spirit in your life, helping you to accomplish something you know you can not do on your own, you understand this mystery. If you have never had this experience, you can.

I will never forget the first time I was asked to speak before my church of about six hundred people. One of my greatest weaknesses and fears had been speaking before a group of people. I prayed and prayed the weeks preceding this occasion. The night before I was to speak I was so nervous and scared that I was actually sick. The next morning, as I was waiting for the moment I was to get behind the podium to speak, I was a wreck; however, the minute I got up to speak and opened my mouth, the peace of God came over me. All fear was gone. I knew that the Holy Spirit had intervened and helped me accomplish the Father's will in a situation where I was extremely weak.

"Christ in you, the hope of glory" means that Jesus through the Holy Spirit has come to dwell within you and will accomplish His will in this world through you and me as we yield to Him. He wants to bring His hope into the lives of people around us by shining His light and accomplishing His works through us. Will you allow Jesus the right to use you today? If so, ask Him to shine His light brightly through you and to let His Spirit bring hope to those close to you.

117

He Will Give You Another Helper

"And I will pray the Father, and He will give you another Helper, that He may abide with you forever" (John 14:16).

Jesus prepared His disciples for His death and resurrection, and He told them that He wasn't leaving them alone or helpless. He shared with them about the Holy Spirit who will be given to them on the day of Pentecost. He called the Holy Spirit the Helper. Another translation for the Greek word parakletos is Comforter. These names for the Holy Spirit give us some understanding of the purpose of the Holy Spirit.

He is called alongside us to help us in all things, and He also brings comfort into our lives when we are in need. A few of the other purposes of the Holy Spirit that are found in Scripture are: to teach, to guide, to anoint, and to give. Truth, promises, grace, holiness, and gifts are some of the things that He has given.

In this particular scripture He is referred to as the Helper. Do you feel as if you need help today? The One who has all the help you could possibly need is available to you now. Not only is He available to you, but He dwells in you. He waits for you to ask Him to provide the help you need in your situation. Jesus did not leave us a Helper for us to ignore Him, but He wants us to avail ourselves of the help that He has provided for us.

Draw close to the Lord today and ask Him to provide for your needs. He is waiting for you to ask. James 4:2 says, "Yet you do not have because you do not ask."

The Spirit of Truth

"The Spirit of truth, whom the world cannot receive, because it neither sees Him nor knows Him; but you know Him, for He dwells with you and will be in you" (John 14:17).

*J*esus told His disciples that when the Helper comes who is also called the Spirit of truth, that the world will not receive Him. We, as Christians, know the Spirit of truth because He dwells within us. Do you sometimes have trouble understanding what is truth and what is not?

In today's world someone will say one thing, and someone else will say just the opposite. They both claim to tell the truth. How do we know the difference? How do we know what is truly correct? As we study Scripture and rely on the Spirit of truth who dwells within us, we will know the truth.

One of the reasons that our Helper has been sent to be with us and live within us is to give us discernment for knowing what is true. We will grow in our ability to understand and to discern what the Spirit of truth is showing us as we spend more time in the presence of our Lord and Savior.

We need to become more sensitive to the leading of the Holy Spirit in our lives. So often in the church world today, we see Christians who have accepted Jesus as Savior but have little understanding of the Holy Spirit who was sent to be His presence in our lives today. Draw close to the Lord today and ask Him to teach you about the Holy Spirit. Ask Him to help you to be sensitive to the leading of the Holy Spirit in your life so that you can "do all things through Christ who strengthens you." We are admonished over and over in the New Testament to walk in the Spirit, to live by the Spirit, and to be led by the Spirit. Let the Spirit of truth be your guide today and every day.

I Will Manifest Myself to Him

"At that day you will know that I am in My Father, and you in Me, and I in you. He who has My commandments and keeps them, it is he who loves Me. And he who loves Me will be loved by My Father, and I will love him and manifest Myself to him" (John 14:20–21).

Jesus assured the disciples that, although He will be cruci-fied, He will live and be with them. In verse 18, He says, "I will not leave you orphans; I will come to you." He tells them that He will come through the Holy Spirit to them. He says that He will manifest Himself to them. Manifest means that He will appear, come to view, or present Himself to the sight of another.

I believe Jesus says to the disciples, and also to you and me today, that He will not only send the Holy Spirit to dwell within us and to be one with us, but He will also reveal Him-self to us in a visible way.

You may be thinking, "What is she talking about?" I be-lieve that one of the ways Jesus makes Himself known to us is by allowing us to see Himself. As we have our quiet time with Him, drawing close to Him, and fellowshiping with Him, we can experience that face to face relationship with Him.

That does not mean that the Lord is literally standing face to face before us. It does mean that, through the eye of our spirit, we can see Him face to face when we are in prayer and in close communion with Him.

Enter into His presence today and seek Him face to face. Let Him manifest Himself to you and experience that one-ness with Him.

In the Spirit

"But you are not in the flesh but in the Spirit, if indeed the Spirit of God dwells in you. Now if anyone does not have the Spirit of Christ, he is not His" (Rom. 8:9).

In Romans, Paul teaches about living according to the Spirit of God. He says that if we have been born again into the kingdom of God, we have His Spirit residing within us. We can choose daily, moment by moment, to walk according to the flesh (what our carnal self desires and wants), or according to the Spirit. He exhorts the Christians in Rome that they are not in the flesh but in the Spirit.

Since His Spirit dwells in believers, we have the potential to walk and live in the Spirit. Life in the Spirit brings victory, peace, confidence, and all good things. Living by the Spirit rather than the flesh allows us to walk in the holiness that was made available to us by the cross of Jesus.

When the Spirit of God comes to dwell in us, a whole new world opens up to us—a spiritual world that cannot be seen by physical eyes but is visible through the eye of our spirits. When we live in eternity in heaven, we will clearly understand the spiritual realm. As long as we are on this earth, we will see and understand the spiritual realm only dimly. First Corinthians 13:12 says, "For now we see in a mirror, dimly, but then face to face. Now I know in part, but then I shall know just as I also am known." We consider what we can see, touch, hear, smell or taste to be reality; however, God's reality is true reality, and His reality is the world in which He lives. He lives in the spiritual realm, and that is the reality that will last throughout eternity.

Choose today to walk according to the Spirit of God. Ask Him to guide you into all truth.

The Spirit Is Life

"And if Christ is in you, the body is dead because of sin, but the Spirit is life because of righteousness" (Rom. 8:10).

The Spirit of God is life! Do you realize what kind of life Paul is talking about? He uses the Greek word zoe, the life of God. When the Holy Spirit dwells within us, the life of God dwells within us! The next verse in Romans 8 says, "But if the Spirit of Him who raised Jesus from the dead dwells in you, He who raised Christ from the dead will also give life to your mortal bodies through His Spirit who dwells in you." Can you imagine that the very life of God dwells within you and gives life to your mortal body? The same life that raised Jesus from the dead dwells in you through the Holy Spirit.

What should that mean to you and me? It means that we have so much to learn about what the Lord holds out to us as believers. When He said, "Greater works shall they do," He really meant that you and I would be able to do what He did when He walked on this earth. We cannot do His works in our own power or strength, but we can do His works because the Spirit of God dwells within us. His life dwells within us, enabling us to be the hands and feet of Jesus extended on earth.

Do you want to be a part of furthering the kingdom of God on this earth? He waits for you to say, "Yes, Lord, use me." Look up today into the face of Jesus and tell Him that you want to be used by Him to share His life with those around you. Then stand back in amazement as you watch the wondrous things that He will perform through you!

More Than Conquerors

"Who shall separate us from the love of Christ? Shall tribulation, or distress, or persecution, or famine, or nakedness, or peril, or sword? . . . Yet in all these things we are more than conquerors through Him who loved us" (Rom. 8:35, 37).

What does it mean to be more than a conqueror? We know that a conqueror is someone who experiences victory. When we go back to the original Greek word that is translated "more than," we find it can also be translated "over and above." More than a conqueror gives the connotation of gaining victory, but also gaining more than victory. How can you gain more than victory?

I believe what the Lord says to us here is that what He holds out to us is so powerful and so wonderful that, even after we gain victory, the blessings we receive are so great that it goes beyond what we can imagine. Ephesians 3:20 says, "Now to Him who is able to do exceedingly abundantly above all that we ask or think, according to the power that works in us."

If you are going through a difficult time, distress, persecution, or tribulation, know that the Alpha and Omega, the Great I Am, the King of kings, and the Lord of lords has told you that you will be more than a conqueror. He tells you that He will do for you exceedingly, abundantly above all that you can ask or think. He dwells within you, and His life is available to you. There is nothing, absolutely nothing, that is too difficult for our Lord. Look to Him today and trust Him to work all things for your good (even better than you could ever think or imagine). What a God we serve!

Unity with One Another

"So we, being many, are one body in Christ, and individually members of one another" (Rom. 12:5).

When we are one with the Lord, we are also one with other believers. As believers in Jesus Christ, we are one body. Scripture refers to the church in several places as the body of Christ. He is the head, and we are the parts or members of the body. If one part of the body is hurt or wounded, it affects the whole body. For example, if I injure my right hand, my whole body is affected. I cannot function normally, and I will need to compensate for the injured hand. If one of our fellow believers is hurt or wounded, we need to treat him as we would want to be treated ourselves. Just as we are one with Christ Jesus, we should have the same oneness or unity with our sisters and brothers in Christ.

First John 4:20 says, "If someone says, 'I love God,' and hates his brother, he is a liar; for he who does not love his brother whom he has seen, how can he love God whom he has not seen?" As we grow in our understanding of the love of God, we cannot help but express love to our sisters and brothers in Christ. The scope of God's love is so immense that it reaches out to cover the sins or weaknesses of others. God's love is unconditional, and we learn more about His unconditional love as we seek Him and receive His love for us.

Seek Him today and let Him shower you with His love in such a way that you become more aware of the need to spread His love among those around you.

Put on the Lord Jesus Christ

"But put on the Lord Jesus Christ, and make no provision for the flesh, to fulfill its lusts" (Rom. 13:14).

If we want to be one with the Lord, we need to put on the Lord Jesus Christ. How do we put on someone? How do we put on someone we cannot even see? I believe Paul tells us that we need to be in close communion or fellowship with Jesus. We need to acknowledge the lordship of Jesus Christ in our life and put our total trust in Him to be our strength. Putting on the Lord Jesus Christ means that we are so close to Him that it is hard to tell who is who. In other words, we take on His nature, and we begin to exhibit His qualities. We act as He would act in the different situations that come up in our lives. He is our life!

Acts 17:28 says, "For in Him we live and move and have our being." Picture yourself putting on a coat. Now as you move about—going out the door, getting in your car, getting out of your car, and going into a building—what is happening to your coat? Your coat is moving with you and doing exactly what you are doing. When we put on Jesus, we will act as He does because He will not be a part of us if we do something contrary to Him. That takes decisions and choices on our part. We must make decisions and choices to live, move, and have our being according to the ways of Jesus!

Make the decision to put on the Lord Jesus Christ today. Live for Him and act as He would as you go about your daily business. Let Him be your strength to be able to act as He would act. It seems so hard at times, but it really is very simple. All we need to do is to let Jesus be Himself through us. Will you let Him have His way in your life?

Through Him We Live

"Yet for us there is one God, the Father, of whom are all things, and we for Him; and one Lord Jesus Christ, through whom are all things, and through whom we live" (1 Cor. 8:6).

We live through the Lord Jesus Christ! He is in us, and we are in Him! When we are in such close communion and fellowship with Him that we are one, we will live as He lives. His ways will become our ways. We will begin to think as He thinks, and we will begin to speak as He speaks. When we find ourselves saying things that sound like Him and His Word, we can know that He is living through us. He is truly having an impact on our lives.

The Christian walk is a process. We grow in our love and knowledge of Jesus, and we grow in our understanding of His Word. We also grow in our fellowship and closeness with Him. As we spend more time with Him, either in fellowship or in studying His Word, the process of growing as a Christian becomes stronger and stronger. If our heart's desire is to walk in close fellowship with the Lord and for our life to be an example of His love and nature, then daily we will need to decide to spend time with Him. We will need to look at our priorities and see if He has that number one spot.

Are you living through Jesus Christ daily? If you are not, all you have to do is to ask Him to be your strength. Ask Him to help you to get your priorities in the right order. He will help you if you will simply take the first step and seek Him with a sincere heart. Let Him know that you want Him first place in your life and that you want Him to live through you and you through Him!

Christ Lives in Me

"I have been crucified with Christ; it is no longer I who live, but Christ lives in me; and the life which I now live in the flesh I live by faith in the Son of God, who loved me and gave Himself for me" (Gal. 2:20).

Jesus says in Matthew 16:24, "If anyone desires to come after Me, let him deny himself, and take up his cross, and follow Me." He tells His disciples, then and now, that just as He went to the cross to die for our sins, we need to take up our cross and die to self. We need to allow Jesus full reign in our lives so that His ways will become our ways.

We talk so often about Jesus being Lord of our lives, but what does that really mean? It means that we seek His guidance in every aspect of our lives. It means that we put aside our desires and our wants and seek His will for our lives. When Jesus tells us to take up our cross, that can mean only one thing—something must die. That something is our will! His will for our lives is far greater than anything that we could ever desire for ourselves.

It is very difficult for us as human beings to give up control of our lives, but that is exactly what Paul tells us to do in this verse. Jesus gave his life for us, paid the price for our sins, and made it possible for us to spend eternity with our Father in heaven. In return, He asks us to give our lives over to Him so that it will not be us who lives—it will be Christ who lives through us.

Will you give Him your life today? You will never regret it because you will find the great joy and peace that only comes through submitting to the Lordship of Jesus Christ.

God Abides in Us

"No one has seen God at any time. If we love one another, God abides in us, and His love has been perfected
in us" (1 John 4:12).

One of the ways that we can know that God abides in us
is to examine the love that we have for others. Do I love
with the love of Jesus? Do I express compassion to those in
need? His love is growing within us as we walk in the process
of sanctification.

Sanctification means being separated from sin, being set
apart for God's purpose, and being purified. When we accept
Jesus as Savior, we receive eternal life, and the process of
sanctification begins. We make decisions, however, that will
determine how close we become to our Lord and how quickly
we will mature.

The Spirit of God comes to dwell within us the moment
we accept Jesus as Savior; however, we can open our lives to
the Spirit of God as much or as little as we choose. Again it
boils down to choices. The decisions that we make daily are
vitally important. We can choose to love, or we can choose to
turn our backs on those who need love. Since the Holy Spirit
resides in us, we can seek His help in responding in the ways
that Scripture teaches. God has made the way for us very simple.
All we have to do is reach out and receive the gift of love that
He holds out to us, and then we need to make daily decisions
to walk with that gift. Our problem is that we get busy in our
ways and our lives, and we do not want to submit.

Be one that responds to our Lord in submission to His will
and His way for your life today. Let Him show you the wonders
of trusting completely in Him and walking in His love.

Abide in Love

"And we have known and believed the love that God has for us. God is love, and he who abides in love abides in God, and God in him" (1 John 4:16).

God's love for us is evident everywhere we turn. We can look at His creation and know that He loves us. When we open our hearts to let His love soak into us, we can begin to see with clearer vision the depth, width, and height of His love. His love is overwhelming and overpowering. When we try to describe His love to someone, words are not adequate. As we receive this wondrous love, our desire to share His love with others will grow. We cannot be in the presence of His love without it affecting our lives. Romans 5:5 tells us that He has poured His love into our hearts by the Holy Spirit.

His love is already there, so how do we begin to apply that truth to our lives? When we are in situations that cause us to be angry, upset, frustrated, or hurt, we need to remember Romans 5:5. We need to ask the Holy Spirit to allow that love that is already in us to come forth in His strength and power. As we begin to act in love (regardless of our feelings), we will begin to see that our feelings will change. That love that seemed so evasive a short time ago suddenly will be real and alive within us! What a joy it is to serve a God who provides for all we need! He makes a way where there seems to be no way.

Have you ever been so angry that you felt there was no hope of being able to respond in a loving way? Many of us have been there; however, with God's help we can respond in love. He has the answer for us—simply to trust in Him and let His Spirit live and love through us!

One in Christ Jesus

"There is neither Jew nor Greek, there is neither slave nor free, there is neither male nor female; for you are all one in Christ Jesus" (Gal. 3:28).

In the world in which we live, we so often notice differences in people. Some focus on distinctions between race, office, or gender; however, in God's eyes there are no distinctions. We are all one in His eyes, and we should all be one in each other's eyes. The amount of money we have, the color of our skin, the language that we speak, the job that we have, or our sex should not be a factor in how we are received by one another. God has a place and a plan for each one of us, and we should look at each other with His eyes, accepting that place and plan.

Psalm 133:1 says, "Behold, how good and how pleasant it is for brethren to dwell together in unity!" Unity means being one in spirit. We may have differences in how we look or speak, and we may have differences in our opinions about some things; however, in the spirit, we are one. We are born-again Christians who love our Lord. When we have differences of opinion, we can agree to disagree agreeably!

This verse in Galatians shows us the importance of accepting our brothers and sisters in Christ for who they are— not expecting them to be like we are!

Come into the presence of the Lord today, and let Him wipe away any prejudice that may exist within you. Let Him shower His love for all into your heart.

I Stand at the Door and Knock

"Behold, I stand at the door and knock. If anyone hears My voice and opens the door, I will come in to him and dine with him, and he with Me" (Rev. 3:20).

Jesus waits for us to open the door of our heart and let Him come in to fellowship with us. He gives us a picture here of a friend or loved one coming to dinner.

Breaking bread together or dining together in the days that Jesus walked the earth was a time of close fellowship. It should still be a time of close fellowship today, but it is not always that way. We live in a world that is so fast-paced that often we do not take the time to sit down at a meal with family or friends to have a time of fellowship and sharing. Jesus wants to be so one with us that we will fellowship together with Him on a regular basis. Mealtime is or should be a regular activity of each day. Jesus wants to spend close time with us daily so that we can grow closer to Him and learn from Him.

Have you reached the place in your Christian walk that you talk most things over with Him? He wants to hear from your heart, and He wants to hear about your day. He knows all that goes on, but He wants you to open up to Him and share with Him. He can be closer to you than any human being. He can be closer to you than your parents, your children, or even your spouse. He will be if you open the door of your heart to spend time in fellowship with Him today and every day of your life. Will you make that decision today? Spending time with your Lord is a life-changing experience that you should not miss.

The Tabernacle of God Is with Men

"And I heard a loud voice from heaven saying, 'Behold, the tabernacle of God is with men, and He will dwell with them, and they shall be His people. God Himself will be with them and be their God'" (Rev. 21:3).

The term "tabernacle" means a dwelling place for God. Have you ever been in a large church or temple that is called a tabernacle? Usually they are very large and ornate because they are considered to be the dwelling place of God. The Jewish temple described in the Old Testament was very detailed and exquisite. We consider a place that would be the dwelling place of God to be something very special.

The scripture for today is a promise of God making His tabernacle with men that points to the time of a new heaven and a new earth; however, God chooses to tabernacle or dwell with His people now. Does that make you feel special? It should, because God Almighty, the Creator of the universe, has chosen you and me with whom to tabernacle! We can come into the very presence of God, and we can fellowship with Him. He has told us in many scriptures that He chooses to dwell within us through the power of the Holy Spirit. Today, however, that fellowship is not constant or continuous. Hopefully we are growing in our relationship and fellowship with our Lord, but we do not spend every moment in His presence. One day, when Jesus comes again, and all things are made new, there will be no interruption to our fellowship with God. We will continually be in His presence, and He will dwell with us always as we glory in the majesty of the new heaven and new earth!

He Would Give You Living Water

"Jesus answered and said to her, 'If you knew the gift of God, and who it is who says to you, 'Give Me a drink,' you would have asked Him, and He would have given you living water'" (John 4:10).

Jesus used water as an illustration of the Holy Spirit to the Samaritan woman at the well. He explained to her that if she knew who He was, she would ask for living water that would give her eternal life. The woman at the well had been married five times, and the man she was living with at the time she met Jesus was not her husband.

Jesus, however, held out to her the way to life eternal. All she had to do was repent of her sins and receive Jesus.

Our Father's love goes beyond anything that we as humans can possibly understand. His desire is that all should follow after Him and be saved. We are shown the way in today's scripture: Jesus says, "You would have asked Him." All we have to do is ask, and He will respond by holding out His living water to us, His precious living water that brings the very life of God into our lives.

Do you have the life of God dwelling within you? If you do not, you can today. All you need to do is repent of your sins and accept Jesus as your Lord and Savior. Pray this prayer to Him right now. "Father, I am sorry that I have not lived my life for You. I know that Jesus is the only way and the only answer for my life. Jesus, come into my heart today and live within me. Let me be Your dwelling place and may my life bring glory to You always!" If you have already accepted Jesus as your Lord and Savior, be an instrument of His light and share with others the good news of Jesus Christ!

Fountain of Water

"But whoever drinks of the water that I shall give him will never thirst. But the water that I shall give him will become in him a fountain of water springing up into everlasting life" (John 4:14).

*T*he picture that Jesus gives us in John 4 is of a fountain springing up. This shows us that the Holy Spirit, who comes to dwell within us when we are born again into the kingdom of God, can well up within us and spring forth to overflowing. We can allow the Holy Spirit room to flow abundantly within us, or we can quench the Spirit of God.

How do we quench the Spirit of God? The term "quench" seems to imply the dampening of a flame of fire. One term in the Bible used to describe the Holy Spirit is fire, which seems to indicate that the Holy Spirit acts as a fire would, burning away chaff and providing heat that warms, enlightens, melts, or consumes. As a fire unleashed within us, the Holy Spirit cleanses us and empowers us to fulfill God's purpose for our lives. When we let the Holy Spirit do His work within us and through us, God's power will be as a fountain springing up within us. The waters of the Holy Spirit bring life into us and into the lives of those around us.

Are you aware of the presence of the Holy Spirit in your life? Seek the Father with all that is within you and let Him fill you afresh and anew with the presence and the power of the Holy Spirit. Ask Him to let His living waters flow through you to those around you. Be open to every opportunity He brings your way to be a witness of His grace and His love.

Let Him Come to Me and Drink

"On the last day, that great day of the feast, Jesus stood and cried out, saying, 'If anyone thirsts, let him come to Me and drink. He who believes in Me, as the Scripture has said, out of his heart will flow rivers of living water'" (John 7:37–38).

We know that we receive the living water of God from Jesus, because He tells us to come to Him and drink. How do we drink from Him? I believe we drink from Him by first receiving Him as our Lord and Savior. Then we continue to drink from Him by studying Scripture, which teaches us more each day about the gift of the Holy Spirit in our lives, and by entering into His presence to spend time in precious fellowship with Him.

As we spend time with Him on a regular basis, and as we study His Word, we will be filled continually with His living water. As we open ourselves up to Him more and more, we allow the Holy Spirit full reign in our lives.

Even though we receive the indwelling of the Holy Spirit when we are born again into the kingdom of God, we need to be continually filled afresh and anew. Do you think it would be enough to drink a full glass of water one day and then never drink any more water again? No, we need water daily to lead a healthy life. We also need the living water of Jesus daily to lead a strong and healthy spiritual life.

Drink of His waters today. Go before Him in all humility and seek everything that He has for you. Let Him pour His Spirit upon you in great abundance and then go forth in His power and strength to let His life shine forth from you.

Out of Your Heart Will Flow Rivers of Living Water

"On the last day, that great day of the feast, Jesus stood and cried out, saying, 'If anyone thirsts, let him come to Me and drink. He who believes in Me, as the Scripture has said, out of his heart will flow rivers of living water'" (John 7:37–38).

In John 4, Jesus talked about a fountain of water springing up into everlasting life. He told us that when we are born again into the kingdom of God, His Holy Spirit comes to dwell within us. If you have ever seen a fountain shooting up, you know that this reference to the Holy Spirit implies that He will rise up within us and then flow out of us. In John 7, however, Jesus refers to the Holy Spirit as flowing "rivers" of living water. Multiple rivers have a great deal more water than in a single fountain.

In the scripture for today, we are being shown that once we have been born again, we can be filled with all the fullness of God's Spirit. We have a choice, however, about how much we will allow the Holy Spirit to work within us. Jesus wants us to be open to allow the Holy Spirit freedom to move and flow in our lives just as rivers flow freely and with mighty power. The living water of God brings His life to us, and then He uses us to allow His life to flow into others' lives.

Let God use you as a vessel that is not only filled to the brim with His Spirit but is also overflowing and pouring out to others. Walk in such close fellowship with Him that you reflect the very essence of His glory!

River in the Tabernacle of God

"There is a river whose streams shall make glad the city of God, the holy place of the tabernacle of the Most High" (Ps. 46:4).

A river is found in the dwelling place of the Lord God Almighty, and that river is the Holy Spirit who brings life to us! Where is His dwelling place? We have found through Scripture that His dwelling place is within His believers. We are the temple of the living God, which means that His river of peace and life dwell within us.

John 7 tells us that out of our innermost being shall flow rivers of living water. God's plan from the beginning of His creation was to send His Son to redeem mankind and send His Spirit to dwell within us. Then we could become His vessels on earth to bring His creation into the knowledge of the saving grace of Jesus Christ.

His living water has been placed in you and me so that we might fulfill His plans upon this earth. Are you aware of His Spirit within you? If not, study His Word, especially John 14–17 and the Book of Acts, and begin to draw close to Him. As you become more aware of His love and grace in your life, you will be able to share His living water with those around you. The world is hungry for something to fill the emptiness inside. Jesus is the only one who can satisfy the aching need in the world today!

Will you let Him spread His love and life through you today as you yield yourself to the Spirit of God dwelling within you? Let His rivers of living water flow through you as you become a part of bringing the answer that is so desperately needed—Jesus!

137

Drink from the River

"They are abundantly satisfied with the fullness of Your house, and you give them drink from the river of Your pleasures" (Ps. 36:8).

In the scripture for today, God's river is referred to as the river of His pleasures. When the Holy Spirit is poured out within us, we truly experience the pleasures of God. He reveals Himself in such a wonderful way to us that we are filled to overflowing with peace and joy. Sometimes it is hard to contain the joy that comes from being in the presence of the Lord and having His Spirit dwelling within. Not only does He dwell within, but He also moves and works through us. The indescribable joy of being used by God Almighty and having His Spirit teach, preach, encourage, or minister through us is overwhelming. To think that the God of the whole universe would choose to dwell within you and me and also to use us as His vessels in others' lives is simply too much to comprehend. And yet, that is His choice. There is no greater pleasure on the face of the earth than to serve our Lord and allow Him complete freedom in our lives.

Are you willing to allow Him that freedom in your life today? Do you want Him to use you, or is that something that frightens or overwhelms you? Do not let fear or feelings of unworthiness rob you of the pleasure of being used by our heavenly Father. Let Him encourage you today by helping you know that you are His, and He is yours. Let Him show you how very special you are in His eyes, and let Him give you what you need to walk in the blessings that come from sharing Him with others. Let the pleasures that come from His river flow through you as you reach out to people in need.

Fountain of Life

"For with You is the fountain of life; in Your light we see light" (Ps. 36:9).

A fountain is in the center of the community where I live. When I read this verse, I immediately picture that fountain, which I usually pass each day. The fountain of water springs upward to great heights from the center, then arches and falls outward down into the lake. When I picture God's fountain of life, I see the living water bursting upward within us, and then pouring out upon others as it falls back into the lake or pool of water. It seems that as it falls back into the pool of water, the living water carries the others it touches to His lake so that they may receive the life that comes from His Holy Spirit.

His Spirit is at work within us, bringing others to the knowledge of His great love and compassion. When we allow His Spirit to spring up within us as a fountain, His living water goes forth to the others around us. They cannot see the peace and joy of His presence in our lives without being affected by His grace. Some may choose to turn their back on Him, but many will not. Many will one day be rejoicing before the throne of God because you and I have allowed His Spirit to spring up within us and then out to them.

Let Him fill you afresh today and let that fountain of His living water spring up within you in greater measure than ever before. Be a living witness of the light and life of Almighty God in the world in which you live.

Waters Shall Burst Forth in the Wilderness

"Then the lame shall leap like a deer, and the tongue of the dumb sing, for waters shall burst forth in the wilderness, and streams in the desert" (Isa. 35:6).

*W*ater tastes best when we are painfully thirsty. When our lives seem to be so dry that we feel as if we are in a desert, the living water of God can quench that terrible thirst. The Spirit of God can rise up so strongly within us that we feel as if we are drenched in the living waters of God. The scripture for today shows us what can happen when we allow the Holy Spirit to rise up within us and have His way—the lame shall leap, and the dumb shall sing. God has placed His Spirit within us so that the works of Jesus can and will continue on this earth. What did Jesus do when He walked on this earth? He healed the sick, cast out demons, taught God's truth, and preached the good news.

Do you believe that you can do the works of Jesus? You cannot do His works in your own strength, but through the power of the Holy Spirit that dwells within you.

First, believe that Jesus meant what He said in John 14:12, "He who believes in Me, the works that I do he will do also; and greater works than these he will do, because I go to My Father." Second, trust Him to work through you rather than trying to figure out what to do yourself and then attempting to work in your own strength. Third, step out in faith and begin to act as if what Jesus said is true. Finally, watch and see what glorious things our Lord accomplishes through you!

Springs of Water

"The parched ground shall become a pool, and the thirsty land springs of water" (Isa. 35:7).

*H*ave you ever noticed what the ground looks like when we have not had any rain for a long time? The ground gets so completely dried out that the surface bursts into a maze of tiny cracks. Then when the rain comes, especially if it is a good soaking rain, the cracks begin to smooth away, and the soil becomes moist and soft again. Then when the soil is tilled, and seeds are planted, we can expect to see a harvest because the soil is soft and supple. This world is made in such a way that nothing will live without water. The earth needs water to produce life, and we as human beings need water to live.

Our Father is holding out to us His living water that brings us spiritual life. We cannot survive spiritually without the water of life. We need to be open on a daily basis to receive the rain of God that pours down upon us and brings life into our spirits. We need to look up into the face of God and let Him refresh us from above.

Are you thirsty today? Do you need the outpouring of His rain upon and within your life? We all need more and more of God's Spirit at work in our lives. No person has reached the place that he or she does not need more of God. Look to Him today and let Him pour out His rain from above upon your spirit. As He does, notice how full and alive you feel as you prepare to move out in the power and strength of His precious Spirit!

I Will Pour Water on Him

"For I will pour water on him who is thirsty, and floods on the dry ground . . ." (Isa. 44:3a).

God has promised us that He will pour water on him who is thirsty. If you are not thirsty, you need to pray that you will be thirsty. We need fresh renewing and refilling each day because just as our physical body continually needs water, our spirit needs to be refreshed and refilled each day with living water. It is easy to know when our physical body needs water because we begin to feel thirsty. It is a little harder to determine our spiritual need for God's living water. We can tell, however, that we are becoming dry spiritually when our prayers do not seem to be getting through or when we do not want to pray. We may find that we do not want to read God's Word or that we begin reacting in ungodly ways. When these things happen, we can be sure that we are in need of the living water of the Holy Spirit.

If you have been having problems in any of these areas, do not be discouraged for our God has promised to pour floods on the dry ground. Look to Him for that rain cloud. Remember the story of Elijah who said it would rain during the drought. He went to the top of the mountain to look for the rain cloud because he knew that it would be there. God did not fail Elijah, and He will not fail you! Look to Him, expecting to receive from Him, and He will open up the windows of heaven and pour out such a blessing of His living water upon you that you will not be able to contain it all. You will have to give some away to those around you.

Rivers in Desolate Heights

"I will open rivers in desolate heights, and fountains in the midst of the valleys; I will make the wilderness a pool of water, and the dry land springs of water" (Isa. 41:18).

Do you feel as if you are in a desperate place? Do you feel as if you do not know where to turn? When we are going through the most difficult trial or tribulation, our Lord is right there waiting for us to call upon Him so that He can pour His living water upon us. His living water brings the life and peace of God into our lives, and it also brings guidance and direction. When things seem to be the worst that they could possibly be, He is at hand ready to refresh us with the Holy Spirit. All we need to do is ask, and we will receive. John 16:24 says, "Until now you have asked nothing in My name. Ask, and you will receive that your joy may be full."

Sometimes we may feel as if we are on desolate heights, deep in a valley, or in a wilderness, but our Lord is promising us the refreshing waters of His Spirit. That means that He brings to us all that we need to be overcomers in this world. He will give us grace to go through the difficult times, and He will also give us victory as overcomers. He does not leave us alone or forsaken, but He is always with us, holding out His hand of compassion and His arm of strength. Nothing is too difficult for our Lord, and He is on our side. Call on Him today, ask, and you will receive all that you need from Him to be an overcomer in your situation!

To Give Drink to My People

"... I give waters in the wilderness and rivers in the desert, to give drink to My people, My chosen" (Isa. 43:20).

Do you believe that you are a chosen one of God? If you have accepted Jesus as your Lord and Savior, you are one of His chosen. Scripture tells us that the Israelites are the chosen people of God, but Ephesians 1:4–5 says, "Just as He chose us in Him before the foundation of the world, that we should be holy and without blame before Him in love, having predestined us to adoption as sons by Jesus Christ to Himself, according to the good pleasure of His will." Clearly, the Gentiles also are adopted by Him to be a part of His family and to be partakers of His promises. We are chosen by Him—think of the magnitude of that statement! And because He chooses us, He gives drink to us, His people. I do not believe He gives us just a sip of the Holy Spirit. He gives us rivers of living water, enough water to fill us, soak us, and overflow us so that we can be used by Him to further His kingdom.

Have you allowed the rivers of living water to fill you up to overflowing, to totally immerse you and soak you through and through? Ask Him to pour forth rivers of His water upon you today so that His life will be so strong within you that it overflows into the lives of those around you. Let Him make you a blessing to a hurting and needy world.

Come to the Waters

"Ho! Everyone who thirsts, come to the waters . . ." (Isa. 55:1).

*A*re you thirsty for more of the Lord in your life? Then here is your answer—come to His waters, and He will refresh you. You may be saying, "How do I know if I am thirsty or not?" If you are thirsty for more of the Lord, you will not be satisfied with your relationship with Him or with your Christian walk. You will know that you need to develop a closer walk with Him in order to fulfill His will within your life.

Sometimes we, as Christians, become complacent in our walk with Him, and complacency is not a Christian trait! Revelations 3:16 says, "So then, because you are lukewarm, and neither cold nor hot, I will vomit you out of My mouth." This is a strong statement that shows how important it is to hunger and thirst for the Lord. If we are feeling satisfied with our Christian walk, we need to begin to seek the Lord and find out what He wants to give us to freshen and renew our relationship with Him. We all need to continually seek more of Him in our lives.

Come to Him today and lift up your face to Him. Let Him pour down upon you the rain of His Holy Spirit that brings such glorious refreshment and growth into our lives. His Spirit fills us with His life in such a way that many others are touched and turned around to serve Him and love Him. How wonderful it will be for you to stand before the throne of grace and know that there are others standing with you because you sought more of Him and witnessed to them of His grace and glory while you were still on this earth!

Draw Water with Joy

"Therefore with joy you will draw water from the wells of salvation" (Isa. 12:3).

When we thirst for more of Him, all we have to do is draw water from Him and know that we will be filled with joy. Do you want more of His joy in your life? We all need His joy and the freedom that comes when His joy rises up within us. Our God is not a solemn God—He is a God who is full of joy! I believe He wants His children to have fun, to laugh, and to enjoy life. I believe He also wants us to enjoy our relationship with Him. We do not have to always approach Him silently or seriously, although there are certainly times to do that. He often waits for us to approach Him rejoicing and expressing the emotions that He has given us. He does not want us to suppress our emotions. He simply wants us to yield our emotions to Him so that they will be led by His Spirit and not flounder out of control.

Proverbs 17:22 says, "A merry heart does good, like medicine." God knows that it is good and healthy for us to express joy. I believe He wants us to laugh and have a good time with Him and with His children. Psalm 126:1–2 says, "When the Lord brought back the captivity of Zion, we were like those who dream. Then our mouth was filled with laughter, and our tongue with singing." Job 8:21 says, "He will yet fill your mouth with laughing, and your lips with rejoicing." Those are just two of many scriptures that talk about laughter and rejoicing.

Receive all of the joy that the Lord has for you today! Go before Him expecting to receive of His nature that is full of joy, rejoicing, and even laughter. Have fun with Him and with those around you.

Springs of Water

"For He who has mercy on them will lead them, even by the springs of water He will guide them" (Isa. 49:10).

Jesus will lead us through the power of the Holy Spirit by the springs of His living water. When we go through difficulties and afflictions, we can look to Him who has all the answers. Not only can we look to Him, we can know that He is ready and waiting to draw us close to Him and to the source of all strength—His living water! Sometimes we struggle and strive, trying to figure out how to get through the problems that face us when all we really need to do is trust Him completely, ask Him to show us His way, and then follow His instructions.

You may ask, "How do I know His instructions?" Listen to Him! That is not an oversimplification—that is truth! When we ask Him for an answer, He will give it. It may come through a sermon, through talking with a friend, reading Scripture, listening to Christian radio or television, or in many other ways. When the answer comes, it will be as if a light comes on in your heart and you will suddenly know that He has given the answer. You will know what to do! Trusting is hard for human beings because we want to be in control of our lives. The one who needs to be in control, however, is Jesus. He has all the answers, and He certainly knows all things. We know so little even when we think we are quite knowledgeable. Let Him guide you by His springs of living water today and bring sweet peace and release into your life.

147

Waters Flowing from the Temple—Ankle Deep

"Water flowing from the temple . . . and he brought me through the waters; the water came up to my ankles" (Ezek. 47:1b, 3b).

Read Ezekiel 47:1–12 and visualize the whole picture that is being related to us by the prophet. This passage gives us a picture of the living water of Jesus pouring out to bring peace, healing, and the work of the Holy Spirit in our lives. The first picture we receive is of the water coming up to our ankles. Think about going to the beach and walking along the shore, splashing in the water where it is ankle deep. That is a fun place to be. The water is not reaching much of our bodies, so we are not fully experiencing the cleansing, soothing effect that comes from its touch. We are still having a good time splashing about in the water however. This image is a picture of the beginning work of the Holy Spirit in our lives. We receive Him with such joy and look forward to moments of fun and adventure with Him.

We cannot mature and grow without first getting our feet wet and beginning the process of walking with the Holy Spirit.

Where do you stand in the process of allowing the Holy Spirit freedom to move and work in your life? Are you splashing in water up to your ankles, or are you beginning to trust more and have His living waters move up to your knees, waist, or even to where you cannot stand? We will look more at the depth of His living waters in our lives tomorrow.

Waters Flowing from the Temple—Waist Deep

"Water flowing from the temple . . . and came up to my knees . . . and up to my waist" (Ezek. 47:1b, 4).

As we continue to look at this picture in Ezekiel of the water flowing from the temple, we see that it begins to rise. Yesterday we looked at water coming up to the ankles, but today we see the living water of the Lord coming up to the knees and then to the waist. This shows us how the Holy Spirit continues to work in our lives, bringing more of Himself and His power and grace as we open ourselves to Him and allow Him free reign within us.

As we begin to walk out into the water, we find that each step becomes more difficult. The pressure of the water pushes against the movement of our legs as we move forward. There is something exhilarating, however, about moving out further into the water. Water brings a sense of cleansing, and it also brings a soothing feeling of peace and contentment. Moving out further and further into water of greater depth becomes a challenge and yet brings great rest and enjoyment as we are lifted and supported by its presence. The Holy Spirit is ready to bring His living water to us at any depth to which we will allow. As we open ourselves more we will find that we experience a greater degree of growth and maturity in the Lord, and we reach a place of rest and peace that is indescribable.

Let the Holy Spirit bring His living water into your life in such great depth that you will experience His peace and rest in a way that you never have before!

Waters Flowing Deep from the Temple

"Water flowing from the temple . . . that I could not cross;
for the water was too deep, water in which one must swim,
a river that could not be crossed" (Ezek. 47:1b, 5).

As we read further in this scripture in Ezekiel 47, we find that the water continues to rise and increase. In the same way, the living water of the Holy Spirit continues to grow in depth in our lives as we yield ourselves to Him. When we get to the point that we are willing to jump in and let His water hold us up, we find His place of great rest. When we are in water that is too deep to stand, what do we do? We either swim or float. I want us to look at floating today.

When we quit fighting the water and allow it to support us, there is a wonderful peace in finding out that the water truly will hold us up. I believe the Lord wants us to come to the place with Him that we simply trust Him to hold us up in His living water as we float in His arms. When we quit struggling and relax in Him, we find that we can simply flow with Him. Just as a river has its natural course and flows along that course, we will flow along the course that the Holy Spirit has for us when we yield ourselves to Him and allow His living water to guide us.

Will you rest in His arms today, fall back in His water, allowing it to hold you up, and flow along His path for you? There is no greater peace and contentment than being in the arms of our Lord and Savior, knowing that what He has in store for you is far greater than anything you could think of or imagine yourself.

Wherever the Rivers Go There Will Be Life

"And it shall be that every living thing that moves, wherever the rivers go, will live . . . for they will be healed, and everything will live wherever the river goes" (Ezek. 47:9).

There is life in the river of God! When we choose to jump in and let His living waters hold us, guide us, and direct our lives, we find that the very life of God is present with us. Can you even begin to imagine what the life of God includes? I find that it completely stretches my imagination and thought process to try to understand the life of God. Yet we are told that when we are in His river, His life is present and available to us.

Are there areas in your life that you want to see renewed? Are there areas in which you want to see something happen? All you have to do is to jump into the river of life that comes from the Holy Spirit and receive what He has for you. You will find that as you jump in, you will experience cleansing that comes from the washing of the water of the Word (Eph. 5:26). You will find that you will begin to understand what the words "trust" and "faith" mean in greater depth as you experience the peace that passes all understanding (Phil. 4:7). You will have greater understanding of God's rest found in Hebrews 4:11. Will you jump in full force today and let the Spirit of God be your source of strength, peace, rest, and cleansing?

Ask the Lord for Rain

"Ask the Lord for rain in the time of the latter rain. The Lord will make flashing clouds; he will give them showers of rain, grass in the field for everyone" (Zech. 10:1).

We need to ask the Lord for an outpouring of His living water. The "latter rain" referred to in the scripture for today is the spring rain, which is usually abundant and expected. This scripture exhorts us to ask for the spring rain and not just assume it will come. This is a lesson to us in asking of the Lord according to His will and expecting to receive from Him. The Lord tells us over and over in Scripture that He will pour out His Spirit upon us, but He also tells us to ask.

James 4:2–3 says, "You do not have because you do not ask. You ask and do not receive, because you ask amiss." We need the living water of the Lord so desperately in our lives, and He has made Himself available to us. We receive the Holy Spirit into our lives when we receive Jesus as Lord and Savior, but we need to open up our lives to let the Holy Spirit rule and reign within us.

If you are going through difficulties and you do not feel that you have the strength, guidance, direction, or wisdom that you need, call upon the Lord and ask Him to pour His Spirit afresh and anew upon you. Ask Him to reveal all that you need to know to be an overcomer in your situation. Ask and you will receive from Him as long as you ask according to His will. Let Him show you the abundance He holds out to you and to all His children.

He Will Come to Us Like the Rain

"Let us know, let us pursue the knowledge of the Lord. His going forth is established as the morning; He will come to us like the rain, like the latter and former rain to the earth" (Hos. 6:3).

This scripture shows us the steadfastness and faithfulness of the Lord. As we pursue the knowledge of Him, He will be as faithful and as steady as the morning. We know that, as sure as there is night, there will be morning. We know this because we experience it every day. We can be as assured of the faithfulness of the Lord as we are sure that morning will come after the night.

We also are aware that rain comes to replenish the earth on a regular basis. Sometimes we go through some dry times, but the rain always comes. Our Father is always there for us. Sometimes we get caught up in the things of this world—busyness, doing our own thing, or simple complacency; and our lives become dry spiritually. As we pursue the knowledge of the Lord, however, He always comes as the rain comes to replenish, refresh, and renew us. How faithful our Lord is to us!

If you are going through a dry time spiritually today, call on Him, and let Him show you the great and mighty things that He wants to do in and through you. Jeremiah 33:3 says, "Call to Me, and I will answer you, and show you great and mighty things, which you do not know." He holds out to us a storehouse of wondrous blessings, which He longs to reveal to us and to use within our lives in order to minister His love to others. Let Him use you today as you draw close to Him and receive the abundance of rain that comes from Him!

He Will Cause the Rain to Come Down

"Be glad then, you children of Zion, and rejoice in the Lord your God; for He has given you the former rain faithfully, and He will cause the rain to come down for you—the former rain, and latter rain in the first month" (Joel 2:23).

The former rain referred to the autumn rain that came at the time of planting, and the latter rain came in the spring at the time prior to harvesting. Spiritually speaking, this scripture refers to the outpouring of the Spirit of God in the last days to bring about spiritual renewal. If you read Joel 2, you will find the scripture from this chapter is quoted in Acts 2 to explain to the people what had happened on the day of Pentecost. There was an outpouring of the Holy Spirit on the day of Pentecost. After He ascended to heaven to sit at the right hand of God the Father, Jesus sent the Holy Spirit. We are assured in Scripture that there will also be an outpouring in the last days before Jesus returns.

Are you ready and prepared to receive all that the Lord has for you today? Do you want to be a part of His plan for fulfilling His kingdom on this earth and in heaven? Look unto Him and let Him bring His refreshing and renewing into your life today. Let Him use you to spread the good news of His Son Jesus Christ and the redemption that He brings to all who will receive and respond to His great gift.

Wisdom Is a Fountain of Life

"The law of the wise is a fountain of life, to turn one away from the snares of death" (Prov. 13:14).

As we have seen in John 4, Jesus tells the woman at the well that when He gives water it will become a fountain of water springing up into everlasting life. In this verse from Proverbs, we are told that wisdom is a fountain of life. When we pursue the knowledge of the Lord Jesus Christ, we receive wisdom that comes from Him. This wisdom comes to us and brings the very life of God into our lives.

We receive eternal life as we accept Jesus as our Lord and Savior, and we also receive a quickening of life from the Holy Spirit when we yield ourselves to Him. The Holy Spirit is a part of the Trinity, and He brings the life of God the Father and also the life of Jesus Christ into our lives. To pursue the knowledge and wisdom that comes from drawing close to the Lord should always be a strong priority in our lives. Spending time in God's Word brings understanding into our lives through the power of the Holy Spirit. As we read His Word, we should be prayerful and open to interpret what we read from the greatest teacher that has ever been or will ever be—the Holy Spirit.

God has given teachers to the Body of Christ to help us understand, but human teachers sometimes make mistakes. Only the Holy Spirit brings the truth of God with complete accuracy. As we listen to the teachers that the Lord has given as gifts to the church, let us always seek to sift what we hear through the Holy Spirit. With God's Word as our guide and the Holy Spirit as our teacher, we can know that the Lord will bring His wisdom into our lives and guide us into all truth!

The Fear of the Lord Is a Fountain of Life

"The fear of the Lord is a fountain of life, to turn one away from the snares of death" (Prov. 14:27).

Yesterday we were told that wisdom is a fountain of life, and today we are told that the fear of the Lord is a fountain of life. Proverbs 9:10 says, "The fear of the Lord is the beginning of wisdom," so clearly the fear of the Lord must be a fountain of life as well.

What does it mean to fear the Lord? The Hebrew for the word "fear" used in Proverbs 14:27 is yirah, which means reverence. It also means dreadful and exceedingly fearful. I believe this scripture tells us that we need to have an exceedingly fearful reverence of our Lord. We do not have fear that He will do something terrible to us, but we do reverence His very nature of holiness and righteousness. We also recognize that there is absolutely nothing on our own that we can do to stand in His presence and be accepted by Him without the sacrifice of Jesus Christ on the cross that opened the way for us to have a relationship with Him.

Do not be fearful of the One who loves you and me with an everlasting love and mercy that is greater than our understanding, but do reverence the great God of the whole universe who loved you and I enough to send His only Son to the cross to pay the price for our sins and give us His righteousness as a gift. Fall on your knees today and thank Him for this great gift that goes beyond anything that this world could ever offer!

Walk by the Rivers of Waters

"They shall come with weeping, and with supplications I will lead them. I will cause them to walk by the rivers of waters, in a straight way in which they shall not stumble . . ." (Jer. 31:9).

When we go through hard or hurtful times, or when we see others going through difficult times, we need to go to the Father in prayer. When we go to the Father in prayer and intercession, He leads us to His rivers of water that bring refreshing and renewing. Every time we come to Him, whether in prayer for ourselves or in intercession for others, we cannot help but be strengthened by His presence.

He is the giver of all things that are good. When we draw close to Him, we begin to see Him in all His glory and all His majesty. We also begin to receive that which He holds out to us—rivers of His living water! Think about rivers—not just a stream, or even a huge fountain, but rivers! He holds out to us that which will enable us to be overcomers in this world and in the world to come. He holds out to us that which will enable us to be His instruments to others around us.

He holds out to us the answer for the world today! Imagine! The whole world looks for answers to all the problems that exist today, and you and I have that answer in Jesus Christ! Jesus has the answer for all things, and He wants to use you and me to pray and intercede for the needs that we see around us. Will you allow Him to use you today? Draw close to Him, seek Him, and let Him show you His plan for using you today to further His kingdom!

Those Who Thirst Shall Be Filled

"Blessed are those who hunger and thirst for righteousness, for they shall be filled" (Matt. 5:6).

As we thirst for more of our Father in heaven, we will be filled. When you are thirsty and want a drink of water, how do you feel? If you are at home, more than likely, you go to the kitchen, pour yourself a glass of water, and drink it. When the thirst is quenched, you go back to what you were doing. If you are out somewhere and something to drink is not easily available, the thirst will begin to grow stronger. When you finally do get to a place where you can get a drink, you feel such relief to have that thirst quenched.

Thirst is not something bad. It is good! Spiritually speaking, thirsting after more of the Lord is a wonderful thing. The Lord wants us to want more of Him, to experience more of His presence, to read and study His Word more, and to enjoy fellowshiping with Him. When that thirst is within us, we can be assured that He will fill that need.

Will you seek Him today, asking Him to fill you with a hungering and thirsting for more of Him in your life? He will be overjoyed to answer that request. Let Him pour His living water upon and within you today so that you can share His goodness and His love with others.

The Lamb Will Lead Them to Living Fountains of Waters

"For the Lamb who is in the midst of the throne will shepherd them and lead them to living fountains of waters. And God will wipe away every tear from their eyes" (Rev. 7:17).

The Lord offers His living waters to us today. But even if we do reach out and receive His waters of refreshing while we are on this earth, He will still lead us to even greater living fountains of waters when we are before Him in heaven. In that day, He will wipe away every tear from our eyes. We have the hope of His victory and overcoming power in our lives today, but we also have the hope and assurance of His grace and mercy for all of eternity.

As long as we are on this earth, there will be tears and there will be sorrow. The day is coming, however, and some believe that it is coming soon, when He will return. When He comes again, there will be one last battle. After that battle will come the Millenium or the reign of Jesus on earth for one thousand years. After the thousand-year reign, a new heaven and a new earth will appear. We will spend eternity rejoicing with our Father where there will be no sorrow, no tears, and only the joy of being totally and completely in His presence.

Are you ready for that day? If not, prepare yourself today. Ask Him to come into your heart and become a part of the family of God—the family that lasts forever and will never let you down!

The Alpha and Omega

"And He said to me, 'It is done! I am the Alpha and the Omega, the Beginning and the End. I will give of the fountain of the water of life freely to him who thirsts'" (Rev. 21:6).

Jesus was from the beginning of creation, and He will exist forever. John 1:1–4 says, "In the beginning was the Word, and the Word was with God, and the Word was God. He was in the beginning with God. All things were made through Him, and without Him nothing was made that was made. In Him was life . . ." Not only is He the beginning and the end, He is everything in between.

The world looks for solutions and for answers, and He is the One who has every solution and every answer. He holds out to us the fountain of the water of life, and we simply do not understand. We continue on our way, trying to figure things out according to the world's system. If only we would put our trust in Him, who is the only way to salvation. When we look at the word "salvation" in the Greek, we find that it means save, rescue, safety, deliver, and health. He holds out to us the very life of God that brings all that we need and gives us the answers necessary to live victoriously in this life.

Will you let Him give you all that He has for you today? Will you allow Him to bring His life into you and show you the way to victory? Come before Him today and let Him pour His blessings upon you as He shows the greatness of His love and mercy toward you and those around you. Be a vessel of His living water and let Him flow from you to others who hunger and thirst to know Him in greater measure.

Take the Water of Life Freely

"And the Spirit and the bride say, 'Come!' And let him who hears say, 'Come!' And let him who thirsts come. Whoever desires, let him take the water of life freely" (Rev. 22:17).

An offer is being made for those who are thirsty to come and take of the water of life freely. That means that we can receive abundantly of the water of life because God holds out His living water to us, and He wants us to receive in great abundance from Him. He wants to give us all that we will ever need to live in the peace and joy that comes from Him. All we have to do is come to Him, seek Him with all our heart, and enter into His presence.

His Word shows us the way to receive what He has for us. His Word brings us direction and wisdom. When we seek to study His Word, trusting the Holy Spirit to be our teacher and guide us into all truth, our eyes will be opened. We will understand the things that seemed so far beyond our reach before. The Holy Spirit will bring illumination and revelation to us so that we can receive all that the Lord has for us to become the man or woman of God that He created us to be.

Are you seeking Him with your whole heart today? Reach up and take hold of His truth and His wisdom today, and let Him become all that you need to fulfill His purposes within you.

Pure River of Water of Life

"And he showed me a pure river of water of life, clear as crystal, proceeding from the throne of God and of the Lamb" (Rev. 22:1).

The river of water of life comes from the throne of God and of the Lamb. How do you and I partake of this river of water of life? We need to seek to enter into the presence of the living God and come before His throne. As we seek Him and look unto Him, expecting to receive from Him, He will not disappoint us. We simply need to spend time with Him and trust Him to draw us close to Him. James 4:8 says, "Draw near to God and He will draw near to you." As we give Him time in our lives, He responds by revealing Himself to us.

Time is probably the most precious commodity today. Once money was more precious, but now it seems that the thing that people need and long for most is more time. God has given us all twenty-four hours each day, and yet we are such busy people that we always run out of time to complete the things on our agendas. We need to look at our priorities and put God first. We need to give Him time each day, and then we will find that our days will go smoother. We will weed out the unimportant things and have time for those things that are truly important in the eyes of eternity.

Will you make the decision today to give Him first place in your life, setting aside time each day to have quality time with Him?

He Leads Me Beside the Still Waters

"The Lord is my shepherd; I shall not want. He makes me to lie down in green pastures; He leads me beside the still waters" (Ps. 23:1–2).

Not only does the Lord our God give us freely of His living water, He also leads us beside still waters. In other words, He gives us peace. Have you ever sat beside a pond of water that was perfectly still? It is such a calming experience. Our God reassures us that He holds out His life to us, and He also offers us His rest and His peace.

When we are going through great difficulties and turmoil, there is One who has all the answers. There is One who will give us peace and release. We do not have to struggle and strive to figure out solutions and answers to the problems that exist in our lives. We simply need to put our trust in Him who knows all things and has the power to overcome in each situation. When we realize that He is enough and He has all the answers, we enter into such a place of rest that we wonder why we could not come to this place before. It seems, however, that this Christian walk is a process, and we must go through trials and tribulations that bring strength and growth into our lives. When we do finally reach that place of rest, the peace truly does pass all understanding.

Seek to enter into that place of rest today and in the days ahead as we look at scriptures that will open our eyes to the wonders of the peace and rest that come from our Lord and Savior!

The Lord Your God is Giving You Rest

"Remember the word which Moses the servant of the Lord commanded you saying, 'The Lord your God is giving you rest and is giving you this land'" (Josh. 1:13).

Joshua is about to lead the Israelites into the promised land, and he reminds them of the commandment of the Lord that came through Moses. The people had been wandering around in the wilderness for forty years, and now they were going to enter into rest by entering into the land that God had promised them. Their time of wandering and restlessness was about to be over. The Lord tells us that we can enter into a place of rest with Him that will bring such peace into our lives that we will be amazed. We do not have to struggle and strive about the issues that face us because we can rest in the Lord and His ability to guide and direct our lives according to His perfect will.

You may be saying, "Yes, but how do I know God's guidance and direction for my life?" You need to be able to trust Him to show you. He will show you, but it may not be immediately or in the way you would expect that direction to come. He can speak to you through His Word, through sermons, through a friend, while you are in prayer, or simply as you drive down the road. As you trust Him, all of a sudden, you will "know that you know" the answer! His rest is amazing, and there is nothing else that can compare to it. Look unto Him who is able to give you the rest and peace that passes all understanding.

Rest on Every Side

"But now the Lord my God has given me rest on every side; there is neither adversary nor evil occurrence" (1 Kings 5:4).

At this point in the history of Israel no adversaries and no attacks were coming against them. Solomon explained that David, his father, could not build the temple for God because he was continually at war. Now, however, there was freedom from warfare, and the Lord was giving rest in order that His temple could now be built.

We sometimes feel as if everything is going against us. We feel as if there are many adversaries and many attacks coming against us. The Lord wants us to know, however, just as Solomon knew, that He will give us rest on every side. He is able to set us free from all our adversaries. He is able to help us become overcomers in this world in which we live. Jesus said, "These things I have spoken to you, that in Me you may have peace. In the world you will have tribulation; but be of good cheer, I have overcome the world" (John 16:33).

We know that we have tribulation because we all experience it, but we can be assured that Jesus came to set us free and to help us be overcomers in this world. There is such rest and peace in knowing that Jesus is Lord. When we allow Him first place in our lives and trust Him with every aspect of our lives, we enter into a place of contentment that penetrates deep within.

Are you struggling with something today that you need to overcome? Give it over to Jesus and let Him provide the answer that will bring that blessed peace and rest into your life!

Rest When We Seek

"And all Judah rejoiced at the oath, for they had sworn with all their heart and sought Him with all their soul; and He was found by them, and the Lord gave them rest all around" (2 Chron. 15:15).

During the reign of Asa, Judah entered into a covenant to seek the Lord God with all their heart and with all their soul. The result of their seeking was to enter into a place of rest. We can come to that place of rest today if we will seek Him with all our heart and with all our soul. Seeking the Lord with all our heart means that we spend time with Him and sincerely seek to be in the center of His will.

Seeking Him with all our soul means that we submit our thoughts, will, and emotions to Him. Second Corinthians 10:5 says, ". . . bringing every thought into captivity to the obedience of Christ." He enables us to bring those thoughts into captivity to His obedience by His strength and His power as we submit ourselves to Him. He is not looking for perfection, but He is looking at our hearts. If our hearts are sincerely longing to be obedient, He will provide what we need to walk in that obedience.

If the idea of submitting your thoughts to Him is new to you, do not expect to turn every thought over to Him immediately. You can begin that walk today, however, by turning over to Him the very next thought that comes to you that you know is not from Him. Ask Him to reveal those thoughts that are not pleasing to Him, and then be diligent to release those that He shows you. See the rest that will enter into your life as you submit to Almighty God!

Rest in the Lord

"Delight yourself also in the Lord, and He shall give you the desires of your heart. Commit your way to the Lord, trust also in Him . . . rest in the Lord, and wait patiently for him" (Ps. 37:4–5, 7a).

These verses give us some insight into resting in the Lord. First David, the author of this psalm, tells us to delight in the Lord. Delight means to give enjoyment, pleasure, or joy. When we seek after the Lord, wanting to give Him enjoyment, pleasure or joy, we will find that all other things in our life that had seemed so important will fade in the wonder of His presence. Once we experience it, delighting in Him will become something that we will seek after regularly.

When we delight ourselves in the Lord, it becomes easy to commit to Him those things that loom so big. Entering into the presence of the Lord and delighting in Him brings about trust, for we begin seeing Him for who He is in all His greatness and majesty and also begin knowing deep within that He who is able is also both personal and caring. When trust enters into the picture, then we are resting in Him. Trust brings about rest and peace that comes from only Him.

Do you want more trust in your life? Simply call upon Him who is able to supply everything that you need. Enter into a place of delighting in Him—enjoying and finding pleasure in your relationship with Him. As you grow closer to Him, spending more time with Him, coming to know Him better, and fellowshiping with Him on a regular basis, you will find that trust will grow in your life. Will you say today, "Here am I, Lord. I want to delight in You"?

This Is the Rest

"To whom He said, 'This is the rest with which you may cause the weary to rest,' and, 'This is the refreshing'" (Isa. 28:12).

In this hurried world in which we live today, do you ever feel as if you need to find a place of rest? Our Father in heaven has such a place for us; and upon finding this place of refreshment and peace, we rejoice. Rest comes when we put our total trust in our Lord. When we put our trust in Him who is able to overcome everything in our lives, all of a sudden those places that have seemed so steep and crooked, or so difficult to overcome, become smooth, level, and even easy to conquer.

We become accustomed to trying to work things out for ourselves. We are a strong-willed and self-sufficient people. We do not like to admit that we need help, and we do not like to ask for others' advice; however, our Lord's plan for us is not that we be independent and self-sufficient, but that we learn to depend on Him for all things. When we put our trust in Him and lean on His power, we will find that the rest that we long for—that often seems so evasive—is right there waiting for us. He wants us to submit ourselves and yield ourselves to Him and to His ways. We find such joy in learning to trust our Lord and Savior, and we find that our life becomes much smoother.

Will you submit yourself to the will of the Father today and let Him reveal His direction for your life? Find that joy and peace that comes from letting Him have complete control of your life, and rest in the assurance that His way is perfect and best!

In Quietness and Confidence Shall Be Your Strength

"In returning and rest you shall be saved; in quietness and confidence shall be your strength" (Isa. 30:15).

There is a reservoir of confidence in finding the rest that comes only from our Father God. When we put our trust in Him, we find a quietness comes over our spirit and also within our soul—the mind, emotions, and will. The soul, that area that is so difficult for us to yield to the Lord, begins to find a place of rest and peace as we lean on Him. Romans 12:2 says, "And do not be conformed to this world, but be transformed by the renewing of your mind, that you may prove what is that good and acceptable and perfect will of God." When we enter into a place of rest and peace, which comes from trusting God completely with whatever life brings our way, we find that we will renew our mind to think as He thinks.

When we are in a place of turmoil and trouble, we need God's Word to bring about peace and rest within us. We find that as we read and study His Word, trust begins to rise within us. We find that our thinking process begins to change as we place His Word into our minds instead of the thoughts that come from the world. It is amazing to experience God's peace in the midst of complete turmoil and chaos. We rejoice in the presence of the One who offers confidence to our souls in the midst of a world that is full of confusion and problems.

Look today to Him who is able to bring sweet peace and rest into your life in a way that you have never experienced before!

Have Rest and Do Not Fear

"'Therefore do not fear, O My servant Jacob,' says the Lord, 'nor be dismayed, O Israel; for behold, I will save you from afar, and your seed from the land of their captivity. Jacob shall return, have rest and be quiet, and no one shall make him afraid'" (Jer. 30:10).

Do you have fear in your life? There is some type of fear in almost everyone's life, but some have fears that are very difficult to overcome. When we come into a place of rest and quiet (quietness of spirit) in the Lord, we find that fear begins to leave.

I know what it is like to experience great fear. I grew up with fear—fear of being adventuresome, fear of people, and especially fear of public speaking. I always ran from the things that I feared, which caused the fear to increase. I did not know that the only way to overcome fear is to trust God and face it. As a young mother, I experienced agoraphobia, which kept me a prisoner in my own home for a time. As my relationship became closer to the Lord, I learned to trust Him with the fear that I was experiencing. After about a year of studying, memorizing, and dwelling on God's Word pertaining to overcoming fear, I was set free from the fear that had plagued me most of my life. What peace and rest came into my life! I cannot explain the joy and contentment that flooded my life as I praised my Father for setting me free. I now know that fear is something that we do not have to live with because our precious Lord and Savior came to set us free from all bondage.

If you need freedom from fear, pray today and ask your Father in heaven to give you the liberty that comes only from Him.

Come and I Will Give You Rest

"Come to Me, all you who labor and are heavy laden, and
I will give you rest" (Matt. 11:28).

There are times in our walk with the Lord that we become laden down with problems, feeling as if we are
carrying a heavy burden; but Jesus tells us to cast our cares
upon Him, and He will give us rest. Does that promise look
good to you today? If you feel the weight of problems and
turmoil, there is an answer for you! Jesus is the answer, and
He tells you and me that He will take our problems and turmoil. He will take the heaviness off us, and He will bring
about the perfect solution to any and every problem.

Nothing that this world or the enemy brings our way is
too much for our Lord and Savior to overcome. He has told
us in His Word that He has made us more than conquerors.
He tells us, "In the world you will have tribulation, but be of
good cheer; I have overcome the world" (John 16:33). No
matter what happens in our lives to bring about anxiety, cares,
or heaviness, He has overcome. All we have to do is to trust
Him, cast our cares upon Him, and walk in the peace and
rest that He holds out to us.

Enter into His presence today and let Him be an overcomer in your life. Cast all your cares upon Him and receive
the beautiful rest that He has for you. Look unto Him who is
greater than any difficulty that exists in this world for you or
for me. Thank Him for His mercy, goodness, strength, and
power that He holds out to you today!

Find Rest for Your Souls

"Take My yoke upon you and learn from Me, for I am gentle and lowly in heart, and you will find rest for your souls. For My yoke is easy and My burden is light" (Matt. 11:29–30).

A yoke is a bar that joins two animals together so that they can work or pull a load in unison. The term has come to mean to couple together or to join intimately. We can assume from this scripture that Jesus tells us that when we are yoked with Him, not only do we learn from Him, but we also receive rest. If He is the One who can overcome any and every difficulty (and He is the One), being yoked to Him can do nothing else for us but bring about rest. He tells us His yoke is easy. If we are yoked with Him, He carries the load. If we walk side by side with Him, then we are on the right path that brings about smoothness, straightness, and the rest that comes from Him.

I am reminded of Isaiah 40:4–5, which says, "Every valley shall be exalted and every mountain and hill brought low; the crooked places shall be made straight and the rough places smooth; the glory of the Lord shall be revealed, and all flesh shall see it together; for the mouth of the Lord has spoken." When we take the yoke of the Lord, we find that glorious rest and peace that comes from walking side by side and hand in hand with Him. When we have that kind of intimate relationship with Him, He reveals His glory to us. When His glory comes upon us, others will see it and want that wondrous relationship with Him that brings about such beautiful rest and peace in our lives. The world is hungry for the rest and peace that comes only from Him.

Enter His Rest

"Therefore, since a promise remains of entering His rest, let us fear lest any of you seem to have come short of it" (Heb. 4:1).

God gives us a promise of entering into His rest, but what does that mean? How can we as Christians fall short of it? Many believe that entering into that rest means that we as Christians fully surrender to the Lordship of Jesus Christ and yield to the Holy Spirit to allow Him complete control in our lives.

I know there are areas in my life where I enjoy wonderful peace and rest. I still seem to struggle somewhat in other areas of my life. I do believe that the more we are yielded to the work of the Holy Spirit, the more we will experience God's rest in our lives. I believe that this process is accelerated as we spend more time with our Lord.

As we enter into His presence, know Him more intimately, spend time in His Word, and fellowship with Him, we will experience the rest and peace that comes with a growing trust in Him. As we know Him in a deeper way, faith and trust will become a more constant and continual way of life. The result of a deepening faith and trust is a way of life that exhibits the rest and peace that the world cannot give—it only comes from a deep and abiding relationship with Jesus Christ!

Will you ask Jesus to be Lord of your life and yield yourself to the work of the Holy Spirit? Enjoy the depth of an intimate relationship with Him that can only bring about such fruit in your life that those around you will seek to receive what you have!

174

Be Diligent to Enter That Rest

"There remains therefore a rest for the people of God. For he who has entered His rest has himself also ceased from his works as God did from His. Let us therefore be diligent to enter that rest . . ." (Heb. 4:9–11a).

In this scripture we are promised and assured that there is a rest for God's people, and we are told that the one who enters that rest has ceased from his works. That does not mean that we no longer go to a job or do physical work; it means that we have entered into a place of trust in God, and we have quit striving to do things in our own power and strength. In other words, we have come to a place of dependence on the Holy Spirit, and we have learned to recognize the direction and guidance of the Holy Spirit in our lives.

The peace and rest that come in this place of trust is truly amazing. This is not something that comes about easily or quickly in our lives as Christians. It is something that comes with submission to the Lord, with devotion to Him and spending time with Him in prayer, in fellowship with Him, and in reading His Word.

Our Christian walk boils down to decisions—decisions that we make on a daily basis. First we decide to ask Jesus to be our Savior. Then we decide to spend time daily with Him.

Will you decide today to walk in obedience to Him and to enter into that rest that comes from placing your trust in Him and His will for your life? Be diligent to enter that rest—there is nothing to compare with it!

175

Rest in Hope

"I have set the Lord always before me; because He is at my right hand I shall not be moved. Therefore my heart is glad, and my glory rejoices; my flesh also will rest in hope" (Ps. 16:8–9).

*W*hen we set the Lord always before us, we enter into a place of rest. We are so strong in our trust of Him that we know that nothing shall move us from His faithfulness and His promises to us. Great joy and rejoicing comes from that kind of rest. One thing we can know and understand through Psalm 16 is that keeping Him at our right hand, or staying close to Him, is essential to entering into that rest.

In Psalm 16, David tells us about the importance of staying close to the Lord, setting Him always before us, and keeping Him at our right hand. David words this in such a way that it helps us to understand the urgency of spending time with the Lord.

There is nothing more important that we can do in one whole day than to spend time with the Lord. When we get up in the morning, we may have a very busy schedule. We may think that there is no way to spend time with the Lord this particular morning; however, if we do not spend that time with Him, our day will not go as well. We need that time with Him more than all those other things that loom so big in our minds.

Make that decision today to spend special time with Him. And then ask Him to show you how you can grow in experiencing His presence all day long in all that you do. As you grow in experiencing His presence continually, you will be greatly blessed!

Lie Down in Peace

"I will both lie down in peace, and sleep; for You alone, O Lord, make me dwell in safety" (Ps. 4:8).

Do you have trouble sleeping some nights? God can give you the peace that you need to find that sweet rest in Him. It is so comforting to know that no matter what you face, the Lord is always with you and that He holds out His peace to you. This is a good scripture to memorize and use when you are having trouble falling asleep at night. As you quote these words over several times, you will find that the peace of God will begin to lull you to sleep.

God's Word is powerful—it brings the very life of God into our lives! Proverbs 4:20–22 says, "My son, give attention to my words; incline your ear to my sayings. Do not let them depart from your eyes; keep them in the midst of your heart; for they are life to those who find them . . ." This scripture tells us that as we keep God's Word before us, both reading it and listening to it, it will bring life to us. When I was in bondage to fear, I memorized three scriptures that promised me freedom from fear. When fear would try to come on me, I quoted those scriptures over and over. As I quoted them, the fear began to lessen until it finally left. There is power in God's Word.

When you cannot sleep, quote Psalm 4:8 over and over several times. You will go to sleep because there is power in God's Word. God is the author of peace and rest, and His desire is for you to find that wondrous contentment that comes from Him. Seek Him today and let Him reveal His peace to you in a way that will bring about such rest within you that others will see and want what you have!

Seek Peace and Pursue It

"Depart from evil and do good; seek peace and pursue it" (Ps. 34:14).

We are told here to pursue peace. Peace is something that we are to go after. It is not something that simply drops into our laps. If something is worthwhile in our life, we will make an effort to achieve it or to go after it. I sometimes wonder if we really understand the importance of peace in our lives. Not only does it bring a sweet contentment within our spirits, helping to calm our minds and emotions, but it also brings health to our physical bodies. Much is being said today about how many diseases are stress-related. Peace is something that we need to pursue. We need to do whatever it takes to have peace in our lives. What does it take? Simply to seek after God, spend time with Him and in His Word, and let trust and faith build in our lives. All it takes is making a decision to put the Lord first in our lives and to make that time for Him.

Are you willing to do that today? Seek after Him with everything that is within you! Pursue Him with all the diligence and energy that you possess! This is a pursuit that will bring such glorious results that you will wish that you had pursued Him much sooner. Do not let anything stand in the way of knowing your Lord in such a way that His peace rules and reigns in your life!

Abundance of Peace

"But the meek shall inherit the earth, and shall delight themselves in the abundance of peace" (Ps. 37:11).

Do you want an abundance of peace in your life? Meekness brings about peace abundantly in our lives. What is meekness? It is something that the world does not look upon favorably, but it is something that the Lord instructs us to have in our lives. Meekness means that we are humble before God, not struggling against Him. It also means exhibiting patience and gentleness. In the King James version of the Bible, meekness is listed as one of the fruit of the Spirit in Galatians 5:22. Meekness is something we should seek after in our lives because its result is an abundance of peace.

If peace is something that seems elusive to you, begin to act in a manner of kindness, gentleness, and patience. Quit struggling with the Lord about the things you do not understand or that go against your will, and let Him supply you with the strength and power to walk in meekness. Look unto Him who is able to provide everything that you need and bring about the peace and rest that comes from only Him. Yield yourself to His way and His purpose for your life and begin to walk in obedience to Him. You will find that meekness will become a way of life for you—yes, even you! All it takes is complete surrender to the King of the Universe, the Prince of Peace, the Lord of lords, the Great Jehovah God! Will you place the whole of your life in His hands today, and then stand back and bask in His presence and in the abundance of peace that He will bring into your life?

179

He Will Speak Peace

"I will hear what God the Lord will speak, for He will speak peace to His people and to His saints" (Ps. 85:8).

Are you one of God's saints? We sometimes have trouble recognizing ourselves as a saint because we know who we are and what is in our hearts; however, according to God's Word, when we are born again into the kingdom of God, we become a saint of God. That does not mean that we live a perfect life, but it does mean that we are redeemed by the blood of Jesus Christ. It means that we have accepted what Jesus did for us on the cross, and we have entered into the family of God.

If you have accepted Jesus as your Lord and Savior, then you are a saint of God! As a saint of God, one of His family, and chosen by Him, He speaks peace to you. His peace that passes all understanding is being spoken to you and to me through His Word and through that very special time when we enter into His presence.

Are you receiving the peace that He is speaking to you today? Let some of those things that loom so big before you fall by the wayside, and spend time seeking Him through His Word and also through meeting Him face to face. As you seek Him, He will respond by revealing Himself to you in such a special way that your life will never be the same again. And you will want to seek Him again tomorrow, the next day, and on and on.

Look unto Him who can bring perfect peace into your life!

Peace for Those Who Love Your Law

"Great peace have those who love Your law, and nothing causes them to stumble" (Ps. 119:165).

God's Word is an essential ingredient in our walk with the Lord. As we spend time in His Word, we will find that peace will grow and become stronger within us. Anytime that we go through difficulties or have needs in our lives, we can find comfort, answers, and direction through reading and applying God's Word.

Yesterday I had a question about an important decision that I needed to make, and I did not know what to do. As I read God's Word, peace began to come over me and envelop me. Before long, not only did I experience peace, but I had an answer about the decision that I needed to make.

So often you and I make our decisions based on what we think and reason or on what other people say. But when we make our decisions based on God's Word and the direction of the Holy Spirit, we "know that we know" what to do. When we base our decisions on God's direction, we will find that we make good decisions—we do not stumble!

If you are faced with making a decision today or you need direction for your life, call upon the One who has all the answers. Ask His direction as you read His Word and find His will for you. Once you walk in obedience to His will, you will find that His peace that passes all understanding will permeate your very being.

The Paths of Wisdom Are Peace

"Her [wisdom's] ways are ways of pleasantness, and all her paths are peace" (Prov. 3:17).

We are instructed over and over in Scripture to seek after wisdom. The kind of wisdom that we are to seek after is God's wisdom, which brings about peace within our lives. Why does God's wisdom bring peace into our lives? I believe it is because with God's wisdom we can accomplish anything that He wills for our lives. We can have the guidance and direction to make good decisions instead of bad decisions that will get us into a lot of trouble or cause problems in our lives.

When we put our trust completely in the Lord, we know that He works all things for our good. We know that we can trust Him to give us what we need to be overcomers in this world. He knows the beginning from the end, and He has all the answers. If we look to Him for wisdom in each situation in which we find ourselves, He will show us what we need to know.

If you are facing a difficult situation today, and you do not know where to turn or what to do, call upon Him who has all the answers—the One who is Wisdom! James 1:5 says, "If any of you lacks wisdom, let him ask of God, who gives to all liberally and without reproach, and it will be given to him." If you are an "any" or an "all," He will surely give you the wisdom to know what to do in your situation. Trust Him today and see what great and glorious things He will do for you as you seek Him for answers in your life!

Peace Like a River

"Behold, I will extend peace to her like a river, and the glory of the Gentiles like a flowing stream" (Isa. 66:12a).

*H*ave you ever sat by the side of a river and experienced the peace and rest that comes from enjoying the gentle flow of the water? Nothing is quite as restful! That same kind of peace is available to us through our precious Lord and Savior. He holds out His peace to us simply because He loves us. Nothing is as elusive in the world that we live in today as peace—the peace that comes from God. Why is it so elusive today? I believe it is because there is such a turning away from God and the things of God. Even Christians sometimes get so caught up in the things of the world that we fail to center upon the only One who can truly bring peace into our lives. We need to spend time in the presence of the Lord and look to Him with such reverence and awe that the things of this world will pale in importance. When we truly are in His presence, the things of the world can do nothing else but fade!

Will you choose to seek Him with all your heart today and enter into that very special place of His presence? You will find that His peace will enter into your life in a new way and the things that have been heavy on your heart will begin to melt away. A new lightness and joy will come as He makes Himself known to you.

I Give You My Peace

"Peace I leave with you; My peace I give to you; not as the world gives do I give to you. Let not your heart be troubled, neither let it be afraid" (John 14:27).

The world cannot give us peace because it comes only from God. The world may give us a momentary sense of satisfaction, happiness, or contentment; however, the moment a crisis or difficult situation comes into our lives, this satisfaction, happiness, and contentment leave. When we have the peace that comes from the Father, crisis or difficulties will not cause our peace to run in the opposite direction. Jesus also said, "These things I have spoken to you, that in Me you may have peace. In the world you will have tribulation; but be of good cheer, I have overcome the world" (John 16:33). This tells us that no matter what happens in our lives, we can have the peace of God that overcomes the difficulties that come our way.

Trusting in God is not always easy, but it brings about a peace that the world cannot understand. Trust comes from spending time reading and studying God's Word, which speaks to every issue that we may face. Many times I have been faced with something that could cause me to be fearful, anxious, or worried. As I read and dwelled on God's Word, the difficulty began to fade in importance. And as I was going through this particular trial, I knew that He was with me, holding my hand and giving me His grace.

If you face a difficult problem at this time, read God's Word, and enter into His presence. Let Him give you that peace and assurance that He is able to take care of you and bring victory in your life.

In Me You May Have Peace

"These things I have spoken to you, that in Me you may have peace. In the world you will have tribulation; but be of good cheer, I have overcome the world" (John 16:33).

When my son was in second grade, he was diagnosed with a memory learning disability. This brought great fear and anxiety into my life and great sorrow and hurt into my son's life. I began to search God's Word for scriptures that would bring peace and comfort into our lives. I also wanted faith to rise up in me to be able to pray according to God's will and believe Him to help my son to overcome. I turned to Isaiah 54:13, which says, "All your children shall be taught by the Lord, and great shall be the peace of your children."

I also found Proverbs 10:7, which says, "The memory of the righteous is blessed." The third scripture that God led me to was 1 Corinthians 2:16, which says, "But we have the mind of Christ." I began to claim and meditate on these three scriptures and to pray these verses over my son in the morning before he left for school and also in the evening as he went to bed. Great peace entered my life, and I knew that my God was able to overcome what seemed like such an impossibility to my mind.

After praying these scriptures and believing for God's intervention in my son's life for five years, a miracle occurred! Much to the shock of his advisors and teachers, my son was able to go from a resource class to a regular classroom and he was making second honors in about six months. To God be all the glory!

Peace Comes with Being Spiritually Minded

"For to be carnally minded is death, but to be spiritually minded is life and peace" (Rom. 8:6).

Do you want peace in your life? The answer is to be spiritually minded. You may ask, "What does it mean to be spiritually minded? How do I become spiritually minded?" To be spiritually minded means to turn your thoughts to the things of the Lord. Read His Word, spend time in prayer and praising Him, and enter into His presence and bask in His glory.

Jeremiah 33:3 says, "Call to Me, and I will answer you, and show you great and mighty things, which you do not know." As we seek Him and call unto Him, He gives us revelation that comes from His Word and from the Holy Spirit. As we learn more from His Word and from His Spirit, we find that we are growing spiritually. We are becoming spiritually minded!

When the things of this world seem to loom big, and we find ourselves dwelling on the difficulties, we need to renew our minds. We need to replace those negative thoughts with the Word of God. Let us look at what God says about the situation instead of what the world is saying about it!

As we look unto Him who is able to give us victory and help us to become overcomers, we will find that the very peace and life of God will rise up strong within us. We will know that there is not one thing that can come against us that God Almighty cannot overcome. Look unto Him today and let that peace that passes all understanding rule and reign in your life!

Pursue Peace

"Therefore let us pursue the things which make for peace and the things by which one may edify another" (Rom. 14:19).

We are told several times in Scripture to pursue peace. Peace can seem evasive at times, but we are to be diligent to run after peace. We are told in Scripture how peace can be a part of our lives, so we need to be obedient to what we learn through Scripture about pursuing peace.

Peace originally comes into our lives when we accept Jesus as our Lord and Savior. But we all know that at times things happen in our lives that seem to steal our peace and joy from us. At these times we need to seek the Lord with all that is within us and to dwell on His Word. When His Word comes in, the enemy (who steals our peace) will have to flee.

I recall a time when I was going to speak at a church. Right before I was to leave my house, fear began to overcome me. I began to walk through my house quoting 2 Timothy 1:7, Isaiah 41:10, and 1 John 4:18 (look them up—it will bless you) with all my might. I was pursuing peace with everything that was within me. Very soon the fear left, and I was encompassed with peace. The Lord showed me that I was to share with the people at the church what had happened to me because what the enemy meant for evil, the Lord was using to bring glory to His name!

Decide to pursue peace today with everything that is within you. Do not let the enemy steal anything from you, but rise up and become the person of God that He created you to be—strong and courageous for Him and full of His peace!

God Is the Author of Peace

"For God is not the author of confusion but of peace, as in all the churches of the saints" (1 Cor. 14:33).

God is not the author of confusion but of peace. If there is confusion in your life, you can be assured that it is not from God. His desire is to bring peace abundantly to you. There are times in all of our lives that confusion seems to be everywhere we turn. When that happens, we need to look at ourselves and recognize that without peace God's purposes cannot be fulfilled. At these times we need to pursue peace with everything that is within us.

David wrote, "In Thee, O Lord, do I put my trust; let me never be put to confusion" (Ps. 71:1 KJV).

David recognized that trust in the Lord cancels out confusion and brings peace. When confusion is in our lives, we cannot think clearly, we cannot make wise decisions, and we seem to be groping for answers. Confusion is a terrible state in which to be.

We need to realize that God is the One who can bring us out of confusion. He is the answer to indecision, muddled thinking, and things that seem to be in great disorder. Our God is an orderly God; and He will bring peace into our situation if we will only look to Him, trust Him, and surrender our minds, emotions, and wills to Him.

Let Him, who is able to bring that peace that passes all understanding, have complete control of your whole being. Watch and see what order and peace He will bring into what seems impossible to you! Our God is a great God and nothing is impossible to Him!

Peace That Surpasses All Understanding

"And the peace of God, which surpasses all understanding, will guard your hearts and minds through Christ Jesus" (Phil. 4:7).

One cannot explain to an unbeliever what God's peace is like. It has to be experienced. It truly does surpass all understanding, for our minds cannot comprehend or explain because words are not adequate.

When God's peace comes into a situation that has been utter chaos, we know that God and God alone has intervened. He not only brings peace into our lives, but He guards our hearts and minds so that we look at the situation through His eyes and respond accordingly.

What should we do if our minds seem to continually dwell on things that bring confusion, fear, or doubt into our lives? We need to renew our minds as Paul tells us in Romans 12:2, which says, "And do not be conformed to this world, but be transformed by the renewing of your mind, that you may prove what is that good and acceptable and perfect will of God." We must pursue peace through being diligent to renew our minds by thinking on those things that are true, noble, just, pure, lovely, and of good report (Phil. 4:8). We find that the results are so wondrous that we never regret the time and effort spent on seeking God's peace.

Come into His presence today and let Him reveal His peace to you in ways that perhaps you have not experienced before. Let Him guard your mind and heart so that you will think on those lovely things that are in His Word instead of all the evil that the world has to offer.

Let the Peace of God Rule in Your Heart

"And let the peace of God rule in your hearts, to which also you were called in one body; and be thankful" (Col. 3:15).

We have no trouble being thankful when the peace of God rules in our hearts. When peace comes in, an attitude of thanksgiving immediately follows because we are so grateful to be rid of anxiety, fear, confusion, doubt and all those things that peace replaces.

This scripture says to let the peace of God rule in your hearts. That means that you must let peace rule in your heart.

You and I have a part to play in this. God does not simply drop peace in our hearts. We must let peace rule in our hearts, and that can happen only when we are completely trusting God. We need to learn to trust Him with every aspect of our lives. If trusting God in some area of your life is a problem for you today, turn to the Bible and find several scriptures that will speak to your situation. You will find that as you read, meditate on, and study these verses, peace will begin to rise within you. Let the Holy Spirit bring these scriptures alive in your spirit. That happens as you read the Word of God, trusting His Spirit to bring revelation and understanding to you.

Let Him reveal Himself to you today through reading His Word, spending time in His presence, and trusting the Holy Spirit to work in your life! Then begin to notice the peace that comes into your life; and rejoice greatly as those shackles of fear, care, and burdens fall away!

The Lord of Peace

"Now may the Lord of peace Himself give you peace always in every way. The Lord be with you all" (2 Thess. 3:16).

This scripture tells us that Jesus Christ is Lord of peace. When we lack peace in our lives, all we have to do is to seek Him. How do we seek Him? We read His Word that brings truth into our lives, we spend time with Him fellowshiping in His presence, and we listen to hear what He speaks to us through the Holy Spirit and through His Word.

When I face something in my life and I do not know what to do, I begin to seek the Lord through prayer. I ask Him to guide me to Scripture that may bring clarity into the situation. I listen to hear what He may be trying to tell me. Sometimes I am impressed with an answer, and sometimes I am not. I begin to read Scripture. When something seems to "jump" off the page at me, I realize that this may be God trying to tell me something or give me direction. When that peace that passes all understanding comes within my heart, then I know that God is directing me. The best way that I know to explain is that "I know that I know that I know." There is no doubt—only peace. I believe that peace is one of the best gauges that we can use to understand God's direction for us. The other reliable gauge is God's Word. He will not direct us to do anything that goes against His Word.

If you need direction in your life today, let Him show you His will and His way for you through His Word and through the peace that will come when you begin to move in the right direction. Remember He wants to give you peace always in every way!

Seek Peace and Pursue It

"Let him turn away from evil and do good; let him seek peace and pursue it" (1 Pet. 3:11).

*A*re you seeking peace and pursuing it? If you are, then you are turning away from evil and you are doing good. Ask yourself, "Is there anything in my life right now that is evil?" Sometimes things that we do not even realize are wrong are standing in the way of peace being within our lives. We need to ask the Lord, and He will reveal to us anything that He may consider sin in our lives that we have overlooked. We sometimes look at sins that we consider "big" sins such as murder, stealing, adultery, etc. and know that they are not a part of our lives; however, sometimes we overlook sins that are operating in us such as doubt, worry, anxiety, fear, a bad attitude, or unforgiveness.

Seek and pursue peace today by letting the Lord reveal whatever may be in your life that He considers sin. There may be disobedience because you have not been willing to answer a call that God has on your life. This may result from a lack of confidence in your ability to do what He calls you to do. It may be because you have a desire to do something else. Whatever the reason, recognize it as sin, repent, and then surrender your will to the heavenly Father. Tell Him that you are willing to do whatever He wants you to do. Then enter into the place of rest and peace that has been evading you for some time. Know that His plan for you is far greater than anything that you could want or imagine for yourself. Also know that whatever He calls you to do, He will provide everything within you that is needed to accomplish His will. Let His peace encompass you as you relinquish everything to Him!

Live in Peace

"Finally, brethren, farewell. Become complete. Be of good comfort, be of one mind, live in peace; and the God of love and peace will be with you" (2 Cor. 13:11).

Paul's letter to the Corinthians is full of instructions about living a Christian life, and in the closing of this letter he tells them and us to live in peace. When God's peace rules and reigns within our hearts, it makes it easier to live in peace with those around us. In preceding days, we have examined how God's peace can become a very real part of our lives. Today we want to look at how we can walk in peace with others.

Unity within believers is a vitally important ingredient for seeing the kingdom of God furthered upon this earth. When we walk in peace with one another and are unified, there is nothing within the will of God that we cannot do. The reason that there is so much in the Bible about peace and unity among the followers of Jesus is because the Lord wants us to work together to fulfill His purposes.

When we choose to walk in peace with those around us, we can be assured that the presence of Almighty God is with us. We are told over and over in His Word to forgive others, even to forgive our enemies! The reason we are instructed to forgive seventy times seven is to show the importance of always forgiving and walking in peace with others.

Will you choose today to forgive anyone that may have hurt you or mistreated you? You will find as you forgive, the peace of God and His presence will rise within you.

The Kingdom of God Is Peace

"For the kingdom of God is not eating and drinking, but righteousness and peace and joy in the Holy Spirit" (Rom. 14:17).

*I*n his letter to the Romans, Paul tells them that the kingdom of God is righteousness and peace and joy in the Holy Spirit. Do you have the Holy Spirit living within you? If you are a born-again believer in Jesus Christ, you do have the Holy Spirit living within you. The Holy Spirit, who is a person of the Trinity, is righteousness, peace, and joy. When He comes to dwell within you, He brings the very nature and attributes of God to live within you.

As we mature in our Christian walk, fruit grows within us; and God's attributes begin to shine forth from us with greater strength. As we grow closer to the Lord through our daily Bible study, prayer, communion, and fellowship with Him, we find that our countenance changes and we are being transformed into His image. As we become more like Him, we find that His peace becomes stronger and stronger within us. Others notice the change within us, and the peace that everyone longs for becomes so evident within us that others begin to ask what is different about us. One reason He places His peace within us is so that we can be examples and witnesses to others of His great grace.

Will you allow Him to make you a witness for Him today? Seek Him and let Him reveal Himself in all His glory to you. As you see Him for who He is, you will be overcome with gratitude for His grace; and you will begin to experience His peace with greater abundance!

God Rested and Was Refreshed

"It is a sign between Me and the children of Israel forever; for in six days the Lord made the heavens and the earth, and on the seventh day He rested and was refreshed" (Exod. 31:17).

On the seventh day of creation God rested and was refreshed. He has a refreshing for us as His children that comes to us when we enter into His presence. Just as He took time to be refreshed, He wants us to take time to be refreshed by Him. He calls us to come aside and spend time with Him in order to know Him with all His glorious attributes.

As we spend time face to face with our Father God, we cannot help but be refreshed in the knowledge that, whatever comes our way, He is able to see us through and help us to overcome and be victorious.

When we trust God, a refreshing comes. This trust enables us to lean completely on the One who has infinite power, might, and strength to provide for our well-being. Notice that the scripture for today says that God rested and was refreshed. Refreshing comes when we rest. We rest in God when we put our total trust in Him and in His abilities, not our own. Trust in God brings about a refreshing that compares with nothing else.

Are you feeling weary and tired? Are you feeling frustrated and worried? Are anger and resentment a problem for you? Place it all at the feet of Jesus and let Him supply that rest and refreshing that only He can give. Put your trust in your Lord and Savior by relinquishing everything to Him. He waits to carry all your burdens and to bring the refreshing that comes like a gentle brook washing over you and within you.

Refreshing in the Presence of the Lord

"Repent therefore and be converted, that your sins may be blotted out, so that times of refreshing may come from the presence of the Lord" (Acts 3:19).

After the day of Pentecost, Peter was on fire for God. He had been filled with the Holy Spirit and was preaching the Word of God with power. Many were being saved, healed, and set free from bondage. In his sermon he said that when we repent and are converted, we can experience the refreshing of the Lord through entering His presence. If anyone needed refreshing, it was the Jewish people who lived during Peter's time. They were under the rule of Rome and did not have the freedom that comes from self-government. The only way that they could experience freedom and refreshing was to submit their lives to Jesus Christ.

Regardless of anyone's situation, Jesus, and Jesus alone, can bring true freedom within and the refreshing that comes from knowing Him in a personal way. Once we turn our lives over to Him, He sends His Spirit to live within us, enabling us to draw close to Him. As we spend more quality time with Him, basking in His presence, we will come to know Him better, and we will be able to place more and more trust in Him. We will find that, as our trust in Him grows, we experience more and more of the refreshing that comes from Him.

Seek to enter into such a close relationship with your Lord Jesus that you will turn more and more of yourself over to Him. Let your trust grow as you come to know Him better, sitting at His feet and worshiping Him for the wondrous God that He is!

See His Face with Joy

"He shall pray to God, and He will delight in him, he shall see His face with joy" (Job 33:26).

Do you want to bring delight to your Father who is in heaven? The scripture for today tells you that when you pray, it brings delight to Him. Does that make you wonder why it is so difficult for His children to find the time or to take the time to enter into prayer with Him? If His children could understand the joy and delight our company brings to Him, I believe we would let nothing stand in the way of spending that precious time with Him in prayer.

When we come before Him face to face during that time of prayer and fellowship, we look upon Him with joy in our hearts. Refreshing comes in His presence, bringing the joy of the Lord into our lives. When His joy is alive within us, we know that there is nothing on the face of this earth that is too great or difficult to overcome with His help. We know in our hearts that "if God be for us, who can be against us?"

Enter into His refreshing today and experience His joy within your soul. Come into His presence with thanksgiving! Let Him delight in you as you express your love and gratitude to Him!

JULY 4

Shout for Joy

"But let all those rejoice who put their trust in You; let them ever shout for joy, because You defend them; let those also who love Your name be joyful in You" (Ps. 5:11).

The joy of the Lord brings refreshing into our lives. When we are filled with joy, we are in a place of great freedom. It rejuvenates our whole being when we are refreshed with the joy that comes from the One who provides all that we need. What brings joy into our lives? The scripture for today tells us that joy comes when we put our trust in the Lord.

Trusting the Lord is something that we as Christians talk about frequently. Do our actions, however, indicate that we truly put our trust in the Lord? If we truly trust Him, we act as if His Word is truth. In other words, we believe His Word and follow through with the instructions within the pages of the Bible. When we are told, "Be anxious for nothing, but in everything by prayer and supplication, with thanksgiving, let your requests be made known to God" (Phil. 4:6), do we overcome anxiety by spending time in prayer before the Lord? Or do we find ourselves continually dwelling on the circumstances that cause anxiety in our lives? We make this choice many times daily. Will we put our trust in God, or will we continue in the way that is natural to us as humans and dwell on those things that bring worry, anxiety, anger, or anything else that is not of God into our lives?

Decide today that you will put your trust in the One who is able to set you free from all that disturbs you, and let Him bring His joy into your life. Let go of all that is burdensome and brings worry and anxiety into your life today. Receive the refreshing that He holds out to you!

In Your Presence Is Fullness of Joy

"You will show me the path of life; in Your presence is fullness of joy; at Your right hand are pleasures forevermore" (Ps. 16:11).

When we enter into the presence of the Lord, we find that we are full of His joy. Nothing revives us as much as being in the presence of God Almighty. If you are hungry for some relief from the burdens of the world, from the chaos and confusion that comes with the busy schedules that are a part of society today, set aside some time to spend alone with your heavenly Father. Let Him restore you and bring about the joy and refreshing that comes from knowing Him intimately.

Psalm 16 shows us that, as we take the time to be still before the Creator of the universe, He will show us direction that leads to life—the life of God! In His presence we find the way to enter into the very life of God. We find out the meaning of being alive in the Spirit of God. We learn the meaning of being able to live like the disciples in the early church. They were continually preaching the Word of God in power, the sick were healed, and the captives were set free. The life of God is awesome in power!

Do you want to know more about entering into the very life of God? Simply spend time in the presence of the Lord, and He will begin to reveal His life to you. The refreshing that will come into your life will be so glorious that you will want to spend time with Him over and over. You will begin to seek Him as never before so that entering into His presence becomes a continual process in your life.

Joy in Your Strength

"The king shall have joy in Your strength, O Lord; and in Your salvation how greatly shall he rejoice!" (Ps. 21:1).

David tells the Lord that he will have joy in the strength of God. David had a very close relationship with the Lord. He spent time in His presence so often that God said, "I have found David the son of Jesse, a man after My own heart, who will do all My will" (Acts 13:22). Being in the presence of the Lord enabled David to grow so close to the Lord that his heart became like the heart of God! Through this closeness David found the strength that comes from God. When he experienced the strength of the Lord, he found a refreshing and joy in his life that was possible only through God.

Do you need the strength of the Lord to enable you to overcome in one or more situations in your life?

If so, all you need to do is set aside time to be still before the Lord and let Him reveal His presence and His glory to you. As you begin to see Him in all His majesty, and yet in all His mercy, you find that His joy will begin to well up within you. The joy of the Lord and the glory of His presence bring such strength into your life that you will know that nothing in this world can come against you or cause you problems that you cannot overcome with the help of the Lord! He is more than able to care for every need in your life. He is more than willing to make you "more than conquerors through Him who loved us" (Rom. 8:37). Seek Him today with all that is within you and let Him reveal His strength and His joy to you as He meets your every need!

Joy Comes in the Morning

". . . Weeping may endure for a night, but joy comes in the morning" (Ps. 30:5).

If you have been in a difficult place for a time, take courage because God promises that joy will come in the morning. Joy is as close as the dawn. Have you ever gone through a night of anxiety or worry when you could not sleep? It seemed as if the morning would never come. But, of course, the morning did come because the sun always rises. God's promise is for you. He tells you that no matter what you go through, He has an answer, and it will come at the right time.

I was praying with a friend recently who had been going through an extremely difficult time. She said to me, "Mary, do you think the night could be just about over?"

She was holding on to God's promise that joy comes in the morning, and she was waiting expectantly for the dawn to come. What happens when the dawn comes? The darkness that has surrounded us begins to fade as the light of the rising sun comes up over the horizon. When the darkness of our circumstances seems the most unbearable, we can know that the joy of the Lord is about to come into our lives as the Son makes His light shine and causes the darkness to flee.

Place your problems in the hands of the One who shines so brightly that there is no room for darkness. May His joy rise up strong within you as you trust in Him!

Humble Shall Increase Their Joy

"The humble also shall increase their joy in the Lord, and the poor among men shall rejoice in the Holy One of Israel" (Isa. 29:19).

If we want an increase in the joy of the Lord in our lives, we need to humble ourselves before God and before men. Humility is not a very attractive quality in the eyes of the world, but in the eyes of God it is one of the greatest qualities that we can have. Jesus was an example of humility to us because He never tried to exalt Himself. In Matthew 18, Jesus was asked the question, "Who then is greatest in the kingdom of heaven?" He called a little child to Him and answered, "Whoever humbles himself as this little child is the greatest in the kingdom of heaven."

Pride is something that we all have to fight in our lives. There seems to be something within us as human beings that cause us to want to exalt ourselves. We want to be noticed by others, and we want others to think well of us. If we do not feel that we are receiving the recognition that we believe we deserve, we so often flaunt our achievements and good qualities before others. Instead of trying to make ourselves look good in the eyes of others, we should concentrate on the goodness and glory of our heavenly Father. When we look at Him in all His glory and power, we begin to recognize that we are nothing without Him. We begin to submit ourselves to Him and His will, and we walk in humility before Him and before others.

Decide today to seek the Lord with all of your being, submitting yourself to Him, and let that glorious quality of humility rise up within you!

The Ransomed of the Lord

"And the ransomed of the Lord shall return, and come to Zion with singing, with everlasting joy on their heads. They shall obtain joy and gladness, and sorrow and sighing shall flee away" (Isa. 35:10).

Who are the ransomed of the Lord? All that have been born again into the kingdom of God are the ransomed of the Lord. We were bought with a very costly price when Jesus went to the cross to pay for our sins. When we recognize the greatness of what Jesus did for us, our hearts are filled with such joy that it is indescribable. When we understand that He took our sins and replaced them with His righteousness, we lift our voices in singing joyful praises to Him. The joy within us spills over into the lives of others because we simply cannot contain the gladness that comes from knowing Him.

If there has been some type of sorrow in your life, meditate on the scripture for today and let the joy of the Lord rise within you. His joy is a gift that the world cannot give you. You may find situations within the world that bring a measure of happiness into your life for a time, but then that happiness will flee. The joy of the Lord is so real and reaches so deep within you that nothing can compare to it. Ask the Lord to fill you with His joy and experience a new depth of relationship with Him, one that will satisfy the longing within your soul!

Break Forth into Joy

"Break forth into joy, sing together, you waste places of Jerusalem! For the Lord has comforted His people, He has redeemed Jerusalem" (Isa. 52:9).

No matter what place you are in today, no matter what your circumstance may be, the Lord God Almighty is able and willing to see you through and to bring you victory. Now that is something to break forth into joy about! Our God is able to comfort us! He is able to provide for anything that we may need! Our God has redeemed us! We are a blessed people because the God of the whole universe loves us. He sent His Son to die on the cross to pay for our sins so that we may have a relationship with Him and be a part of His family. Our God is a loving God who holds out His mercy, grace, and comfort to us.

We so often get discouraged and depressed because of the circumstances around us. We have a wondrous Lord, however, who has told us in 1 Corinthians 15:57, "But thanks be to God, who gives us the victory through our Lord Jesus Christ."

Do these verses encourage you today in whatever circumstance you find yourself? As you read and meditate on these scriptures, you will find that the joy of the Lord will begin to rise within you. In the beginning that joy will be as a small seed, but as you continue to dwell on the meaning within these scriptures, you will find that His joy will grow and grow within you until you feel as if you cannot contain it. It is then that you will begin to break forth with joy, and your mouth will begin to sing praises to the Lord of the universe who loves you with an everlasting love!

You Shall Go Out with Joy

"For you shall go out with joy, and be led out with peace; the mountains and the hills shall break forth into singing before you, and all the trees of the field shall clap their hands" (Isa. 55:12).

Do you long for some peace and rest? In the scripture for today, the Lord promises peace and joy to you and all His children. As a matter of fact, we shall have such joy and peace that it will seem as if all God's creation is breaking forth into singing before us.

You may ask, "How can that be true in my life? She does not know what I am going through." No, I do not know what you are going through, but I do know that, no matter what you or anyone else is going through, our God is bigger! If God was able to deliver Shadrach, Meshach, and Abednego from the fiery furnace, He is certainly able to deliver us from whatever difficulty confronts us.

Shadrach, Meshach, and Abednego were inside a fiery furnace that was so hot that the men who threw them into the furnace were killed. Can you imagine the joy and peace that they must have experienced when they saw the fourth man walking around in the furnace with them, and they were not being consumed by the flames? Can you imagine the joy and peace that they must have felt when they were taken out of the fiery furnace completely well and intact? God is able to provide everything that you need to help you overcome in whatever faces you today. Trust Him as Shadrach, Meshach, and Abednego did so long ago, and receive the joy and peace that He holds out to you today!

Joy of the Lord Is Your Strength

"Do not sorrow, for the joy of the Lord is your strength"
(Neh. 8:10).

When we go through difficult times, it seems as if everything and everyone is against us. We feel defeated and
beaten down. We can, however, know that it does not matter what we are going through. Our God is more than enough
to bring us victory! Romans 8:37 tells us, "Yet in all these
things we are more than conquerors through Him who loved
us." It is enough to be conquerors, but our God tells us that
we are more than conquerors! When this truth becomes in-
grained within us, the joy of the Lord wells up within us, and
we are strengthened.

I find that when I am going through very difficult times,
it helps me to meditate on scriptures such as the one for
today, and also to think on those times in the past when
the Lord has strengthened me and brought me victory.
Sometimes the victory would be almost instant. Other times
the victory would be a long time in coming, but the Lord
would sustain me and give me grace as we went through the
difficulty together. I have also found that the times when
the victory did not come easily or quickly, I grew stronger
in my walk with the Lord and in my dependence and trust
of Him. His strength allows us to go through a difficulty
with grace and dignity as we place our total trust in the
One who is greater than all things.

Will you place your problems and burdens in His hands
and let Him fill you with His joy and strength? Be refreshed in
His presence today as He provides His grace in all you face!

Your Word Was Joy to Me

"Your words were found, and I ate them, and Your word was to me the joy and rejoicing of my heart; for I am called by Your name, O Lord God of hosts" (Jer. 15:16).

The scripture for today gives us understanding of the importance of God's Word in our lives. We need to find God's Word for our lives each day. That means we need to pick up our Bible and read it. We need to study and seek to understand it. We also need the help of the Holy Spirit in bringing the Word of God alive in our spirits.

I believe that the meaning of "eating" God's Word is the same as we might express in today's vernacular as "devouring" God's Word. In other words, we need to keep it before us in such a way that it truly changes our lives. When God's Word has that kind of importance in our lives, we find that His joy rises up strong within us. We find ourselves rejoicing before Him continuously.

If you have been slack in reading and studying your Bible, make the commitment today to let the Word of God be a strong priority in your life. But it is not enough to read or even to study your Bible. You need to let the Holy Spirit guide, teach, and admonish you through Scripture. When the Holy Spirit guides your reading and studying, you will find that the Word of God comes alive within you in such a way that you will live and experience what you are reading. Your life will take on new excitement and joy as you are refreshed by the life that comes from within the pages of the Holy Bible!

Rejoice When You Are Reviled

"Blessed are you when men hate you, and when they exclude you, and revile you, and cast out your name as evil, for the Son of Man's sake. Rejoice in that day and leap for joy! For indeed your reward is great in heaven, for in like manner their fathers did to the prophets" (Luke 6:22–23).

I used to read this passage and think, How in the world can one rejoice when he or she is being reviled and excluded by others? I had a very clear answer to that question some years ago when I was with a group of women. Most of us were young mothers at the time, and we were standing together after a meeting discussing children, homes, etc. I made a comment about how the Lord had blessed me, and one of the women looked at me incredulously. She turned her back on me which excluded me from the circle of women. To my great surprise, the feeling that was going through me was pure joy as I recalled the same scripture that we are using for our devotion today. I realized at that moment that God is able to supernaturally enable us to respond to exclusion and rejection with great joy when it is for Jesus' sake.

Do not be afraid to share your love for Jesus. Do not be afraid to tell others about all that He has done for you. Know that, even if others reject you or persecute you in some way, your reward will be great in heaven. As you spend time with your Lord today, ask Him to fill you with such joy in His presence that when He brings opportunities your way to be a witness to others, you will not hesitate. The joy that is within you will rise and spill over so that others will experience the goodness and grace of the Lord.

Your Joy May Be Full

"These things I have spoken to you, that My joy may remain in you, and that your joy may be full" (John 15:11).

Jesus speaks words that bring joy into our lives. In John 15, He spoke about the vine and the branches. He tells us that He is the vine, and we are the branches.

The branches cannot do anything without the vine. He shares with us the importance of our dependence upon Him, and He tells us that as we receive these words and begin to live them in our lives, His joy will be made full within us.

We need to draw so close to the Lord that we know Him for who He is. We need to learn more about His nature and His attributes, and we need to seek Him with everything that is within us. He calls out to us to come unto Him. He reaches out to us with open arms, and He longs to draw us close to Himself. As we spend time reading His Word and resting in His presence, our lives will be changed. We will find His joy bubbling up within us like rivers of living water, and that joy will affect the lives of those around us. Joy is contagious! When His joy flows out of us, others' lives cannot help but be touched and changed.

Will you draw close to the Lord today, and let Him fill you with the fullness of His joy? Ask Him to use you to spread His joy among the people around you. Expect His joy to rise up strongly within you as you reach out to others in His name.

No One Will Take Your Joy From You

"Therefore you now have sorrow; but I will see you again and your heart will rejoice, and your joy no one will take from you" (John 16:22).

Jesus told His disciples and followers that He will leave them, but He will return again. He said that when they see Him again, they will rejoice, and no one will take their joy from them. When Jesus gives us joy in our lives, no person can take it from us. It is a gift from the Lord. As long as we keep our eyes upon Him and trust in Him, His joy will remain strong within us.

When there are times of sorrow in our lives, we need to look to the One who can bring peace and joy within us. I have found in my own life, during times of sorrow, that I find comfort and strength by reading and meditating on God's Word. The words of the Bible bring peace, comfort, and joy even in the darkest times that beset us. Knowing that Jesus is with us and will never leave or forsake us brings comfort. Knowing that He has come to set us free and give us victory brings deep and lasting joy into our lives.

If you are going through a difficult and sorrowful time in your life today, open up your Bible and turn to 2 Corinthians 1:3–4a, which says, "Blessed be the God and Father of our Lord Jesus Christ, the Father of mercies and God of all comfort, who comforts us in all our tribulation . . ." As you meditate on this scripture and others on comfort, see how the Lord will fill your heart with His joy. Watch Him with wonder as He turns your sorrow into joy!

Ask That Your Joy May Be Full

"Until now you have asked nothing in My name. Ask, and you will receive, that your joy may be full" (John 16:24).

Jesus told us to ask in His name. What does it mean to ask in the name of Jesus? It does not mean simply saying in a prayer, "In the name of Jesus." It means asking in the will and nature of Jesus. It means to ask as He would, not as we desire.

When we do ask according to His will, we can know that He will answer our prayer. What joy that brings into our lives when He answers our prayers! To think that Jesus, the King of kings and Lord of lords, hears our requests and answers! That certainly is reason to be joyful!

Have you had a prayer answered recently? How did you feel when you realized that the Lord had heard and answered your prayer? If you have not had a prayer answered recently, perhaps you need to determine what His will is before you pray. When you pray according to His will, you can be assured he will hear and answer. First John 5:14–15 says, "Now this is the confidence that we have in Him, that if we ask anything according to His will, He hears us. And if we know that He hears us, whatever we ask, we know that we have the petitions that we have asked of Him." There is no doubt about it—your prayer will be answered.

Place your trust in Him today, seek His will, and pray accordingly. Then rest in the assurance that in God's time your prayer will be answered. Expect your answer and expect to receive the fullness of His joy!

Finish My Race with Joy

"But none of these things move me; nor do I count my life dear to myself, so that I may finish my race with joy, and the ministry which I received from the Lord Jesus, to testify to the gospel of the grace of God" (Acts 20:24).

Paul faced chains and tribulations, but the thing that was most important to him was fulfilling the call of the Lord on His life. What brought joy into his life was testifying to the gospel of the grace of God. He knew that the Lord had a call on his life, and he was determined to walk in obedience to Him even if that meant being thrown in jail, beaten, or killed. He knew that the greatest joy that can be experienced comes from fulfilling God's calling upon one's life. Paul was a man who knew the importance of obedience to his Savior.

Obedience is a word that we sometimes do not like to hear. I have learned, however, that it can bring great joy into my life and also into yours. I have experienced times when I knew God was calling me to do something that I was afraid to do. I realized, however, that doing His will would bring great peace and joy into my life.

As I moved in obedience to Him, the fear left. I also found that my desires changed, and I was greatly blessed by being obedient to His will and His call upon my life.

If you know that God has a call on your life (and He does because He has a call on everyone of His children's lives), and you do not want to fulfill it, trust Him. Begin to move in obedience to Him as Paul did and experience the great joy that comes from fulfilling the call of God on your life!

Power of the Holy Spirit

"Now may the God of hope fill you with all joy and peace in believing, that you may abound in hope by the power of the Holy Spirit" (Rom. 15:13).

As we believe the truths of God's Word and begin to live in accordance with His promises, we are filled with joy and peace. We are also filled with the power of the Holy Spirit. There is great joy in knowing that the Holy Spirit resides within us. There is also great joy when we begin to experience the power of the Holy Spirit at work within us as He uses us to witness and minister to others.

The greatest joy that I have experienced has come as I have submitted myself to the Lord and allowed His Spirit to minister to others through me. I have been absolutely amazed at what He does. I know that I cannot do anything on my own. I know that I am not capable of the kind of mercy that comes forth. I know that it is the Holy Spirit of God using me to meet the needs of others. What joy that brings to my soul!

Will you submit yourself to the Lord today and let Him reveal His plan for using you in the power of the Holy Spirit? Do not miss out on the joy of seeing others blessed as He uses you to witness and minister to those in need. The greatest joy and blessing that you can experience in this world is to lay down your desires and your plans and follow God's call in your life to reach out to the needs of others through the power of His Holy Spirit.

Joy in Giving

"Moreover, brethren, we make known to you the grace of God bestowed on the churches of Macedonia: that in a great trial of affliction the abundance of their joy and their deep poverty abounded in the riches of their liberality" (2 Cor. 8:1–2).

Although the church of Macedonia was financially poor, they experienced an abundance of joy because they were generous and liberal in their giving. This shows us the importance of giving regardless of the lack that we experience financially. As we give out of our need, we find that God blesses us in return.

Philippians 4:15–17 says, "Now you Philippians know also that in the beginning of the gospel, when I departed from Macedonia, no church shared with me concerning giving and receiving but you only. For even in Thessalonica you sent aid once and again for my necessities. Not that I seek the gift, but I seek the fruit that abounds to your account." Notice that Paul talked to the church at Philippi about not just giving but about giving and receiving. He told them that when they give, it is fruit accounted to them. There is no greater fruit that we can experience than the joy that comes into our lives as we seek to meet the needs of others.

If there is someone who you know that has a great need in his or her life, seek the Lord about how He would use you in meeting that need. As you reach out to others in giving either financially or in some other way, you will experience joy unspeakable!

The Fruit of the Spirit

"But the fruit of the Spirit is love, joy, peace, longsuffering, kindness, goodness, faithfulness, gentleness, self-control. Against such there is no law" (Gal. 5:22–23).

The fruit of the Spirit comes from the Holy Spirit, and it is something that we cannot produce by our own efforts. When the Spirit of God is in control of our lives, we will exhibit the character and nature of God Almighty. The fruit of the Spirit is the character of God! This wonderful fruit is produced within us as we seek Him with all our hearts and submit more and more of our lives to Him.

When an apple tree is planted, does an apple instantly appear ripe, red, and juicy? No, the apple begins as a blossom and then slowly develops into the juicy fruit that we pluck off the tree or buy in our grocery store. The fruit of the Spirit develops in our lives in much the same way. As we start to draw close to the Lord and yield ourselves to Him, we begin to see and experience more love, joy, peace, and the other characteristics of the fruit of the Spirit. As our walk with the Lord continues and we grow in His image, we will exhibit more and more of these characteristics. Hopefully, we are more joyous today than we were last year, and we should expect to be even more joyous next month than we are today.

Do you read this list of characteristics of the fruit of the Spirit and think to yourself, I am really lacking in some of these areas? If you need to see the fruit of the Spirit growing in greater degree in your life (and we all do!), draw close to the One who is the producer of fruit and yield yourself to Him. Let Him reveal Himself and His character to you in such a way that you begin to receive His nature within yourself.

Joy Is in the Presence of Jesus

"For what is our hope, or joy, or crown of rejoicing? Is it not even you in the presence of our Lord Jesus Christ at His coming?" (1 Thess. 2:19).

The scripture for today brings great excitement and joy into my heart because I believe that joy comes from being in the presence of the Lord. Has Jesus Christ come into your life? If He has, then you can experience the joy that comes from being in the very presence of the Lord. His presence is always with you and me, but there are times that we draw so close to Him that we experience His manifest presence. In other words, we feel literally immersed in the very presence of God. We know that He has promised that He will always be with us, but sometimes His presence becomes so real to us that it is overwhelming. We feel and experience His presence so strongly that immeasurable joy rises within our spirits and overflows to those around us.

If you need the joy of the Lord to be real and alive within you, decide today to draw close to the Lord. Enter into His presence with thanksgiving and offer a sacrifice of praise to Him. You will begin to experience the joy of the Lord in your life in a mighty way as His manifest presence becomes a reality to you. Be determined and do not give up! Seek Him until you are truly aware of His presence in your life today!

Count It All Joy

"My brethren, count it all joy when you fall into various trials" (James 1:2).

You may say, "How in the world can I count it all joy when I am in the midst of a trial? What is joyful about being in a trial?" To be perfectly honest, nothing is joyful about the trial itself, but we can be joyful knowing that passing through the trial will produce spiritual growth in our lives. We can be joyful knowing that our Lord will bring good out of the trial, and we will be stronger as a result.

When a trial comes along in our lives, we need to seek the Lord and ask Him, "What can I learn from this situation?" We need to have ears to hear from Him. We need to stay spiritually in tune with our Lord by reading our Bible and keeping ourselves open to the direction of the Holy Spirit. When a Bible verse that is relevant to our situation seems to "jump out" at us as we read, we need to take it to heart. We need to begin to practice what the scripture says. If it says to "put away wrath," then we need to repent of anger. If it says "be not anxious," then we need to repent of worry and begin to dwell on God's strength and power instead of dwelling on the circumstance.

If you are in the midst of a trial today, decide to "count it all joy." Seek the Lord by reading His Word. Ask the Holy Spirit to guide and direct you and seek to learn from the Lord. Let Him bring wisdom and understanding into your life and shape you into a stronger follower of Jesus!

Joy Inexpressible

"... Jesus Christ, whom having not seen you love. Though now you do not see Him, yet believing, you rejoice with joy inexpressible and full of glory" (1 Pet. 1:8).

*B*elieving in Jesus Christ and what He has done for us on the cross brings great joy into our lives. Even though we cannot see Him with our physical eyes, we know by His revelation to us in His Word about His grace and His goodness to us. Receiving more understanding in His Word through the revelation of the Holy Spirit of the plan of Jesus brings greater and greater joy in our lives.

What is joy inexpressible? The King James version of the Bible says, "unspeakable." It means that joy is so strong within us that we cannot describe to someone else what we are experiencing or feeling. Words are not adequate to convey the greatness and glory of the joy of the Lord in our lives.

Have you ever experienced joy to the point that you could not describe what you were feeling? Have you ever been in a worship service where the presence of the Lord was so overwhelming that you were overcome with joy? Have you ever experienced a time alone with the Lord when He manifested His presence to you in such a way that you knew He loved you with an everlasting love? Have you ever received an answer to prayer that was so significant that you were overcome with joy, knowing that the Lord of the whole universe heard and answered your prayer? If you have not experienced even one of these precious times with the Lord, please believe that you can! Seek Him with your whole being today and let Him know that you love Him with all your heart. Let Him bless you with His love and presence in your life!

Exceeding Joy

"But rejoice to the extent that you partake of Christ's sufferings, that when His glory is revealed, you may also be glad with exceeding joy" (1 Pet. 4:13).

Do you want to partake of Christ's sufferings? Probably your initial response would be "no" because none of us wants to suffer. When we partake of Christ's suffering, however, we know that there are blessings that await us. John 15:20–21 says, "Remember the word that I said to you. 'A servant is not greater than his master.' If they persecuted Me, they will also persecute you. . . . But all these things they will do to you for My name's sake, because they do not know Him who sent Me." Since Jesus suffered, we can expect that if we walk in obedience to Him, we will also suffer.

The kind of suffering we can expect to happen in our lives as we follow the teachings and ways of our Savior will probably be rejection or some other kind of persecution. It may be a minor rejection or it may be something very significant. We might find that we need to take an unpopular stand on an issue at work and risk losing that job. Whatever happens in our lives as a result of our obedience and commitment to Jesus Christ will eventually bring us great joy because He always honors obedience. James 1:2 says, "Count it all joy when you fall into various trials." No matter what comes our way, we can have the fullness of joy residing within us. What a multitude of blessings accompany faith in Jesus Christ!

Refresh My Heart in the Lord

"Yes, brother, let me have joy from you in the Lord; refresh my heart in the Lord" (Philem. 20).

Paul wrote to his friend Philemon. I believe that what
he said to his friend shows us that we are to refresh
each other in the Lord. His joy can be transferred from one
believer to another. Have you ever been around a Christian
friend who spilled over with the joy of the Lord? When you
left that person's presence, you probably felt great joy yourself. There is something contagious about the joy of the Lord!

One thing we can learn from Paul in the scripture for
today is to share our joy with others. We need to testify to
the goodness of God in our lives. We need to share with
others His answers to our prayers. We need to share with
others what it is like to commune with our awesome Father
in heaven. We need to tell our friends and acquaintances
how the Lord has set us free from bondage in our lives. As we
share our experiences of the grace and goodness of the Lord
with others, they will see and understand the joy that is a
part of our lives. They will want to experience the closeness
with the Lord that is evident within our lives. We have great
opportunities to be witnesses to those around us. My prayer
is that we will take these opportunities and walk through the
open doors that the Lord provides in all of our lives each day.

Shout for Joy!

"Be glad in the Lord and rejoice, you righteous; and shout for joy, all you upright in heart!" (Ps. 32:11).

*H*ave you ever been so filled with joy in the Lord that you wanted to shout to Him? Have you ever shouted? There is something so refreshing and freeing about shouting to the Lord. I am a very reserved person. I have grown up in a mainline denominational church where we do not shout. I have, however, experienced tremendous joy both alone at home and in services where there is freedom to shout. When I have let go of my inhibitions and shouted with joy unto the Lord, it has always been a wonderful experience, releasing my feelings and emotions to my heavenly Father.

I do not believe that we as Christians should base our beliefs on emotions, but I do recognize that God is the one who gave us these feelings. Although we should not allow emotions to control our lives, I firmly believe that God intends for us to express them in many ways. As a matter of fact, we find within the pages of Scripture direction and admonishment to shout unto the Lord, sing unto the Lord, clap our hands unto the Lord, and even to dance before the Lord. Finding the freedom to express my emotions of love and joy unto the Lord has brought greater feelings of peace, contentment, and joy into my life.

If you have never allowed yourself to shout, sing, or clap unto the Lord, you may want to try expressing your emotions to the Lord the next time you are in awe of His goodness.

To God My Exceeding Joy

"Then I will go to the altar of God, to God my exceeding joy; and on the harp I will praise You, O God, my God" (Ps. 43:4).

*W*here is the altar of God? The altar of God is wherever you meet God, wherever you are when you worship Him. You could meet Him in your prayer closet, or you could meet Him in your car as you drive to work or run errands. You could meet God in a worship service in your church, or you could meet Him when you are at a prayer meeting or a Bible study. No matter where you are in an attitude of worship, you can experience exceeding joy in His presence.

Do you have a harp? Do you play a harp? Well, neither do I, but we do not have to play a musical instrument to praise God. We can praise Him to express the joy that dwells within us by lifting our voice in verbal praise. We can begin to sing praises to Him, or we may even lift our voice and begin to shout our love and adoration to Him. We may simply want to whisper in great reverence our love for Him. There are many ways we can express praise to our Father in heaven, and the important thing is not how we do it, but that we do it!

Will you offer praises to your Father God today and tell Him how much you love Him? Do not be afraid to express your adoration for Him with great abandonment! Enjoy the closeness that comes between you and your Savior as you open up from the depths of your feelings and express them to Him.

That Your Joy May Be Full

"And these things we write to you that your joy may be full" (1 John 1:4).

John wrote to the believers about the love, light, and life of Jesus Christ. He wanted to reveal truths about walking in fellowship with other believers. The scripture for today indicates that the things John wrote to the believers will bring them a fullness of joy. We need to understand that the more we know Jesus Christ, the more we will be filled with His joy! This understanding makes me want to know Jesus better and better. It makes me want to draw close to Him and worship Him with every ounce of my being. It makes me want to listen to Him and hear what He has to say to me personally. It makes me want to spend precious time with Him so that I will be transformed from glory to glory into His image.

Do you share my desire to know Jesus in a greater way? If you do, spend time reading 1 John and receive the joy of the Lord as He is revealed to you in greater measure. Ask the Lord to give you greater insight into His truth about Himself. Expect to be transformed as you know Him better and as He reveals to you the things in your life that He would like to change. Offer yourself to Him without any reservation. Give Him full rule and reign in your life and know the fullness of joy that John writes about in his letter to the believers.

Joyful in My House of Prayer

"Even them I will bring to My holy mountain, and make them joyful in My house of prayer" (Isa. 56:7a).

Isaiah spoke a word from the Lord in which He told His people, Israel, that He will bring His salvation to all people. When He says in the scripture for today that He will bring them to His holy mountain, He refers to the Gentiles. He makes His holy mountain (or in other words His very presence) available to all nations and all peoples who will receive Him. He says that He will make them joyful in His house of prayer.

Some of the most joyful moments I have spent with the Lord have been as I yielded myself to Him in prayer. Praying for the needs of other people or nations has brought great joy into my life. As I spend time in prayer for others, I also am drawing closer to my Lord. Spending time in His holy mountain or in His presence brings such joy that words cannot describe it. As I spend glorious moments with Him in His presence, I find myself wanting to spend more and more time with Him. Nothing compares to the absolute joy and rapture that comes from being in the presence of the Most Holy One!

Will you decide today to enter into the presence of the Lord God Almighty and experience the joy and awe that comes from knowing Him better? Let Him take you in His arms and share the wonders of His love and grace with you!

Presented Before the Presence of His Glory

"Now to Him who is able to keep you from stumbling, and to present you faultless before the presence of His glory with exceeding joy" (Jude 24).

Our Lord told us that He is able to bring us blameless before Him in worship.

You may ask, "How can He bring me before Him blameless? I know who I am, and I know what I do." He brings you before Himself blameless because of the sacrifice and shedding of blood on the cross by Jesus Christ. We have the assurance that we truly can enter into the presence of the Lord God Almighty because Jesus made a way for us by His sacrifice. What joy that should bring to us! We can enter a relationship with the God of the universe! We can know Him, talk to Him, receive from Him, hear from Him, and we can fellowship in His presence just as Moses did. We can know Him face to face as a friend and become "people after His own heart" like mighty King David. We can enter into a beautiful worship experience and praise Him for who He is! We can enter into such a close relationship with Him that gradually we are transformed into His image!

Will you take the time today to enter into a truly wondrous relationship with Him and know the joy that exceeds anything you have ever experienced before? Will you talk with Him as you would a friend? Will you listen to Him as He shares His love for you?

Let this day be a day of transformation as you receive the goodness and grace of a close face to face relationship with the Giver of life!

The Son Gives Life

"For as the Father raises the dead and gives life to them, even so the Son gives life to whom He will" (John 5:21).

Jesus gives life! He gives physical life, and He gives spiritual life. What is life? All of us know what physical life is because we experience it. Isaiah 44:2 tells us that the Lord made us and formed us in the womb. He is the one who gives us physical life. The Lord breathed life into Adam, and He is the one who provides breath to us today. Do you remember the vision that God gave Ezekiel about the dry bones in Ezekiel 37? He showed him a valley of dry bones and then commanded Ezekiel to prophesy to the dry bones. The bones began to come together and flesh came upon them. Ezekiel then began to prophesy breath to them, and the breath of God came into them and they lived!

Spiritual life comes from the Lord Jesus also. He came to give us eternal life so that we can live with Him in heaven always. The scripture for today says that He will give life to whom He will. To whom do you believe Jesus wills to give life? I believe He wills that none should perish, but that all should have eternal life.

Have you accepted the eternal life that Jesus holds out to you? If you have, will you make a commitment today to share His love and grace with those around you? Ask the Lord to place one person on your heart and mind today who needs to know about the saving grace of Jesus Christ. Ask Him also for the courage, boldness, and the words to be a witness to that person. Know the great joy of spreading the love of Jesus to others!

Passed from Death into Life

"Most assuredly, I say to you, he who hears My word and believes in Him who sent Me has everlasting life, and shall not come into judgment, but has passed from death into life" (John 5:24).

*H*ave you ever seen life ebb out of a person? Have you ever seen a person who is dead? One moment that person is alive, and the next moment he is dead. Death is final, and nothing can bring that person back to life (except a resurrection miracle from God). We become aware of what a precious gift life is when we experience the death of someone we know. We also become aware of the fact that life is something we cannot control. There is a source of life that goes beyond human reasoning or understanding. That source is Jesus Christ!

We are assured in the scripture for today that when we believe on the One who sent Jesus Christ, we pass from death to life. Do you remember what your life was like before you accepted Jesus Christ as your Lord and Savior? There was emptiness and a void within. There was dissatisfaction and a longing for something more. When you accepted Jesus Christ, the emptiness and dissatisfaction left. You were filled with joy and contentment within, and could not wait to tell someone else about your decision.

If you would like a fresh touch from the Lord today, pray this prayer. "Father, I pray that the joy and excitement that existed in my life when I first accepted Jesus will be restored today. I pray that You will fan the flame that dwells within me and cause great revival to come within. Use me to spread the good news of Jesus Christ to those around me. Amen."

The Spirit Gives Life

"It is the Spirit who gives life; the flesh profits nothing. The words that I speak to you are spirit, and they are life" (John 6:63).

The Spirit of God gives life. When we read God's Word, and it seems to come alive within us, we know that the Spirit of God is at work. Many times I have read the Word of God but it was nothing more than words on a page. Other times, however, when I read the Bible, passages seemed to "jump off" the page at me. When this happens, I know that God is speaking directly to me through His Word. The Holy Spirit is at work bringing the written Word alive in my spirit to give me direction, comfort, strength, or whatever I need at the moment.

Notice in the scripture for today that Jesus said, "The words that I speak to you are spirit, and they are life." No matter what we are going through, He has an answer for us in His Word. We can receive teaching, correction, reproof, direction, or whatever we need from the Bible. We need to read God's Word daily, learning and absorbing the truth within its pages, but we also should go to the Bible in times of need, expecting to receive answers for each situation.

If you have not begun a daily routine of Bible reading, make that commitment today. Let the Holy Spirit speak to you through the pages of the only book on earth that truly is alive! Read, expecting to receive answers to your needs, and move into a place of excitement and joy as you listen to your Savior speak to you through the pages of His Holy Word!

Light of Life

"Then Jesus spoke to them again, saying, 'I am the light of the world. He who follows Me shall not walk in darkness, but have the light of life'" (John 8:12).

When the lights go off in your home at night, and you are surrounded by darkness, how do you react? How do you feel? If you try to move around to see if you can find a flashlight, more than likely you will run into something and bump your knee or stump your toe. It is very difficult to do anything in the dark. We all need light to function well and complete our tasks. The time we really feel comfortable surrounded by darkness is at night when we are asleep. Sleep hardly counts as "being alive" because in that state we are not aware of what goes on around us. To really enjoy and experience what life is all about, we need light in our lives.

My husband and I decided to remove the ceiling light in the bedroom to put in a ceiling fan. We have three lamps in the room, but they just do not give the same type of light as a ceiling light. Many times I cannot see things in that room as clearly as I would like, and I wish I had my ceiling light back. Like a powerful, well-placed light fixture, the Light of Life brings clarity into our lives. We can see and understand the things of God better when we allow the light of God's truth into our lives. He holds out to us all that we need to live a full and satisfying life with Him.

Is your life more than an existence? Do you know the joy and satisfaction of living in the light of the truth of Jesus? Draw close to Him today and let Him reveal His life to you in greater measure.

Gives Life to the Dead

"(As it is written, 'I have made you a father of many nations') in the presence of Him whom he believed—God, who gives life to the dead and calls those things which do not exist as though they did" (Rom. 4:17).

The scripture for today refers to Abraham, the father of many nations. Abraham believed God when He promised him a son and many descendants. Abraham and Sarah were too old to have children, but Abraham knew that if God had promised a child, then God was able to give life. God called forth a son even though the possibility of a son did not exist, and Abraham did not have any more sense than to believe that God could do the impossible! We like the story of Abraham and think that He truly did have faith, but we usually fall short when it's our turn to believe and respond as Abraham did. How many of us are willing to let go of our "sense" and believe God for something that is impossible? If it is something that God has promised us and is within His will, then we should be just like Abraham and believe God.

Is there something in your life that looms big and impossible? Seek the Lord today and find out what His will is for you. Take a step of faith and believe God can and will do the impossible in your life. Let Him prove to you what a powerful and loving Father you have in heaven! As He moves in your life, do not keep the news to yourself. Go out and shout from the housetop that the God you serve is a mighty God!

Life of Jesus

". . . Always carrying about in the body the dying of the Lord Jesus, that the life of Jesus also may be manifested in our body" (2 Cor. 4:10).

Paul speaks about the weaknesses in our lives in this verse. He shares that as we acknowledge our weakness, the power of God will be at work within us. Paul knew that he could expect to be put to death at any time as he traveled from town to town with the good news of Jesus Christ, but he also knew that in his suffering he was following in the footsteps of Jesus. No matter what he faced or how difficult the situation was in his life, Jesus Christ lived within him in all of His strength. He knew that the life of Jesus Christ would give him grace to face any and all trials. He also had the hope of resurrection when he faced physical death. He waited with expectancy and joy for life eternal!

Did you know that the life of Jesus Christ dwells within you? You never have to rely only upon yourself and your own strength. Jesus gives His life to you so that you may continue on this earth fulfilling His kingdom. What are you doing to fulfill His kingdom in your life today? Meditate on that question and then ask the Lord to reveal to you how He wants to live His life through you. Do not fear being a witness for Jesus Christ. Simply let His light and life shine through you daily. You may be saying, "How can I do that?" As you enter more and more into His presence and come to know Him for who He is, then you will exhibit more of His traits, and His life will truly shine forth from you!

God Gives Life to All Things

"Fight the good fight of faith, lay hold on eternal life, to which you were also called and have confessed the good confession in the presence of many witnesses. I urge you in the sight of God who gives life to all things . . ." (1 Tim. 6:12–13a).

God gives life to all things! When you look at a newborn baby, are you not overwhelmed by the knowledge that only God can give life? To look at the innocence and the intricacy of an infant is breathtaking. Have you ever just sat and watched a baby breathe and wonder in awe as he or she takes each breath? To look at those tiny fingers and watch them move and curl about your own finger brings such joy! Life is an amazing gift that we too often take for granted.

I do not see how anyone can look at a newborn baby and not believe in God. His life is there bringing new life into the world. As that child grows, he or she has a choice to make: to accept the life of God through Jesus Christ or reject Him. If he accepts God's life, a change will come upon him. His countenance will glow as God's life floods through his spirit. When each child is born, he receives physical life from God, but that is not all that God holds out to him. He also offers spiritual life, and that brings the glow from within. When the life of God comes into a person's life, a radiance bursts forth that the world cannot understand or provide.

If you know someone who needs the radiance that comes from accepting Jesus Christ as Lord and Savior, will you ask the Lord to give you the opportunity and the courage to share His life with that person? Receive the joy that comes from being used by the Lord to reach out to someone else today.

Water of Life

"And the Spirit and the bride say, 'Come!' And let him who hears say, 'Come!' And let him who thirsts come. Whoever desires, let him take the water of life freely" (Rev. 22:17).

*W*hat is the water of life? It is the living water that comes from the throne of God to nourish and sustain us. Many scriptures in the Word of God talk about the water of God. God wants to refresh us and give us His life abundantly by supplying His living water to us. Water is symbolic of something that we all can relate to and understand.

What happens to a tomato plant in your garden if it does not rain and you do not water it? It will begin to wither; eventually it will die. What happens to a person lost in a desert with no water? After a time that person will become dehydrated and eventually die. Because water is essential for life, the Lord has used it as a symbol of life to help us understand the depth of what He holds out to us. Water is essential for life, but it is also something that brings a refreshing into our lives when we are dry and thirsty.

If you are in a place of dryness and you are thirsty for more of God, reach out to Him today. Ask Him to fill you to overflowing with His living waters, and experience the refreshing and life that comes from your Father in heaven.

Your Word Has Given Me Life

"This is my comfort in my affliction, for Your word has given me life" (Ps. 119:50).

No matter what we go through, we can find peace and life through God's Word. When we go through difficulties, nothing else can compare to the comfort, strength, peace, and joy brought into our lives when we spend time in God's Word. We have been told that God's Word is alive, and I certainly believe it because I have experienced it!

Many years ago I suffered from such great fear that I had panic attacks whenever I was in a crowd or out among people. I knew that what I was experiencing was not the abundant life that Jesus came to give me. I sought the Lord to receive His help. I believed that He was leading me to memorize 2 Timothy 1:7, Isaiah 41:10, and 1 John 4:18a, which all reveal that fear is not from God and that He is always available to help us. Then whenever fear and panic began to rise within me, I quoted these scriptures. As I quoted them over and over, peace began to overcome the fear and panic. They faded away, and I was free to carry on. Believe me, I felt as if I was passing from death into life! God's Word is alive and well, and it will bring the very life of God into our lives!

If you are going through something that seems to overpower you, seek the Lord and ask Him to lead you to something in His Word that will bring comfort, strength, and victory into your life. Read and meditate on God's particular word for your situation more than once. Keep it before you often, and you will experience the life and victory that God holds out to you!

I Set Before You Life

"Now you shall say to this people, 'Thus says the Lord: "Behold, I set before you the way of life and the way of death"'" (Jer. 21:8).

God sets before us the way of life and also the way of death. It is our responsibility to choose life. The choices we make daily determine if we are living in the life of God or not. When we accept Jesus Christ as Savior, we are born again into the kingdom of God, and we choose to receive the life of God into our lives. We can walk in that life on a day to day basis, or we can choose to walk in darkness. If we have a personal relationship with Jesus Christ, when we choose to walk in darkness, God's conviction comes upon us. We then choose if we will repent or if we will continue in darkness.

If we decide not to repent in a certain situation, our heart becomes hardened. The next time we need to repent, it will be easier to ignore the call to repentance. Our heart will become hardened even more. If this process continues, we could find ourselves in a position of not hearing God. We lose that sensitivity to His voice and His direction.

Psalm 139:23–24 says, "Search me, O God, and know my heart; try me, and know my anxieties; and see if there is any wicked way in me, and lead me in the way everlasting." Psalm 51:10 says, "Create in me a clean heart, O God, and renew a steadfast spirit within me." Will you pray those prayers from the Psalms today and let the God of the universe reveal anything in your life that may have hardened your heart? Let Him set you free to receive all that He has for you!

Fountain of Life

"For with You is the fountain of life; in Your light we see light" (Ps. 36:9).

*W*hat do you think of when you see a fountain? A picture of water gushing forth with great force may come to your mind. The scripture for today brings to mind a picture of the greatness and power of the life of God. He holds out to you the power of His life, and all that you have to do is receive it. When you receive His life within, you become a vessel He can use to release His life to others. Do you believe a fountain of God's life can well up within you in such a way that others' lives will be affected in such a way that they will also become fountains of the life of God? That is possible for you!

As we draw close to the Lord on a daily basis we will look at others with His compassion. We will have a word of wisdom for a friend who is going through a difficult time. We will begin to reach out to those who are hungry and need clothing for their families. We will pray for the sick as Jesus did, and according to Mark 16:18, they will recover. When we live as Jesus lived and do the works that He did, we are examples of His fountain of life at work in this world.

Do you believe that you can live as Jesus lived? John 14:12 says, "Most assuredly, I say to you, he who believes in Me, the works that I do he will do also; and greater works than these he will do, because I go to My Father." You can do the works of Jesus and be a fountain of life to those around you. Draw close to Him today and let Him fill you with His nature and His ways so that you will show His life in this world!

Life Is More Than Food

"Life is more than food, and the body is more than clothing" (Luke 12:23).

*H*ave you ever heard the saying, "Do you live to eat or eat to live?" The scripture for today is certainly an answer for those of us who may have a problem with eating. We are told that life is more than food. You may be the type of person who responds to this statement with: "Of course life is more than food!" Many, however, have a problem with eating too much and cannot seem to control it.

Our lives revolve around what is most important to us. As Christians, our lives should revolve around the Lord, and our responses to situations that arise in our lives should reflect His nature and character. When someone cuts in front of us on the interstate, we should ask God to bless them and protect them (and those around them) instead of griping or complaining. When someone says something hateful to us, we should respond in a loving way instead of arguing with him or her. When we have been deeply hurt, we should forgive rather than holding on to the hurt until it turns into bitterness.

What are your priorities? What do you think about most? How do you spend your time? If there are areas of your life that you need to turn over to the Lord in order to place Him number one on your list of priorities, will you do that today? If you live to eat or are burdened with some other obsession, ask the Lord's forgiveness and ask Him to help you have victory in this area of your life.

Bread of God

"For the bread of God is He who comes down from heaven and gives life to the world" (John 6:33).

In Scripture bread represents that which sustains us or gives us life. Without proper nourishment to our physical body, we would eventually die. Bread or food is something we need to keep our physical body functioning properly. In the scripture for today, John tells us that God came down from heaven to give life to the world. We know that God came as a baby upon this earth, and His name was Jesus. How did He bring life to the world? He brought His life to us by atoning for our sins when He died upon the cross. Having lived a perfect, sinless life, He descended to hell to pay for our sins, and then He gloriously ascended into heaven to sit at the right hand of God the Father. This sacrificial act on His part enables us to have life eternal. When we accept Jesus Christ as our Lord and Savior, His life is imparted into us. We receive His righteousness even though we do not deserve it.

Do you know someone who has not received Jesus as Lord and Savior? Would you commit yourself to pray for that person daily and to be used according to God's will as a witness for His saving grace? Be a part of bringing the life of God into the life of someone else or hopefully the lives of many others!

Jesus Is the Bread of Life

"And Jesus said to them, 'I am the bread of life. He who comes to Me shall never hunger, and he who believes in Me shall never thirst'" (John 6:35).

What a beautiful promise the scripture for today brings to us! When we come to Jesus and believe in Him, we shall never hunger or thirst again. Before we turned our lives over to Jesus Christ, a void within caused us to continuously look for something else. Our spiritual hunger and thirst could not be filled by anything except God alone.

When the Lord comes to live within us, the joy and peace are hard to describe. Let us look at how we may have felt at sometime when we had gone a long time without eating. Perhaps we had been fasting or perhaps our circumstance kept us from being able to eat for some time. We were extremely hungry. We wanted something to eat so badly that was about all we could think about. How did that food taste as we took our first bite? It was delicious! We kept on eating and filling that hunger until we could eat no more. When we were finished and sat back, there was such a good feeling of satisfaction. That still cannot describe the feeling that we receive when we accept Jesus Christ as our Lord and Savior. No earthly feeling of satisfaction can compare with the peace and contentment that comes from knowing Jesus!

Pray today for that person whom the Lord has put on your heart who needs to know Jesus Christ as his or her Lord and Savior. Be persistent and do not give up. Pray that your friend, relative, or acquaintance will come to know the peace that passes all understanding that only comes from a personal relationship with Jesus Christ!

AUGUST 15

Everlasting Life

"Most assuredly, I say to you, he who believes in Me has everlasting life" (John 6:47).

What does it mean to have everlasting life? It means that we will spend eternity with our Father in heaven. We will join with the angels before the throne of God, praising and worshiping Him with every ounce of our being. Have you ever thought it might be boring in heaven if all we do is praise God. I've wondered that myself at times, and I have heard others express the same concern. I believe that we tend to think that way because we have not even begun to understand the greatness of God. If we had the slightest inkling of what He is really like, we would know that praising Him in His throne room will be so incredibly glorious that we may find ourselves wanting to praise Him all the time. I believe there will be other things for us to do in heaven. I heard someone say the other day that we will be doing three things in our eternal home: praising God, worshiping God, and serving God. Most of us have experienced only a very small taste of what praising and worshiping God will be like in heaven. That is something we can look forward to with great excitement and anticipation.

Begin today to enter into a deeper praise of the Lord. Lift your voice and express from your heart feelings of gratitude for all that He has done for you. If that is difficult for you, begin to thank Him for life itself. Thank Him for the beauty of the earth. Thank Him for the sunshine, the rain, the mountains, the beach, and everything else that you love about His creation.

Words of Eternal Life

"But Simon Peter answered Him, 'Lord, to whom shall we go? You have the words of eternal life'" (John 6:68).

If our life lacks something, there is only one place to go. We need to go to Jesus, who has words of eternal life. Where do we find the words of Jesus? The Bible, of course, is the place where the divine words of Jesus are recorded. When we take His words, read them, study them, and begin to apply them to our lives, we will find that our lives are radically changed! What seemed so lacking and empty before, now feels full of excitement and life. How do we describe life? It is very difficult. One definition found in Webster's dictionary is "a vital force."

Do you remember a time in your life when everything seemed very "humdrum," and there was no vitality and no excitement? There seemed to be only an empty hole. On the other hand, can you remember a time when you were in a worship service and the music or the message was so anointed of God that something seemed to "leap" within you? That was the life of God rising within your spirit to witness to the life of God coming forth in that worship service. The life of God is contagious. He wants you and me to share that life with others. Will you make a commitment not to suppress His life within you but to let that life flow out of you to those around you? Experience the joy of being used by God to bring His life into the lives of others.

Life Comes from Humility

"By humility and the fear of the Lord are riches and honor and life" (Prov. 22:4).

Humility or submission to God is a trait that brings life to us. Submitting ourselves to Him and worshiping Him for who He is brings about an aliveness within us that is overwhelming! Humility or its counterpart, meekness, is something the world looks upon with disdain. As Christians, humility reveals our love, trust, and obedience to the Lord. Micah 6:8 says, "He has shown you, O man, what is good; and what does the Lord require of you but to do justly, to love mercy, and to walk humbly with your God?"

In this day that we live in, independence and living our own way are encouraged everywhere we turn. "Do your own thing" and "Be good to yourself" are expressions that we hear on talk shows, read about in books, and see on commercials. Being surrounded by this philosophy makes it difficult for us to receive the truth that comes to us from the Word of God, but we must realize that God's truth is greater than what comes from the mind of man. His truth shows us that submission to Him and releasing our wills to His will is an expression of our complete trust in Him. When we respond to Him according to His Word and His way rather than the world's way, we acknowledge that He is God. We express our faith in Him.

Place your trust in Him today by being obedient to Him. Let Him know that you are willing to follow Him regardless of what the world tells you to do. Step out in faith and let Him show you what a great and glorious God you serve!

Jesus Is the Way, the Truth, and the Life

"Jesus said to him, 'I am the way, the truth, and the life. No one comes to the Father except through Me'" (John 14:6).

Jesus is life! He tells us that no one can come to the Father except through Him! When Jesus tells us that He is life, He reveals to us that He is the life of God. He gives us the life of God when we believe that He is the Son of God, God in the flesh, and that He came to save us. There is no way to receive the life of God without knowing the truth about God and following the way to God. Jesus is the way, the truth, and the life. He is the only way!

I have been in services or classes in church where the scripture for today has been questioned. Many people seem to have trouble accepting what Jesus said because they are concerned about people who may not have had the gospel preached to them. They may also be concerned about someone they know who is Muslim, Hindu, or some other religion. They may feel that this person is a good person and should go to heaven. This is why the Lord gave us the great commission in Matthew 28:19, which says, "Go therefore and make disciples of all the nations . . . teaching them to observe all things that I have commanded you." We need to be ready and willing to spread the good news of Jesus Christ so that all will have the knowledge and understanding that Jesus is truly the way, the truth, and the life!

Would you be willing today to let the Lord use you as a witness of the saving grace of Jesus Christ? Ask Him to bring an opportunity your way and give you the courage and boldness to witness for Him.

The Living God

"My soul thirsts for God, for the living God. When shall I come and appear before God?" (Ps. 42:2).

The psalmist cries out for the living God. When we come into the presence of God, we find the kind of life that exists only in Him! We need to seek God with all that we are. We need to thirst for Him with a longing that can only be quenched by meeting Him face to face. He waits for us to come unto Him just as we are. He does not ask us to become perfect, but He waits with open arms for us to seek Him and spend time with Him. As we spend time with Him, we find that we are being changed. We do not have to change ourselves, for when we enter into the presence of God, He brings about a transformation in our lives. We cannot look upon the face of God without seeing ourselves for who we are. We will cry out with the psalmist, "Create in me a clean heart and a right spirit" (Ps. 51:10).

If you find that you have been feeling satisfied or complacent in your relationship with the Lord, call out to Him today as the psalmist did. Ask Him to fill you with a deep thirsting for more of Him in your life. Wait upon Him, and you will find that He will draw you close unto Himself. He will reveal the wonders of His truth to you in such a way that His life will spring up within you afresh and anew!

He Gives to All Life

"Nor is He worshiped with men's hands, as though He needed anything since He gives to all life, breath, and all things" (Acts 17:25).

God gives us all life and breath! Yes, He even gives life and breath to the atheists and agnostics. It does not matter what we think or believe, God has already put His plan into practice. He has made the earth and everything within it. He created man and woman and breathed the breath of life into them. Everyday, when we awake in the mornings, we need to thank God for life and breath. We take our lives for granted, but we would not be here if God had not chosen to create us.

Since God arranged for you and for me to live, He must have a plan for our lives.

I know what His plan for my life is at this time. He may reveal more of His plan to me as the days go by, but for now I know that His plan is for me to teach His Word, write this book (with His help!), intercede for others, and to be open to minister to the needs of others with His love as He brings them across my path. The greatest joy I have is to share God's Word and see people's lives change as a result.

Do you know God's plan for your life? You will experience great joy and fulfillment when you come to know His purpose and follow His plan. Call upon Him today and ask Him to reveal His purpose for your life. As He begins to show you, walk in obedience to that plan. Go through the doors that He opens for you and be blessed as you see the fruit that comes forth for the kingdom of God!

In Him We Live

"For in Him we live and move and have our being, as also some of your own poets have said, 'For we are also His offspring'" (Acts 17:28).

Because we are the offspring of Jesus Christ, we live and move and have our being in Him. How much we live and move and have our being in Him depends upon how much we submit ourselves to Him. The more we surrender our lives to Him and walk in obedience to His direction for our lives, the more we truly experience His life within us.

Have you ever gone through a time when you felt as though you were just existing? Nothing you did seemed important, and you could not get excited about anything. Did you have questions such as, "Why am I here? What is the purpose for my life? Is there more to life than this?" I trust you have received the answers to those questions and will now be God's instrument in revealing His answers to others who are still questioning. If you have not received, open yourself to the answers God would speak to you today. He has given you life for a purpose. That purpose is to receive Jesus Christ as your Lord and Savior and to be filled with His Spirit so that you can be a witness to others. When you walk in fulfillment of His purpose for your life, you will know the joy and excitement that comes from living, moving, and having your being in Him. Nothing compares with walking in oneness with the Almighty God!

Finding Life

"He who follows righteousness and mercy finds life, righteousness and honor" (Prov. 21:21).

Do you want the life of God in your life? If you do, you need to follow after righteousness and mercy. "How do I do that?" you might ask. To seek righteousness and mercy, we must simply seek that which is of God. When we look at Jesus, His life on this earth, and His words to us through the Bible, we look at righteousness and mercy in action. We need to follow after Jesus, His ways, and all that He teaches us.

We need to read the Word of God, but we also need to let His Word become alive and real to us. We need to seek Him and His presence in our lives so that we can understand His Word and His purposes for our lives. In other words, we need to have a very real and close relationship with the King of kings and the Lord of lords so that we can receive from Him all that He holds out to us. We will be able to receive from Him when we are communicating with Him—really hearing what He is saying, understanding His direction in our lives, and responding in obedience to Him. He is righteousness and mercy!

We need, therefore, to seek after Him with everything that is within us.

Look to Him who is your example and let Him reveal Himself in all His righteousness. Let Him show you His mercy today so that you can find and understand the life of God that is within you. Be aware as that life begins to bubble up within you with new wisdom, love, mercy, and acts of kindness. Allow Him who is righteousness to live through you!

In Him Was Life

"In Him was life, and the life was the light of men"
(John 1:4).

The apostle John tells us that the life of God is found in Jesus, and that life brings light to mankind. Jesus is the one whom we need to keep our eyes upon. Jesus is the one who brings the life of God into our lives so that we can share that life with others. When we allow Jesus full reign in our lives, His light will shine forth from us in such a way that those around us cannot help but notice that there is something different about us. They will begin to ask questions about why we are different. They will want to know how they can receive what we have.

The best way to be a witness for Jesus Christ is to draw so close to Him that we begin to be changed and transformed into His likeness. When we enter into His presence with praise and worship, we begin to see Him in all His glory. We find ourselves looking at our lives very differently. Our priorities begin to change, and the things of God start to take first place. The change that comes to us is not something that we cause to happen; it is something that comes from the hand of God. That change is so evident to others that they will be drawn to us and to Jesus who lives within us. Witnessing is easy because it is simply a way of life! It is living so close to Jesus Christ that others can see the light that comes from Him!

Will you decide today to draw close to the One who holds out life to you and to those around you? Let His light shine forth from you as you grow in awareness of His presence in your life!

I Am the Resurrection and the Life

"Jesus said to her, 'I am the resurrection and the life. He who believes in Me, though he may die, he shall live'" (John 11:25).

Jesus spoke to Martha, the sister of Lazarus, after Lazarus had died. Martha knew that if Jesus had been there sooner, her brother would not have died. Jesus spoke words of comfort and life to Martha. These same words are used over and over again to bring comfort and strength to those who face the loss of a loved one. They remind us that our loved one has gone home to be with Jesus, and that this is a promise for all of us. We can know that when our physical bodies give out, there is life eternal in heaven with our Lord. We will receive a new body in the resurrection, and we will live forever.

Jesus is the way to life eternal. He was the first to receive His resurrected body, and one day we also will have a new body suitable for eternity. We will receive this new body when Jesus comes again. First Corinthians 15:51–53 says, "Behold, I tell you a mystery: we shall not all sleep, but we shall all be changed—in a moment, in the twinkling of an eye, at the last trumpet. For the trumpet will sound, and the dead will be raised incorruptible, and we shall be changed. For this corruptible must put on incorruption, and this mortal must put on immortality."

Are you ready for that great day when Jesus shall return for His own? Are you ready to receive an incorruptible body that will be yours throughout eternity? Do you have friends and loved ones who are not ready? Let the Lord use you to share the good news of Jesus Christ with these so that they will not be left behind!

Life Giving Spirit

"And so it is written, 'The first man Adam became a living being.' The last Adam became a life-giving spirit" (1 Cor. 15:45).

Who is the last Adam? The last Adam is Jesus Christ who came to restore what had been taken from mankind in the Garden of Eden. When the first Adam sinned, death entered the world. Jesus (the second Adam) came to restore life to mankind. First Corinthians 15:49 says, "And as we have borne the image of the man of dust, we shall also bear the image of the heavenly Man." What a promise! Do you want to bear the image of Jesus Christ? I certainly do! I want to be all that He wants me to be, and I know this truth can come from only Him. I can do nothing on my own, but "I can do all things through Christ who strengthens me." (Phil. 4:13). Colossians 1:27b says, "Christ in you, the hope of glory." When Christ came to dwell within me, He enabled me to bear His image. The more I open my life to Him, the more I will bear His image.

Do you want to bear the image of Christ in your life? Do you want His life to be so real in you that others see and know that you belong to Jesus Christ? Thank Him today for coming to dwell within you, and commit yourself to Him so that His life can reach out through you to others. Be the hope of glory that Paul talks about in Colossians!

This Is Eternal Life

"And this is eternal life, that they may know You, the only true God, and Jesus Christ whom You have sent" (John 17:3).

Knowing God and Jesus Christ is eternal life! How do we know God? How do we know Jesus Christ so that we can experience eternal life? We know Him through His Word and through the Holy Spirit. As we read the Word of God, we find that the life of God begins to come forth from the pages. We gain understanding of God, and we gain understanding of Jesus Christ, the Son of God, who came in the flesh to reveal God the Father to us.

When we look at Jesus Christ and His life on earth through Scripture, we see a picture of the character and nature of God. We see righteousness and mercy at work in this world. We see a God who cares so much for His creation that He sent His Son to live and die for us. We see a God who allowed His Son, who was free from all sin, to suffer on a cross to pay for our sins. We see a God who provided a way for us to have a relationship with Him and to be a part of His family. We see through the life of Jesus Christ kindness, goodness, holiness, purity, justice, compassion, supreme love, and so much more! All that we see and understand about God the Father and Jesus Christ brings the very life of God into our lives!

Do you want to experience more of the life of God in your life? Read about Jesus Christ in Scripture and spend time fellowshiping with Him each day. Know Him better through the Word and through His Holy Spirit who draws you ever closer unto Him!

Life Is in His Son

"And this is the testimony: that God has given us eternal life, and this life is in His Son. He who has the Son has life; he who does not have the Son of God does not have life" (1 John 5:11–12).

The life of God comes through Jesus Christ! Do you have the life of God within you? Do you know how to identify the life of God? Although the life of God is eternal, it is more than endless life. It is something that we can experience now in this present time. We can experience a quality of life on a daily basis right here on earth that is truly supernatural!

Knowing God and experiencing His life through Jesus Christ bring a peace that passes all understanding into our lives. It brings joy unspeakable into our everyday experience. Knowing the God of the universe, knowing Him personally and spending time with Him is such an overwhelming experience that it is very difficult to even put into words. Who can describe what happens within us when we have complete trust in Him? Who can give an account of what it means to have a confident assurance that Almighty God loves us and is our friend? Who can put into words the feeling of walking, talking, and knowing intimately the King of kings and Lord of lords? We can experience the glory of God on this earth as well as throughout eternity, and He is waiting right now for us to seek Him with every ounce of our being!

Will you draw near to the Lord today and experience the pure joy of being in His presence? Know and enter into the very life of God as you walk with Him and talk with Him. Let Him reveal the wonders of His glory to you as you enter into a more intimate relationship with Him today and in the days ahead!

You Will Live Also

"A little while longer and the world will see Me no more, but you will see Me. Because I live, you will live also" (John 14:19).

In the scripture for today, Jesus told His disciples that they will live because He lives. He prepared them for His death and resurrection. Because He was resurrected and received a new body, we have the promise of life eternal, and we know we will receive a new resurrected body as well.

Probably one of the greatest fears that man faces is the fear of death. Without Christ, death is an extremely fearful thing to face. Some believe that after death there is nothing. Some believe there is an eternity, but they do not know what eternity holds for them.

For the Christian, death means our physical body dies, but we live throughout eternity with the Lord where there are no more tears, pain, or sickness. For the Christian death should bring rejoicing instead of fear. Paul said in Philippians 1:21, "For to me, to live is Christ, and to die is gain."

How do you feel about death? Can you say with Paul, "To live is Christ, and to die is gain"? If you have any fear at all of the prospect of death, ask the Lord to give you an assurance of the joy and peace that will fill our eternity with Him. Read in Revelation 4 about the glory that surrounds His throne in heaven where you one day will be!

Breath of Life

"And the Lord God formed man of the dust of the ground, and breathed into his nostrils the breath of life; and man became a living being" (Gen. 2:7).

We are alive because God Almighty breathed His breath into us. When God breathed into Adam, the first man, it was the life of God that came into him. What does it mean to have the breath of God within us? It means that we are able to understand and communicate with God Almighty! We can have a relationship with Him that enables us to live a life on this earth filled with the goodness, strength, joy, and peace that comes from God.

Because we live in a world that is full of sin, much around us is not of God. (Sometimes ungodly influences even creep inside us.) We need to push that all away and keep our minds on the things of God. Philippians 4:8 says, "Finally, brethren, whatever things are true, whatever things are noble, whatever things are just, whatever things are pure, whatever things are lovely, whatever things are of good report, if there is any virtue and if there is anything praiseworthy—meditate on these things." The more we renew our minds with the things of God, the more the life of God will be evident in our lives.

If the things of this world become too strong in your life, meditate on the scripture in Philippians that I quoted above and also on Romans 12:1–2. As you think on these scriptures, you will find that they will begin to come alive in your life. You will find yourself drawing away from the things of this world and turning closer and closer to the things of the Lord!

You Shall Live

"'I will put My Spirit in you, and you shall live, and I will place you in your own land. Then you shall know that I, the Lord, have spoken it and performed it,' says the Lord" (Ezek. 37:14).

God gives us physical life, and He also gives us spiritual life. We receive physical life when our mothers give birth to us, but we receive spiritual life when we are born again into the kingdom of God. We are born again when we make the decision to accept Jesus Christ into our lives. We experience a quickening within that comes from the Spirit of God as He brings the spirit that He has placed within us to life. His Holy Spirit comes to dwell within us, and suddenly we begin to understand things that we have never understood before!

We have a choice about how much we open our lives to the Spirit of God who dwells within us. We can grow in our walk with the Lord by allowing the Holy Spirit to rule and reign in our lives, or we can quench the Spirit of God and continue on as usual.

First Thessalonians 5:19 says, "Do not quench the Spirit." Here we are told not to dampen the fire of the Holy Spirit. Instead we need to fan the flame within us by reading the Word of God, spending time in close communication with the Lord, and being obedient to His will for our lives.

Let the breath of the Holy Spirit bring greater life into you today by fanning the flame of the Holy Spirit that resides within you! Seek to hear and then respond to His direction for your life today. Let Him reveal to you someone with whom you can share or someone for whom you can pray. Give Him your time and your thoughts and receive from Him!

Choose Life

"I call heaven and earth as witnesses today against you, that I have set before you life and death, blessing and cursing; therefore choose life, that both you and your descendants may live" (Deut. 30:19).

We have a choice to make! We can choose to walk in the life of God, or we can choose death. That means we can choose to accept Jesus Christ as our Lord and Savior or not. I believe we can take it a little further though. I believe that as Christians we can choose the life of God in daily decisions or we can choose death. We can choose to walk in the aliveness of the Spirit of God, or we can choose to make our own decisions and lose out on the joy, peace, and light that comes from being submissive to our Lord.

As human beings we so often want to do things "our way," but we can never know the aliveness that comes from God when we do our own thing. We need to learn submission! We need not only to realize in our minds that God knows best, but we need to live like we believe that God knows best. Good intentions do not mean much in this thing called living. We need to put into action those things that God instructs us to do.

If you have had some good intentions about the things of God, begin today to put into practice your good intentions. Choose today to live life to the fullest and walk in submission to the One who knows all things. Let Him reveal His plan for your life and then be obedient to Him. Know the joy that comes from choosing His way!

Light of Men

"In Him was life, and the life was the light of men. And the light shines in the darkness, and the darkness did not comprehend it" (John 1:4–5).

When Jesus came to this world as flesh and blood, He brought light to men. He brought the very essence of light to those who would receive. What is the essence of light? The essence of light is Jesus Christ! When we accept Jesus Christ as our Lord and Savior, we begin to understand spiritual things that evaded us before. It is as if a "light" comes on in our lives. Our understanding grows in such a way that we know that we can take no credit for it.

Let us think for a moment what it is like to walk into a dark room. There is no light, and we cannot see anything. What do we do? We usually grope around trying to find a light switch so that we can see where we are walking. Being in darkness is not a pleasant thing for us. The same thing is true for us spiritually. When we are in spiritual darkness, we, in like fashion, grope around trying to find some light. Sometimes we may "stump our toe" or we may "stumble and fall." As we continue to search as Christians, however, we will find the light that brings great illumination and direction into our lives.

Do you feel that there is darkness and lack of understanding in your life today? Are you groping around trying to find answers to some of life's big questions?

Go before the Creator of light and ask Him to give you revelation and illumination so that you will be able to fulfill His purposes in your life.

Gives Light to Every Man

"That was the true Light which gives light to every man coming into the world" (John 1:9).

Jesus came to give light to every man and woman on the face of the earth. Does that mean that every man and woman will receive His light? No! Everyone is given the choice of receiving His light into their lives. Many, however, refuse to accept the wondrous light that is held out to them. He brings illumination and understanding to those who do believe in Him, and He enlightens the conscience of those who do not believe in order that they may make the choice to turn to Him.

Those of us who have made the choice to believe in Jesus Christ can look forward to growing in our understanding of Him and His plan and purposes. Growth, however, is also related to our choices. We can choose to read and study the Bible, pray on a regular basis, fellowship with other believers, and seek a close relationship with Him daily. We can, on the other hand, choose to go about our busy schedules day by day and not spend time with Him. The amount of His light that increases within our lives depends on the choices that we make.

Let me encourage you today to choose to spend precious time with Him. You will never regret growing in your relationship with Him because your understanding of the true purpose of life will grow. You will find contentment and peace through your growing knowledge of Him that will not compare to anything else on the face of this earth! Draw close today and worship Him without reservation. Share from your heart, and receive from Him wondrous revelation of His glory!

Have the Light of Life

"Then Jesus spoke to them again, saying, 'I am the light of the world. He who follows Me shall not walk in darkness, but have the light of life'" (John 8:12).

*A*re you following Jesus? If you can answer "yes" to that question, you have the light of the world bringing illumination and understanding to you. You can be assured that you do not have to walk in darkness. What does it mean to walk in darkness? It can mean that you lack knowledge and direction for your life. It can also mean that there is sin in your life.

No one is completely free from sin; but we have the promise that when we follow Jesus, we shall not walk in darkness. By paying the price on the cross for our sins and enabling forgiveness to come into our lives, Jesus has made the way for us to overcome all darkness. What a joy and a privilege it is to follow the Lord Jesus Christ! We can walk in the knowledge that when we sin and repent, Jesus forgives us. We can walk in the knowledge and understanding that comes from a close relationship with Jesus Christ. All we have to do is accept Jesus Christ as our Lord and Savior and draw close to Him on a daily basis. He makes it so simple for us; and still, so often, we will not make the choice to draw close to Him daily.

Will you make that choice today to spend some time with Him, learning from Him, and letting Him share His wonders with you? I believe that, as you spend quality time with Him, holding back nothing, and sharing your heart with Him, you will find that you will want to give Him more of your time. Words cannot describe the overwhelming, gentle presence of the Lord—you can only experience it! Will you experience His presence and His light today?

261

Sons of Light

"While you have the light, believe in the light, that you may become sons of light. These things Jesus spoke, and departed, and was hidden from them" (John 12:36).

When we believe in Jesus wholeheartedly, His light will shine so brightly within and through us that we will truly be considered "sons and daughters of light." Believing in Jesus means more than mental assent. It is having the conviction that Jesus is the Son of God and that He came to bring His life and light into our lives. When we believe with our hearts as well as with our minds, action will follow. We will believe that His Word is true, and we will begin to be obedient to the instructions and directions that are found within it.

Sons and daughters of light will have a glow about them. They will be expressions of everything that is good and pure. The fruit of the Spirit will be in evidence in their lives, and they will express the love of Jesus to others. They will even be expressions of His love to those who are difficult to love. They will see with the eyes of Jesus, be sensitive with the compassion of Jesus, and respond with the outstretched arms of Jesus.

Are you a son or daughter of light? Do you allow the love and compassion of Jesus to rule and reign in your life? If you believe that you lack in any area of expressing the attributes of Jesus, reach out to Him today and ask Him to fill you afresh with His presence and His nature. As you enter into the very presence of God Almighty, let His light so permeate your being that you become an example to those in your family, at work, and in your daily surroundings.

Men Loved Darkness Rather Than Light

"And this is the condemnation, that the light has come into the world, and men loved darkness rather than light, because their deeds were evil" (John 3:19).

It is hard to believe that Jesus came into the world bringing the very light of God, and yet men and women love darkness more. As we look around the world today, we can see that plenty of people love darkness more than the light of Jesus. This darkness is evidenced by murder, prejudice, violence, hatred, homosexuality, abortion, and many other sins that are listed in Scripture.

What can you and I do about the darkness in the world today? First, we can decide not to participate in deeds of darkness. Second, we can enter into intercession for those around us who are obviously involved in darkness. Sometimes we take prayer and intercession too lightly. We pray, but we do not really expect our prayers to be answered. Is that scriptural? No! Mark 11:24 says, "Therefore I say to you, whatever things you ask when you pray, believe that you receive them, and you will have them." We need to enter into prayer for others who are in darkness, believing that God hears our prayers, and that He will answer!

Ask the Lord to place on your heart someone who is walking in darkness, and enter into intercessory prayer for that person. Pray for his salvation and pray for him to be set free from the darkness that surrounds him and has him in bondage. Pray, believing, and you will see answers to your prayers. Be a part of the furthering of God's kingdom by praying for your family, neighbors, those at work, and any that you come in contact with daily.

Let Your Light So Shine

"You are the light of the world. A city that is set on a hill cannot be hidden. Nor do they light a lamp and put it under a basket, but on a lampstand, and it gives light to all who are in the house. Let your light so shine before men that they may see your good works and glorify your Father in heaven" (Matt. 5:14–16).

In the scripture for today, we are told not to hide our light under a basket but to let it shine before men. Begin to picture a room with a light. Now picture that light being covered with a basket. What happens to the light in the room? It begins to dissipate and the room is dark. Jesus told us that we need to put our light on a lampstand; or, in other words, we are to let the light of Jesus be so visible within us that others readily see and experience His light. We are like a city that is set on a hill, clearly visible. We are to let the light of Jesus shine so brightly that His love and nature are easily evident within our lives.

How do we let our light shine? When we allow Jesus to live through us, expressing His nature and attributes, then others will see the good works and deeds that come forth from Him through us; and He will be glorified. The way to allow Jesus to live through us is to study His Word daily, seek Him, spend time with Him, know Him better, draw close to Him in prayer, and commune with Him.

Will you spend time with Him to allow His light to grow brighter and brighter within you so that others' lives will be touched and changed? You cannot outgive God. The more that you give of yourself and your time to Him, the more your life will be blessed and changed by being in His glorious presence!

A Light Shone Around Him

"As he journeyed he came near Damascus, and suddenly a light shone around him from heaven" (Acts 9:3).

Saul of Tarsus was nearing Damascus when a light shone around him. This light was Jesus, Himself, appearing to Saul. Saul had a decision to make. Would he accept Jesus Christ as his Messiah, or would he turn away? Having experienced the glorious light of the presence of Jesus Christ, he was compelled to choose to follow Jesus Christ.

We know Saul of Tarsus as Paul, the apostle who lived a life that shone forth with the light of Jesus in such a powerful way that churches were established in many towns, many lives were saved and changed, and many miracles occurred. The man who once persecuted the Church of Jesus Christ became one of His strongest followers and witnesses.

Paul is a wonderful example to us of what a difference the light of Jesus can make in a person's life. Paul, who once was filled with darkness, hatred, and persecution, was turned around to be filled with love, compassion, strength, and wisdom. Can that happen to us today? Of course it can!

Think of a person in your life who seems to be far away from living a Christian life. Begin to pray for that person, expecting God to change that person from darkness to light. Be open to any opportunity that the Lord may bring your way to share the love and truth of Jesus Christ with that person. Do not try to make things happen, but trust the Lord to open doors and bring you or another person the opportunity to witness to him. Get ready to experience the joy and delight that will come into your life as you see your friend or family member turn his life over to the King of kings and Lord of lords!

I Am Jesus of Nazareth

"So I answered, 'Who are You, Lord?' And He said to me, 'I am Jesus of Nazareth, whom you are persecuting.' And those who were with me indeed saw the light and were afraid, but they did not hear the voice of Him who spoke to me" (Acts 22:8–9).

Paul recounts his Damascus road experience to a mob in Jerusalem after he was arrested. When this light appeared to Paul, he asked the question, "Who are You, Lord?" And Jesus answered him, "I am Jesus of Nazareth, whom you are persecuting." This statement not only shows that Jesus is great light; but it also shows us that when Saul was persecuting the Christians, Jesus took that so personally that He told Saul that he was persecuting Jesus, Himself. He, who is great light and brings His light into our lives, feels and experiences the persecution that we go through. What a wondrous Lord we serve! He gives us His light that guides and directs our lives, and He gives us His presence that comforts and strengthens us when we go through difficult times.

Are you going through difficult times today? If you are, go to Him who is Light and share your problems with Him. He not only feels and understands what you are going through, but He also has an answer for you. He desires to bring victory into your life by helping you overcome your problems. Romans 8:37 says, "We are more than conquerors through Him who loves us." Jesus of Nazareth still provides all that we need to overcome in this world. Let Him reveal His wondrous light and strength to you today as you enter into His presence face to face.

Light of the Glory of God

"For it is the God who commanded light to shine out of darkness, who has shone in our hearts to give the light of the knowledge of the glory of God in the face of Jesus Christ" (2 Cor. 4:6).

What a glorious promise our scripture for today brings to us! The same God who spoke light into existence when He created the heavens and the earth shines His light into our hearts, giving us knowledge of the glory of God. We can see and understand the glory of God through coming into a face to face relationship with Jesus Christ. How do we come into a face to face relationship with Jesus Christ? We come by simply allowing Him time and place in our lives. As we draw close to Him, seeking Him with all that is within us, we can enter into such an intimate relationship with Him that we can actually hear Him speak to us.

We can look into His face and see the glory of His countenance. As we see Him in all His glory, we begin to be changed into His image. As His light shines upon us, it begins to penetrate and reveal the things that are not pleasing to God. As we see these things, sitting in His presence, we can do nothing less than repent and ask for forgiveness.

Will you seek to enter into His presence today face to face? Will you look unto Jesus and allow Him to bring His light into your life in such a way that it reveals the things that are not of Him? Will you look to Him with a repentant heart, asking forgiveness for your sins? Now as that forgiveness flows to you, look up into the face of your marvelous Lord who is truly worthy to receive all your praises!

Walk as Children of Light

"For you were once darkness, but now you are light in the Lord. Walk as children of light" (Eph. 5:8).

We all have experienced darkness because we come into this world needing to know Jesus Christ. When we accept Him as our Lord and Savior, the darkness flees; and He gives us His light. Do we always live as children of light? You and I both know that we do not. We are learning and growing in the Christian walk that we have entered into. The fact that we do not always make the choices that express the light of Jesus does not mean that His light does not dwell within us. It means that at that moment we put our light under a bushel, and we quench the Spirit of God who dwells within us.

In order to walk as children of light, we need to choose on a daily basis to read and study God's Word. We also need to take that choice a step further and be obedient to what we are studying. As we study the Bible, we read truth that will bring the light and life of Jesus Christ into our lives. We will be convicted of the ungodly practices in our lives, and we will be encouraged to reach out and act in the love and grace of our Lord. God's Word is a "lamp unto our feet" that brings revelation and understanding about ourselves and God's plan for our lives.

Choose today to enter into a regular and meaningful study of God's Word that will bring clarity and direction for walking as a child of light. Open up the pages of the one book that is alive and powerful, and watch the changes that it will bring in your life.

Called into His Marvelous Light

"But you are a chosen generation, a royal priesthood, a holy nation, His own special people, that you may proclaim the praises of Him who called you out of darkness into His marvelous light" (1 Pet. 2:9).

*B*ecause you have been called out of darkness into His marvelous light, you can and should proclaim praises to Him. Are you excited about your relationship with Jesus Christ? If you are, then there is nothing that can hold you back from sharing and proclaiming His grace and His glory. If you are not excited, then you can be! Ask the Creator of the whole universe to set you on fire with excitement and zeal! Ask Him to place within you a hunger and thirst for more of Him.

Make a commitment to Him today to study His Word and to spend time with Him. Be open to the opportunities that He will bring your way to be a witness for Him. Be sensitive to the needs around you. If you have friends or family members that are hurting or in need, offer to pray for them. Share with them how the Lord has met your needs. If they need something material to help them over a hump, search for a way to meet that need. God will provide for them, and He will also provide a way for you to be a part of providing for them. That does not mean that you have to give everything that is needed out of your own resources. It does mean, however, that God will show you a way for the provisions to come. Know the joy of being used by the Lord to meet the needs of others and bringing joy into their lives. Know the excitement of sharing the good news of Jesus Christ with others and seeing their lives change!

Speak in the Light

"Whatever I tell you in the dark, speak in the light, and what you hear in the ear, preach on the housetops" (Matt. 10:27).

In another translation, the scripture for today says, "Shout it from the housetops." Jesus instructs us to shout or preach from the housetops what He shares with us in secret or what He whispers in our ear. The picture that we have here is us spending precious time alone with Him to receive His truth and be built up and edified. When we spend this time with Him, we will receive more and more of His light so that we can go out into the world around us.

Where is your world? It is your neighborhood, home, school, work, and wherever you spend your time on a daily basis. You and I are to share with others the revelation and knowledge that Jesus gives to us. If that seems like a difficult task for you, ask the Lord to show you how you can begin to move in the direction of sharing His love and truth with others. You do not have to begin by going out on a street corner and preaching or by climbing on your roof and literally shouting to all of your neighborhood. You may begin by choosing one neighbor to pray for on a daily basis, asking the Lord to open an opportunity to share with that neighbor. You will be amazed at the opportunity that will come your way. When that time comes, begin to share with boldness whatever the Holy Spirit brings to your mind. He will give you the words, and He will prepare the heart of your neighbor to receive the truth of Jesus Christ. Begin your time of prayer for your neighbor today and know the joy that comes from being used by the Kings of kings and the Lord of lords!

Shine as Lights in the World

"That you may become blameless and harmless, children of God without fault in the midst of a crooked and perverse generation, among whom you shine as lights in the world" (Phil. 2:15).

When you look around, do you feel that you are in the midst of a crooked and perverse generation? The scripture for today was written approximately 2,000 years ago, but it seems as if it were written only yesterday. So much in our world today is full of darkness and sin, and we are instructed to shine as lights in the midst of the darkness.

Consider the darkness of a cloudy night when the moon and stars are not visible. It is pitch-black, and we cannot see anything. Suddenly the clouds begin to move, and we see a star shining brightly in the sky. Then the moon becomes visible, and light begins to come forth. There is something exciting about light coming forth in the midst of darkness. When the sun begins to rise in the eastern sky and the darkness begins to dissipate, we know that another day is dawning. Hope and joy comes with the light of a new day.

We are to shine as lights in this world that is full of darkness. We are to bring hope and joy to others in the knowledge that Jesus is Lord of all. When others look at us, they should see such peace and joy that they want to receive what we have.

Will you be a light shining in the midst of a crooked and perverse world? Share with others the wonders of turning your life over to a Savior who is not only filled with victory and power but also love and mercy!

The Lord Is My Light

"The Lord is my light and my salvation; whom shall I fear? The Lord is the strength of my life; of whom shall I be afraid?" (Ps. 27:1).

We do not need to fear anyone because the Lord is our strength and light. No matter what someone might say or do to us, we have the assurance that Jesus has the answer. He is there to help us and protect us, and He will reveal to us through His light exactly how we can overcome. We need not be afraid of anyone! Romans 8:31 says, "If God be for us, who can be against us?" When God is on our side, there is absolutely nothing that can come against us that we cannot overcome with the strength, light, and wisdom of God Almighty!

If you are in an extremely difficult situation, would you rather have the advice of a good friend or revelation from the Lord? You may say, "I can at least hear and understand what my friend would say to me." That is true, but it is also true that you and I can hear from God. When we do hear from God, nothing can take that wondrous experience from us, and nothing on the face of the earth can compare with the truth and wisdom that will come from Him! We can be assured that what He speaks to us will be the exact and perfect answer to the problem that we face.

Will you seek the strength and light of the only One who has every perfect and good answer to the problems that you may face today? Will you draw close to Him and listen for His guidance and direction for you? Be strong and courageous because the Lord that you serve is greater than any person or circumstance that may be causing you to be afraid!

The Light of God's Countenance

"For they did not gain possession of the land by their own sword, nor did their own arm save them; but it was Your right hand, Your arm, and the light of Your countenance because You favored them" (Ps. 44:3).

The Israelites did not gain possession of the Promised Land by their own strength or their own abilities, but strictly by the strength and power of Almighty God. They were strongly outnumbered by their enemy, and they were not armed with strong weapons. They were simply armed with the presence and might of their Jehovah God.

We can rely on the light of Jesus Christ to see us through any difficulty, trial, or tribulation. As we look to Him, He will reveal to us what steps to take in a given situation, and He will guide and direct us through times that look impossible to the natural eye. He has every answer to every question and can reveal to us what we need to know to overcome in this world. He has placed us in this world to be a reflection of His light to others.

As we trust Him with our lives and all that comes our way, we will be an expression of the peace that comes from total trust in Him. When we face circumstances that seem overwhelming to us, and we place our trust in Him, the light reflected from our lives will draw others into His presence.

Will you place that difficulty that you face into His strong right hand and His arm so that He can bring you victory in the battle that is raging against you? As you do, you will see that others around you will be drawn to the light that reflects from your countenance. Look to your wondrous Lord and Savior for the light of His countenance and receive from Him!

273

God Gives Us Light

"God is the Lord, and He has given us light . . . You are my God, and I will praise You; You are my God, I will exalt You" (Ps. 118:27–28).

We are told over and over in Scripture that God is light. In the verses for today, we are told that He gives us light. Can you imagine? The God of the whole universe gives to you and me His light. We can receive from Him revelation and understanding of anything that we need to know and understand. Does that make you want to praise and exalt God Almighty?

When I think of all that He holds out to me and His goodness and mercy, I can hardly contain myself. I want to praise Him and worship Him with every ounce of my being. He is more than worthy to receive praise and worship from you and me. Instead of spending time on all the busyness of this world, we need to go before Him and tell Him how we feel about Him. As we communicate with Him, sharing our feelings, we need to be open to receive from Him. He waits to share with us His love for us and His direction for our lives and to encourage us about every aspect of our lives.

Will you take the time today to enter into the glorious light of His presence and to worship and exalt Him with all that is within you? Let Him be such an encouragement to you that you will rise up and take the place that He has for you. Go forth in the strength and power of His Spirit and reach out to those around you. Be an instrument in His hands to further His kingdom on this earth!

A Light to My Path

"Your word is a lamp to my feet and a light to my path"
(Ps. 119:105).

Thank You, Lord God, that You have blessed us with Your Word. Thank You that Bibles are available to us in abundance. Help us, Lord, to take the precious gift of Your Word and hold on to it with great perseverance and diligence. Help us to decide daily to read, study, and meditate on Your Word. I thank You, precious Jesus, that as we read the Bible, You will bring understanding and revelation to us through Your Spirit. Thank You that there is no question that we can ask that cannot be answered through Your Word. Help us to put our faith so completely in You and Your Word that we will ask and receive, seek and find, and knock and it will be opened to us.

We praise You that You are continually shining the light of Your Word upon us, bringing direction and guidance into our lives. No matter where we are or what our circumstance may be, You are there with every answer. Help us to listen and receive Your answer for us. May we walk in obedience to Your direction for us just as Mary did when she said, "Be it done unto me according to Your Word."

Lord, You truly are a wondrous God! May Your blessings be so strong upon us that we cannot contain our praises and thanksgiving for You. May we spread Your love and blessings wherever Your path may take us. May we spill over with excitement, zeal, and joy because of Your presence that resides so strongly within us. May the world around us see Your light within us and be changed. Use us as Your instruments to bring Your kingdom upon this earth! Amen.

Walk in the Light of the Lord

"O house of Jacob, come and let us walk in the light of the Lord" (Isa. 2:5).

Since God's Word is a "light unto our path," we need to walk in that light that He gives to us. We need to spend time with His Word, and then we need to decide to walk in obedience to His Word. Reading the Bible alone is not enough for a strong Christian walk, but walking in obedience to the light of His Word is what strengthens us.

If you have never read through the Bible in a year, you may want to give that a try. Many plans are available as helps for reading through God's Word. When you begin your reading plan, do not rush through it. Take the time to study, meditate, and ponder the meaning of what you are reading. Ask yourself questions as you read. What is this scripture saying to me? How can I apply this to my life today?

Be sensitive to the Holy Spirit as He teaches, corrects, convicts, and encourages you through the Word of God. When He brings a particular situation or person to your mind as you are reading, ask Him how you can respond to that particular need or person. Be alert and aware of the direction and guidance of the Holy Spirit to use you in the lives of others. Walking in the light of the Lord is a daily adventure that will bring great joy and excitement into your life.

Have Seen a Great Light

"The people who walked in darkness have seen a great light; those who dwelt in the land of the shadow of death, upon them a light has shined" (Isa. 9:2).

The light of Jesus is so powerful and so bright that it can overcome any and all darkness and death. When we are surrounded by the darkness of the world, we can know that the light of Jesus that resides within us will dispel the darkness. The light of Jesus dwells within us, but we need to let it shine forth. We need to seek Him with all our strength so that His light will shine brightly from us.

Have you ever befriended someone with the expectancy of being a witness and an example to them, only to find that they influenced you in the wrong way? I believe that has happened to all of us at some time in our lives. When we are around people who walk in darkness, we need to be strong in the Lord. We need to be so in tune to Him that we radiate His light so brightly that those in darkness will find the darkness melting away. Just as darkness fades when we turn on a light in our home at night, darkness that dwells within nonbelievers will begin to fade as they are exposed to the light of Jesus. They will find that they are so drawn to the Savior they will turn their lives over to Him and be totally changed.

Would you like to be a part of the Savior's plan to help draw someone into His kingdom? Seek Him with all your heart, let Him live big within you, and let His light shine so brightly from you that others' lives will be changed. Know the joy of being used by your wondrous Lord and Savior, and see your friends' and loved ones' lives being changed by His glorious love and light!

Light to the Gentiles

"I, the Lord, have called You in righteousness, and will hold Your hand; I will keep You and give You as a covenant to the people, as a light to the Gentiles, to open blind eyes, to bring out prisoners from the prison, those who sit in darkness from the prison house" (Isa. 42:6–7).

Jesus was given as a covenant for you and for me. He went to the cross to pay the price for our sins and to give us His righteousness. He, who lived a perfect life without sin, took our sins upon Himself to make a way for us to be a part of the family of God.

A covenant is a solemn agreement or promise that is binding. The promise that God has made to us through Jesus Christ is complete and final. God will never go back on His promise or covenant with us. We, as human beings, do not understand the finality and completeness of God's promise. We do not always keep our word, and we often break our promises. We can be assured, however, that whatever our Lord promises, He will do.

The light that comes with God's covenant is so brilliant that blind eyes will be opened and prisoners will come out of dark prisons. We can expect that His light will illuminate us so that we will have understanding in areas where we have been blinded and be set free from areas of bondage and darkness. As we turn our lives over to the Lord, He will use us to help bring His light into the lives of others.

Draw close to Him today and let His light shine brilliantly from you into the lives of those close to you. Be a reflection of the grace and mercy of the One who brings His light into your life as you yield yourself to Him!

I Will Make Darkness Light Before Them

"I will bring the blind by a way they did not know; I will lead them in paths they have not known. I will make darkness light before them, and crooked places straight. These things I will do for them" (Isa. 42:16).

The Lord promises us that when He brings His light into our lives, He will give us direction that will keep us on a straight path. We often, however, find ourselves choosing to go down a path that God has not placed before us; and when we do, we find ourselves in trouble. We so often wonder why nothing seems to be going right and everything seems to be in such a state of turmoil. It could be because we are out of the will of God and doing our own thing. Our daily decisions make the difference in whether we walk in peace or confusion.

The Lord waits upon us to yield ourselves to Him and to seek His ways. He wants to change the crooked path that we are on to a straight path that leads to peace, fruitfulness, and total well-being in Him. The joy and contentment that come from submission to Him are worth everything that we think we are giving up.

Are you ready to submit the things in your life that are holding you back from the straight path that leads to peace and contentment? Pray this prayer to our heavenly Father: "Father, help me to submit my whole life to You. I want to be in the center of Your will and walking down the straight path that You have placed before me. In Jesus' name. Amen."

Light of the World

"As long as I am in the world, I am the light of the world" (John 9:5).

*I*s Jesus still in the world? Yes, He is in the world through the work and presence of the Holy Spirit. He is still the light of the world. He is my light, and He is your light! We need to lean on Him and receive from Him all that He has for us now, on this earth. He holds out to us revelation and understanding that the world longs to have. The world does not know to whom to turn in order to receive understanding that would bring peace and joy to them. We, as Christians, have the answer—we belong to the One who has all the answers! Why do we fail to look to Him and receive what He has for us?

We are such busy people that we fail to turn to the God of the whole universe who holds out His arms and His light and revelation to us. We also doubt that God would speak to us. If we could only grasp the enormity of what is available to us because we have turned our lives over to the Lord God Almighty, we would truly be lights shining upon a hill. We would shine so brightly that those around us would be amazed at the illumination that comes from us.

Would you be willing today to reach out to Him who has all the answers?

Listen and hear from your Father who is in heaven. Pick up your Bible and expect His Word to speak to you. Be sensitive to the teaching and preaching that is within your church. Know that Almighty God is able to reveal to you all that you need to know to function on this earth and to fulfill His plan for your life!

A Light into the World

"I have come as a light into the world, that whoever believes in Me should not abide in darkness" (John 12:46).

Because Jesus has come as a light into the world, we as believers do not have to abide in darkness. That means that He gives us the strength and power to overcome darkness that would try to infiltrate our lives. What kind of darkness would try to infiltrate the life of a believer? So often darkness can come very subtly and over a long period of time. We can be conditioned to accept the things of darkness when we choose to watch certain types of television programs and movies that have ungodly influences. There are all kinds of temptations to the believer besides television and movies. All of us continually face peer pressure.

The strength to battle temptations and darkness that come against us is available to all believers. We need to be strong in God's Word, walking in close communion with Him through prayer and time spent with Him, and walking in close fellowship with other believers. When we come together encouraging and building one another up, we find nothing that we cannot face with the help of God. We need to always be open to share our needs with one another and be willing to pray for each other.

If you face some type of temptation today, let the light of Jesus shine forth upon you through spending time in His Word and, also, by spending time with a special Christian friend whom you can trust to be a prayer support for you.

281

Light to the Gentiles

"For so the Lord has commanded us: 'I have set you as a light to the Gentiles, that you should be for salvation to the ends of the earth'" (Acts 13:47).

When Paul and Barnabas were preaching about Jesus to both the Jews and the Gentiles in Antioch, the Jews began to oppose them. In the scripture for today, Paul quotes from Isaiah 49:6, which prophesied that Jesus would be sent as a light to the Gentiles. In other words, Jesus was sent to the whole world, to both the Jews and the Gentiles. He was sent in order that anyone and everyone who turned their lives over to Him would be saved.

What does salvation mean? Salvation means to be whole, to have complete well-being, peace, and security. When we accept Jesus Christ as our Lord and Savior, we receive eternal life with the promise of wholeness, complete well-being, and total peace and security in heaven. We can also expect to receive wholeness and peace on this earth as well. It is nothing compared to what we will experience in heaven, but it is wonderful because we are receiving freedom in the midst of so much turmoil.

Are you receiving all that Jesus holds out to you? Are you experiencing peace in the midst of a storm? Are you experiencing a feeling of total well-being even though the circumstances around you are difficult? If you cannot answer yes to the above questions, you need to turn to Jesus with an expectancy and ask Him to give you peace. Ask Him to reveal to you what is holding you back from receiving all that He has for you. Receive His salvation in fullness now as well as for all eternity!

Sons of Light

"You are all sons of light and sons of the day. We are not of the night nor of darkness" (1 Thess. 5:5).

Are you a son or daughter of light? If you have accepted Jesus Christ as Lord and Savior, you are a son or daughter of light. That means that the light of Jesus dwells within you. You have available to you understanding and revelation that come from the Holy Spirit. He will speak to you through Scripture, bringing them alive within you so that you understand those things that you have never understood before. Your mind and heart will be illumined with the truth of Jesus Christ.

When we walk in the light of Jesus Christ, we no longer need to or should be a part of darkness. In other words, we need to make decisions based on what God's Word tells us rather than on our desires or other peoples' influences. When it seems difficult to make decisions based on God's Word, we need to draw close to our heavenly Father and let Him encourage us. We need to draw into the light that brings comfort, strength, and all that we need to overcome in this world. We need to let Numbers 6:24–26 come alive to us. It says, "The Lord bless you and keep you; the Lord make His face to shine upon you, and be gracious to you; the Lord lift up His countenance upon you and give you peace." When He shines His face upon us and His light permeates our very being, there is no way that we will give in to the darkness of the world.

Let Him shine His face upon you today. Enter into His presence and seek Him with all that is within you. Expect to enter into a face to face relationship with Him so that you can receive His light into your life. Turn away from darkness and receive the glorious light of Jesus Christ!

A Light That Shines in a Dark Place

"And so we have the prophetic word confirmed which you do well to heed as a light that shines in a dark place, until the day dawns and the morning star rises in your hearts" (2 Pet. 1:19).

In the scripture for today, Peter refers to the prophetic word that came during the Transfiguration when a voice from heaven spoke and said, "This is My beloved Son, in whom I am well pleased." When the light of Jesus comes into a life or a situation, darkness has to flee. Jesus spent His life on earth taking His light into dark places. When He met the woman at the well, He shed His light into a life that was filled with darkness. Her life was changed, and she became the first recorded evangelist when she went back into her town and began to tell the people about the "Man" who told her all about her life. Many lives were saved and changed as a result of Jesus taking His light into dark places.

Are we supposed to take the light of Jesus Christ into dark places today? Yes, Jesus was our example! We need to be open to every opportunity that comes our way to share the grace, mercy, and love of Jesus with those who walk in darkness.

Will you be open today to any opportunities that Jesus may bring across your path to share His goodness and light with someone? If your answer is yes, then pray this prayer: "Father, in the precious name of Jesus, I ask You to give me an opportunity to share Your grace with someone today. May I be sensitive to the leading of the Holy Spirit as You open a door for me today. Thank You. Amen."

God Is Light

"This is the message which we have heard from Him and declare to you, that God is light and in Him is no darkness at all. If we say that we have fellowship with Him, and walk in darkness, we lie and do not practice the truth" (1 John 1:5–6).

This is a hard scripture to receive because it tells us that if we walk in darkness and say that we have fellowship with the Lord, we lie. It is so easy to say that we have fellowship with the Lord, but the real test of that statement is found in our actions. Are we truly following His ways and walking in light? Are we showing His love to those around us? Are we able to forgive those who have wronged us? Do we turn the other cheek when someone is mean to us? Are we glad when someone we know is promoted or has something good happen to him, or are we envious or jealous? Do we find ourselves telling others tidbits of gossip in the guise of being "prayer requests"?

Sometimes we think of "darkness" as something foreboding such as murder, adultery, stealing, or homosexuality. We frequently want to overlook the fact that darkness can also be found deep within as sins that are not observable to the outward eye. We, as Christians, need to be aware of the darkness that tries to take hold in our lives and firmly stand against it.

Let the Lord reveal to you today if there is any form of darkness residing within you or even trying to get a foothold in your life. Trust Him to set you free and help you to be "more than a conqueror."

Fellowship with One Another

"But if we walk in the light as He is in the light, we have fellowship with one another, and the blood of Jesus Christ His Son cleanses us from all sin" (1 John 1:7).

Sometimes we think that there is no way that we can walk in the light as Jesus is in the light. The scripture for today, however, tells us that we can. And when we do walk in the light, we have fellowship with one another. How often do we find ourselves out of fellowship with someone else? Unfortunately more often than we would like to admit. When we are out of fellowship with others, that means that we are not walking in the light of Jesus. We need to take inventory of our lives and see if our relationships are all in order or if there is someone with whom we are having a problem.

Christianity is all about relationships—first, our relationship with Jesus Christ and second, our relationship with others. We cannot have a close relationship with Jesus without being aware of the needs in our relationships with others. As we draw closer and closer to Him, we will begin to see ways that we can restore and reconcile strained relationships. Jesus is in the reconciliation business, and we are the ones He uses to bring reconciliation to the world. We cannot bring reconciliation to a lost and dying world if we are in wrong relationship with those close to us.

Draw close to Him today and let Him bring reconciliation into your life. Let Him use you to bring reconciliation into the lives of others. He waits with open arms to help you set your life straight and to restore those relationships that have been difficult and a problem. Will you trust Him today to set you free and use you to further His kingdom?

Christ Will Give You Light

"Therefore He says: 'Awake, you who sleep, arise from the dead, and Christ will give you light'" (Eph. 5:14).

Do you sometimes feel as if you are asleep spiritually? The scripture for today is an admonition to wake up and arise from the dead. If you are in a place of dryness and seemingly deadness, take heart! Jesus is ready to pour out His light upon you. His light is available in an abundance. He is not wanting to hold back the brightness of His truth from you or me. He waits for us to reach out and receive all that He has for us.

How do we reach out and receive His light from Him? I believe as we read His Word with an open heart, He reveals truth to us. As we draw close to Him in prayer and communion with Him, He shines so brightly upon us that we begin to be a reflection of His light. We can also receive His light by being in fellowship with other believers who are strongly committed to Him. They will have a good influence in our lives, and we can share with one another about the goodness and grace of our Lord.

If you have been slack in reading your Bible, make a commitment today to read faithfully, expecting to receive insight and revelation from the Holy Spirit. If you have not been spending time alone with the Lord in prayer and communion, go before Him right now and bask in the joy of His wonderful presence. If you have neglected fellowshiping with other believers, choose today to join a Bible study, prayer group, or some type of small group where you can grow and be strengthened in your walk with the Lord. Give the Lord every opportunity to work in and through your life so that you can be a strong reflection of His glorious light!

287

The Glory of the Lord Is Risen Upon You

"Arise, shine; for your light has come! And the glory of the Lord is risen upon you. For behold, the darkness shall cover the earth, and deep darkness the people; but the Lord will arise over you, and His glory will be seen upon you. The Gentiles shall come to your light . . ." (Isa. 60:1–3a).

When we spend glorious time in the presence of the Lord, basking in His glory, we will be so filled with His light that others will come to us. They will want to know why our life radiates such peace, contentment, and joy. They will want to experience the same light that has arisen upon us. Those who are surrounded by darkness long to know how to come out of the darkness. So often their lives are in a rut, and they do not know any way of life except the one in which they are involved. They need to see and be surrounded by people who walk in the light of Jesus. They long for someone who can tell them how to be set free and how to overcome.

We, as Christians, have the answer for which the world is longing. We need to overcome the fear of rejection, apathy and indifference, and wrong priorities. We need to get out in the world and let the light of Jesus radiate so brilliantly that those in darkness will flood into the light. We need to be willing to feed the hungry, pray for the sick, visit the prisoner, and clothe those who are cold. We need to go where there are needs and be an instrument of the Lord in providing for those needs. We need to go with such a winsome countenance that those in darkness will know that we meet their physical needs because of the One who can meet their spiritual needs. Let us go in unconditional love and spread the beautiful light of Jesus until there are multitudes responding to His call!

Love One Another

"A new commandment I give to you, that you love one another; as I have loved you, that you also love one another" (John 13:34).

The direction of Jesus in the scripture for today is two-fold. He not only tells us to love one another, but He tells us to love one another as He has loved us. How has Jesus loved us? He has loved us unconditionally. No matter what we may say or do, He loves us. That does not mean that He approves of everything that we do or say, but He loves us anyway.

Is it easy to love someone who says ugly or cruel things? Of course, it is not easy, but "[we] can do all things through Christ who strengthens [us]." Loving as Jesus loves does not come easy, but it is something that must be possible because He has instructed us to love as He loves. How can we love as He loves? We can love as He loves only through the power of the Holy Spirit who resides within us as Christians. Romans 5:5 says, ". . . the love of God has been poured out in our hearts by the Holy Spirit who was given to us."

Would you be willing today to let the Lord express His love to a difficult-to-love person through you by the power of the Holy Spirit? Trust Him to show you how to reach out to this person in such a way that he (or she) will see such an expression of love that he (or she) will be drawn close to Him. Rejoice as the Lord changes a strained and difficult relationship into a beautiful friendship. You will know that this has come from the outpouring love of Jesus.

OCTOBER 2

Keep My Commandments

"He who has My commandments and keeps them, it is he who loves Me. And he who loves Me will be loved by My Father, and I will love him and manifest Myself to him" (John 14:21).

In 1974, when Jesus became Lord of my life, I was filled with such a strong love for Him that I wanted to do anything and everything that I thought He wanted me to do. I began to read and consume His Word because I knew that it held the key to understanding His will and direction for my life. As I read the Bible, I saw areas of my life that were not lining up with His commandments. My heart was filled with grief that I was not pleasing Him in these different areas. I repented and then began to see changes occur in my life as I would trust Him to help me obey Him. This process of growing and walking with Him continues today as I still seek to keep His commandments because I love Him more and more as each day passes. What a joy to know and love the Lord of lords and King of kings!

Are you keeping the commandments of the Lord as an expression of your love for Him? Go before Him today and ask Him to help you to be obedient to His Word. Let Him reveal any areas of your life that are not pleasing to Him, and then trust Him to give you the strength and power to overcome in those areas. Bask in His presence as He manifests Himself to you and pours out His love upon you!

We Will Make Our Home with Him

"Jesus answered and said to him, 'If anyone loves Me, he will keep My word; and My Father will love him, and We will come to him and make Our home with him'" (John 14:23).

Do you want Jesus the Son and God the Father to come and make their home with you? Can you imagine what that would be like? If you love Jesus and keep His Word, you can expect that They will come and dwell with you. They will make themselves known to you in such a way that you will actually experience their presence in your daily life.

When we spend time in God's Word and decide to follow God's Word, we find that we draw closer and closer to the Lord. We begin to take on His character and attributes in such a way that our lives will be changed. As we follow in obedience to God's Word, we find ourselves seeking to spend more and more time in the presence of the Lord. We truly become aware that His presence is not something "way out there" that is available only on rare occasions. We find, however, that He is available to us always. He has enough time for each one of us on a regular basis. He wants to spend time and make His home with us continually. All we have to do is to love Him and keep His words.

Will you take time today to read, study, and meditate on God's Word? As you do, be open to the opportunities that He brings your way to walk in obedience to His Word. As you read, study, and act on the Bible, you will find that your love for Him will grow stronger and stronger. His love is so great and His mercy is so enduring that, as you read about His nature, you cannot help but grow in your love for Him!

Abide in My Love

"As the Father loved Me, I also have loved you; abide in My love" (John 15:9).

This scripture instructs us to abide in the love of Jesus. I believe that we abide in the love of Jesus by knowing Him better through His Word and spending time with Him in prayer. Prayer is communication between God and us. Not only do we need to share our hearts with Him, but we need to listen to Him, to receive from Him, and to respond to Him.

Talking to the Lord and then hearing from Him can be an awesome and overwhelming experience. When we have prayed about something important to us or someone we know and then receive an answer, we can hardly contain ourselves. To think that the God of the whole universe would take the time to listen to us and then to answer! It is just as awesome and overwhelming to be talking to Him in prayer and then to actually "hear" a response from Him. How do we "hear" from God? Usually it is a still, quiet voice deep within our spirit. Our spirit seems to be deep within the center of our being. In the New American Standard Version of the Bible, John 7:38 says, "From [the believer's] innermost being shall flow rivers of living water." We should always test what we think we are hearing with God's Word and with spiritually mature Christians whom we can trust.

Go before the Lord in your quiet time today, expecting both to "hear" from Him and to receive an answer to your prayer. Rejoice as your Lord begins to share great and wondrous things with you personally!

Greater Love

"Greater love has no one than this, than to lay down one's life for his friends" (John 15:13).

*I*f you are reading this devotional today, you have not laid down your physical life for a friend. Does that mean, however, that you have never laid down your life for a friend? No! If you have ever given up something important to you so that you could meet a need in a friend's life, then you have "laid down your life" for your friend. In other words, you have put your friend and his needs first before your own needs or desires.

I have a dear friend who is involved in a homeless ministry. She lays down her life several times a week to go out on the streets and help those in desperate need. Even on days when there is snow on the ground and the temperature is below freezing, she takes food, something warm to drink, blankets, sweat shirts, coats, and toboggans to those who are cold and hungry. Some would not have lived through the night if Maxine had not gone and "laid down her life" for people whom she does not know but for whom she cares deeply. She shares the love of Jesus by meeting physical needs as well as by telling them about her Lord, Jesus Christ.

Have you ever "laid down your life" for someone else? Ask the Lord today to show you someone who has a great need in his life. Be willing to be the Lord's instrument in meeting that need. Let the Lord use you to spread His love to those who are in great need and, perhaps, are not easy to love. You will be so mightily blessed by "laying down your life" that you will want to be used by God again and again in others' lives.

OCTOBER 6

Feed My Sheep

"He said to him the third time, 'Simon, son of Jonah, do you love Me?' Peter was grieved because He said to him the third time, 'Do you love Me?' And he said to Him, 'Lord, You know all things; You know that I love You.' Jesus said to him, 'Feed My sheep'" (John 21:17).

Jesus asked Peter to express his love for his Master by being obedient to His instruction to him. We are told over and over in Scripture that obedience is an act of love. When we obey the words of Jesus, we walk in love to those around us. We feed the hungry, clothe the cold, visit those in prisons, care for widows and orphans, and express His love in other ways to those who are in need.

Are the only people in need the ones who are poor and possibly homeless? Of course not! There are many needy people in the world, and some of them live in expensive houses in nice subdivisions. Their need may be different than the need of the poor but just as real. Many alcoholics and addicts live in nice neighborhoods. Many suffer from depression and even have thoughts of suicide. The need in this world is overwhelming to us, but not to our God. All things are possible with our Lord, and He wants to use us in the lives of those who are hurting. We need to be sensitive to the needs of people all around us. The Lord brings opportunities to us each day to be an example of His love. We need to ask Him to help us be more sensitive to His Holy Spirit so that we can trust Him to speak and act through us in expressing His love.

Love of God Poured Out in Our Hearts

"Now hope does not disappoint, because the love of God has been poured out in our hearts by the Holy Spirit who was given to us" (Rom. 5:5).

Did you know that the love of God actually dwells within you? Do you feel as if the love of God is within you? God's Word tells us that His love dwells within us, yet we do not always feel as if His love is within us. How do we grow in our knowledge and expression of that love that dwells within us?

I believe we grow in experiencing God's love and sharing it with others by drawing close to the Lord. He is love. As we draw close to Him, we begin to understand and experience that glorious love that can be found no other place. He is the One who expresses love in such a way that our lives are changed by it. As we seek Him face to face and bask in the glory of His love, we receive His glory that changes us into His image. Can we even begin to imagine what His image is like? Spending time in His presence reveals the greatness of His love in such a way that we find ourselves becoming more and more a reflection of His love to others. Those who have been so difficult to love and understand suddenly become easier to love. Our lives will be transformed, and the Lord will use us as His instruments in helping to bring about transformation in others' lives.

Will you draw close to the Lord today and seek His presence—where you can be changed by His powerful love? You will find yourself reaching out to others in ways that you never before even considered. Let your life be an expression of that wondrous love that has been poured out in your heart by the Holy Spirit!

Who Shall Separate Us from the Love of Christ?

"Who shall separate us from the love of Christ? Shall tribulation, or distress, or persecution, or famine, or nakedness, or peril, or sword?" (Rom. 8:35).

*A*bsolutely nothing can separate you from the love of God! God's love is everlasting and eternal. No matter what problem may exist in your life today, your God is greater and His love is ever-present. Your situation may be so drastic that you feel there is no hope.

Even when we feel that God is not near and we are in a desperate situation, the love of God is at work in our lives. Sometimes we feel as if we are praying to a brick wall and there probably will be no results. That is not true! We cannot rely upon our feelings, but we must put our trust and belief in God's Word. His Word is full of promises to us that He loves us and cares about what is happening in our lives. Revelation 1:8 says, "I am the Alpha and the Omega, the Beginning and the End," and His love is in every niche and corner between beginning and end. There is no place that we can go to escape the love of God.

Would you like to curl up in the arms of Love today? Put aside all the busy things you feel that you need to do, and find a place of quiet. With your Bible open before you, begin to seek the Lord. Let Him show you how very precious you are in His sight. Receive all the love that He has to pour out on you and then let His light and love shine forth from you into the lives of others.

Give Preference to One Another

"Be kindly affectionate to one another with brotherly love, in honor giving preference to one another" (Rom. 12:10).

Sometimes giving preference to someone else is easy, but at other times it is very difficult. When the person to whom we give preference is angry, uncaring, or ungrateful, we usually find our mind telling us to forget about being kind. That person, however, is the very person who needs to see someone care enough about him to show him some kindness.

Giving preference is not something that happens very much in the world in which we live. The world tells us to think about ourselves. "If it feels good, do it" is a phrase that we hear often. It is the premise of many television commercials. Putting ourselves and our own needs first is something that surrounds us constantly. As Christians, in order to counteract this way of thinking that is so prevalent, we need to be strengthened and encouraged by God's Word and each other. We need to spend time with the Lord, letting Him show us through His Word that His way is best. His way tells us to give preference to others. We also need to spend time in fellowship with other believers who are strong in God's Word so that the influences in our lives will be godly.

If you find it difficult to give preference to one or many people in your life, go before the Lord today and ask Him to help you. Ask Him for His strength and power to walk in obedience to His Word. Enter into His presence and let Him reveal His love to you so that you can be an instrument of His love in every relationship in your life, including any difficult ones.

Eye Has Not Seen

"But as it is written: 'Eye has not seen, nor ear heard, nor have entered into the heart of man the things which God has prepared for those who love Him'" (1 Cor. 2:9).

When we love God, we have no idea how great and wondrous are the blessings that He has in store for us. Ephesians 3:20 says, "Now to Him who is able to do exceedingly abundantly above all that we ask or think, according to the power that works in us."

Our imagination and our thinking are not great enough to comprehend the goodness and greatness of our God and His love for us.

First Corinthians 2:10, the verse that follows our scripture for today, says, "But God has revealed them to us through His Spirit." We cannot understand naturally all He holds out to us, but we can understand spiritually if we are in tune with Him. When we listen to Him through His Word, in prayer, and through other believers, we find He reveals hidden things that bring great joy, wisdom, and peace into our lives. We have greater understanding through Him to be able to reach out and help others as they go through times of desperation and despair. Instead of feeling hopeless and inadequate when a friend comes to us with a seemingly impossible situation, we look to our loving Father for His solution and response.

Are you wanting to know some of those things that God has prepared for you? Open up to Him with a heart filled with love and trust, and receive the glory of His beautiful presence in your life!

Faith Working Through Love

"For in Christ Jesus neither circumcision nor uncircumcision avails anything, but faith working through love" (Gal. 5:6).

In Hebrews 11:6, we are told that "without faith it is impossible to please Him," and 1 Corinthians 13:2 says, "And though I have all faith, so that I could remove mountains, but have not love, I am nothing." Faith is vitally important in our walk with the Lord. Faith without love, however, is totally meaningless.

His love is so overpowering and magnificent that we simply cannot comprehend the depth and scope of it. Yet He has placed that love within us so that we can be to those around us as He would be to them if He still walked on this earth. Whenever He brings an opportunity, we are to be His hands and feet extended here and now to express His love and compassion. Those opportunities are all around us. Jesus wants us to reach out by His love and bring His comfort, encouragement, truth, and love into the lives of those in need. He reveals to us all that needs to be done; how to do it; and then He gives us the strength, boldness, and power to accomplish His purpose.

Is someone coming to your mind as you read this devotional today? Perhaps it is someone who has a child in deep trouble, someone who has marriage problems, someone who is very sick, or perhaps someone who is very angry. Begin to pray for this person and be open to how the Lord would use you to bring His love into this person's life.

Through Love Serve One Another

"For you, brethren, have been called to liberty; only do not use liberty as an opportunity for the flesh, but through love serve one another" (Gal. 5:13).

One of the motivational gifts found in Romans 12 is the gift of service. People strong in service love to help other people. When they see a need, they immediately want to help in meeting that need. They often are very practical and hospitable people. They are the ones who immediately begin to cook a meal if someone is sick. They may go over to the sick person's house and begin to clean it. They are wonderful people, and the church cannot do without them.

Not everyone is strong in the gift of service, but everyone is called to serve in some capacity. People gifted in other areas can serve in the ways that they are most effective. A teacher may serve by giving of his time to prepare lessons and teach others about the need to love each other. An administrator may serve by taking charge of a project that eventually brings many into the kingdom.

No one person is exempt from service, and there may be times that a person must meet a need in an area toward which he is not strongly motivated. God's liberty calls each to serve—to serve as designed by Him and to serve out of love rather than out of obligation.

Do you know your strongest motivational gift? If not, read Romans 12:6–8 and ask the Lord to reveal those things in which you are most effective. Begin to move out in those areas of service, and enjoy the great pleasure that comes from serving God through serving His people!

Love for All the Saints

"Therefore I also, after I heard of your faith in the Lord Jesus and your love for all the saints, do not cease to give thanks for you, making mention of you in my prayers" (Eph. 1:15–16).

Paul was so pleased by reports that the church at Ephesus was showing love to all the saints that he gave thanks for them to the Lord. Who are all the saints? We know that they are the fellow believers within our own local church or denomination (and even denominations similar to ours), but do they also include the people down the street who worship in a different style from us? As long as they profess Jesus Christ as Lord and Savior, then they are also saints, and we need to express the love of Jesus to them.

What do you think would happen in this world if we accepted and loved those who are Christians even though they are different from us? When there is unity within the body of Christ, there will be nothing that we cannot accomplish together. That does not mean that we need to agree on every single point in the Bible, but it does mean that we are in unity because Jesus Christ is Lord. If we dwell on the major issues in God's Word rather than our differing opinions, we find that the internal accusations and "pointing of the finger" will be gone. It is then that we can work together to accomplish God's perfect will on this earth.

Do you have any prejudices against other churches or denominations? Ask the Lord to help you to walk in unity and love with all believers so that His will and purpose will be accomplished with the body of Christ on this earth!

301

Rooted and Grounded in Love

"That Christ may dwell in your hearts through faith; that you, being rooted and grounded in love . . ." (Eph. 3:17).

Do you want to be rooted and grounded in love? I believe that we all, as Christians, have that desire in our hearts. How can we be rooted and grounded in love? We need to draw close to the Lord, closer than we have ever drawn before. We need to know Him in His fullness and experience the joy that comes from a close and intimate relationship with Almighty God. That kind of relationship comes from spending time reading and studying His Word and from daily deciding to walk in obedience to His Word.

Closeness and intimacy also come from spending time in prayer and communion with Him. Prayer opens our heart to Him and then opens our spirit to receive what He shares with us. When we believe that we can experience the same closeness that those in the Bible experienced with Father God, then we find ourselves beginning to move into that intimacy. As we meet Him face to face, we find that we want to be obedient to the instructions and commandments found in His Word. We realize that walking His way is the only way real peace and contentment can dwell in us. We find that, besides peace and contentment, there will also be joy unspeakable and great excitement!

Are you ready to be rooted and grounded in love? Seek Him with all that is within you. Soak in His presence and in the joy and peace that comes from taking His Word seriously in your life. Make a commitment today to walk in obedience to all that He has revealed and is revealing to you through His Word and your time spent with Him.

Filled with All the Fullness of God

"That you may be able to comprehend with all the saints what is the width and length and depth and height—to know the love of Christ which passes knowledge; that you may be filled with all the fullness of God" (Eph. 3:18–19).

The love of Christ surpasses knowledge! When we know His love, we realize that no earthly knowledge can begin to compare with His love. When we truly know His love—its width, length, depth, and height, we are being filled with the fullness of God. What does that mean in our lives?

To be filled with the fullness of God means that we have become so close to Him that we have begun to take on His ways and His appearance. Have you ever seen a couple who has been married many, many years, who begin to sound the same and even look the same? They have become so much a part of each other's lives that they say the same things and do the same things. When we spend more and more time with our Lord, we begin to take on His ways. We find ourselves saying those things that we hear Him saying in His Word. We will find ourselves doing those things that Jesus did when He walked on this earth.

Do you want to be filled with the fullness of God Almighty? All you have to do is to spend time with Him. Time is a precious commodity. You may think, I do not have enough time to spend with Him to truly be one with Him and receive His fullness. If you can grasp the magnitude of what a difference spending time with Him will make, not only in your life, but in the lives of others around you, I believe you will make the time to enter into His presence in such a way that His fullness becomes a part of your life!

OCTOBER 16

Bearing with One Another

"I, therefore, the prisoner of the Lord, beseech you to walk worthy of the calling with which you were called, with all lowliness and gentleness, with longsuffering, bearing with one another in love" (Eph. 4:1–2).

*W*hat does it mean to bear with one another in love? I think of David and his relationship with Saul. David loved and respected Saul as king even though Saul tried to destroy David because of jealousy. God had chosen David to become king in the place of Saul. When Saul came against him, David had several opportunities to hurt or kill Saul. He always refrained from hurting Saul because he knew that at the appropriate time he would be placed on the throne through God's power and not through his own.

Is there a Saul in your life? Perhaps your situation with a Saul is not as drastic as David's situation was, but you still can learn from David about bearing with this person in love. Take this person to the Lord in prayer on a daily basis. Ask the Lord to show you how to pray for him or her. Be open to any and every opportunity the Lord brings your way to express the love of Jesus to your "Saul." Your expressions of love may be the very thing that will bring a turning in this person's life. His seeing you consistently share the unconditional love of Jesus will be a witness that cannot be ignored.

You will find that your heart will be filled with "feelings" of love and acceptance toward this person, replacing the "feelings" of frustration and anger. Let the Lord use you to bring His love into the life of that someone who is difficult to love, and then be blessed as He changes your feelings and attitude toward that person into genuine love.

Speaking the Truth in Love

"But, speaking the truth in love, may grow up in all things into Him who is the head—Christ—from whom the whole body, joined and knit together by what every joint supplies, according to the effective working by which every part does its share, causes growth of the body for the edifying of itself in love" (Eph. 4:15–16).

*I*s speaking the truth in love easy for you? We, as Christians, want to think that we always tell the truth, but how often do we say "yes" when we really mean "no"? How often do we avoid telling someone how we really feel about something because we do not want to make waves? How often do we avoid confrontation because we are afraid of being rejected? We need to learn how to be honest and truthful in a loving and caring way. The truth is not always easy to hear because the truth has a way of revealing some things about ourselves that we sometimes would rather forget or deny.

If we avoid speaking the truth into someone's life, we are not being fair to them or honest with ourselves. When we speak the truth in love to someone, that person may not like it at first. That person will, however, have to deal with the truth that he or she has heard and often will be grateful within time.

Is there someone in your life to whom you have avoided speaking the truth? If there is, ask the Lord to reveal to you how to approach this person and how to express the truth in a way that he or she can receive it. Continue to pray for this person on a regular basis and watch as the Lord brings about transforming changes.

Walk in Love

"And walk in love, as Christ also has loved us and given Himself for us, an offering and a sacrifice to God for a sweet-smelling aroma" (Eph. 5:2).

The scripture for today encourages us to walk in the same sacrificial love that Jesus walked in when He was on this earth. We get some insight into this sacrificial love by reading in God's Word about the kind of life that Jesus led. He went about teaching, preaching, healing the sick, setting people free from bondage, and doing mighty miracles, such as raising Lazarus from the dead. When He saw needs within the people, He had compassion on them and met their needs. He was constantly thinking about the needs of others.

Do you think it is possible for you to walk in this kind of sacrificial love? You may think, "There is no way I could do all that!" In your own strength, there is no way you can do what Jesus did. You can, however, with the power of the Holy Spirit that resides within you, begin to move and walk in sacrificial love little by little. The Lord does not expect you to be a giant Christian in one day, one week, or one year. He knows that it takes time in His presence and growth in His Word to enable you to be able to trust Him enough to walk in sacrificial love toward others. He waits, with arms outstretched, for you to begin to take steps toward Him, expecting Him to fill you to overflowing with His love. Let His love be poured out in such magnitude from your life that those around you will be amazed!

Having the Same Love

"Fulfill my joy by being like-minded, having the same love, being of one accord, of one mind" (Phil. 2:2).

When we, as Christians, walk in the same sacrificial love of Jesus, we will have the same love. His love is in you, and His love is in me. Because we are individuals with different personalities, it may look a little different in each one of us. His love within us brings unity to the body of Christ. When we love our fellow Christians, we are not going to be gossiping about them. We will not be criticizing or judging each other. We will not be jealous or envious of each other's accomplishments.

Unity is not something that naturally comes because we are Christians. It comes as we decide to love and trust one another and walk in the footsteps of Christ.

He gives us discernment to know those things that are of Him and those things that are not of Him. He does not ask us to compromise our beliefs, but He does ask us to understand and accept other Christians who may interpret a scripture a little differently than we do. There is not one perfect Christian walking this earth today, and, therefore, there is always room to learn and grow. Those who interpret a scripture differently from us may be more correct than we are. If they are wrong, Jesus is able to correct them. He is also able to correct us when we are wrong. Let us love one another with the same love, being in unity, even in our diversity.

Love in the Spirit

"As you also learned from Epaphras, our dear fellow servant, who is a faithful minister of Christ on your behalf, who also declared to us your love in the Spirit" (Col. 1:7–8).

*E*paphras, having seen God's love expressed in the lives of the people in Colosse, shared that good news with Paul. I believe that this scripture for today can be an encouragement for us to always look for God's love in others and to share the good news of His love being in the lives of others. So often we tend to dwell on the negative and hear of all the bad things that go on. When we dwell on the good and look for the good, our lives and the lives of others are edified. We are encouraged and strengthened by hearing good reports and testimonies.

The Colossian church was strong in faith and in love. Because of their faith working through love, much fruit was brought forth for the kingdom of God. We need to look at our lives today and see if we are walking in love in such a way that others are noticing and are being blessed and encouraged. Is there fruit coming forth that will increase and strengthen the Body of Christ? We need to ask ourselves, "What am I doing to show the love of Jesus?"

If your heart is being drawn to walk in greater love for the Lord and His people, ask the Lord to show you ways that you can express His love. Be open to the ideas and opportunities that come your way. Sometimes those opportunities are totally unexpected, and sometimes they are very subtle. Ask the Lord to help you to be sensitive to His leading in your life. Be His instrument in bringing an increase of His love into the lives of those around you!

Remembering Your Labor of Love

"Remembering without ceasing your work of faith, labor of love, and patience of hope in our Lord Jesus Christ in the sight of our God and Father" (1 Thess. 1:3).

Paul encouraged the people in Thessalonica by recounting their strength in faith, love, and hope. When we see others who are strong in love, we need to encourage them by expressing our gratitude for their love. All of us need encouragement to continue to grow and be strong, and Paul was very wise in the way he encouraged the churches that he had planted. When writing to them, he continually uplifted them by expressing his gratitude for their walk of love.

The believers in Thessalonica were not only walking in love; they were laboring in love. What is the difference between walking and laboring? Laboring requires a great deal more effort. We have to put all our strength into laboring whereas walking can be almost effortless. The people in the church at Thessalonica went the extra mile, and they did not leave anything to chance. They made sure that the people around them were loved in such a way that whatever it took to meet their needs, they would do it.

The result from their labor of love was that many others were drawn to know Jesus Christ.

Are you laboring in love for the Lord? Would you be willing to exert whatever effort is needed to express the love of Jesus to others? Enter into the presence of God Almighty, and let Him fill you with such overpowering love that you would be willing to do whatever it takes to let His love be poured out into the lives of others!

Abound in Love

"And may the Lord make you increase and abound in love to one another and to all, just as we do to you" (1 Thess. 3:12).

Paul's prayer for the church at Thessalonica is one that we should be praying for ourselves and for the Body of Christ. We need to increase and abound in love to one another and to all! One of the reasons that many people are not drawn to come to church is because they see how church people treat each other. We need to be an example of the love of God to each other so that those outside the church will see and want to come in.

Lord, help us to know You so intimately that we will be filled to overflowing with Your love for one another. May that love spill forth from us to those outside the church. May we be such an expression of Your compassion and mercy that many will see and come into Your kingdom. Show us how we can reach out to those who would never come inside a church door. Let us be consumed with Your desire and burden for the lost. Let us be an answer to the prayer "to send out laborers into His harvest" (Matt. 9:38).

Make us aware of where the "harvest fields" are for us. Open our eyes to the needs around us and then fill us with such love that we will not back down or turn our backs. May we go forth in the strength and power of Your Holy Spirit, pouring forth Your love to the broken-hearted, hungry, rejected, abused, and indifferent. May Your love break through all barriers that keep people from receiving You.

God Has Given a Spirit of Love

"For God has not given us a spirit of fear, but of power and of love and of a sound mind" (2 Tim. 1:7).

Most of us experience some type of fear in our lives. There is fear everywhere we turn in the world around us. How do we overcome the fear that is so prevalent today? We need to turn to Jesus because He has promised us that He has not given fear, but He has given us power, love, and a sound mind. Love is an opposite of fear. First John 4:18 says, "There is no fear in love; but perfect love casts out fear." We can gauge our need for more love in our lives by checking how much fear is present. Love conquers fear, and we need to receive the love of Jesus so strongly in our lives that fear begins to fade away.

When we fear the opinion of people, that shows we care about what people think more than we love God. As we seek Him with all our hearts and grow closer to Him, we find His love growing in us. We also find ourselves becoming more and more free of fear—fear of what people think, fear of rejection, and all kinds of fear that come from making others a priority over God. God's love brings power in our lives to be strong and to be the kind of person that can help others grow in their walk with the Lord.

If there is fear in your life today, draw close to the Lord. Let Him show you how to be a true friend who speaks the truth in love and is not afraid to be open and honest. Bask in the joy that comes from growing in your relationship with Him and, thus, growing in your relationship with others.

Stir Up Love

"And let us consider one another in order to stir up love and good works" (Heb. 10:24).

Love is an action! If we truly love with the love of Jesus, we will do works of love. Sometimes we need to stir up love in our hearts. There are times that we all get sluggish in our walk as Christians. We find that we think of ourselves more, or we find that we are caught up in the things of the world and do not want to spend time with God's people or with Him. Also we get busy doing those things that others seem to expect of us, motivated by a sense of obligation rather than of love.

When we find ourselves in that sluggish place, how do we stir up love and good works? I believe we stir up love by deciding to spend time with God, both reading His Word and in prayer and communion with Him. We also need to spend time with God's people because they will encourage us to be strong in the Lord and to walk in His love. We also need to look for opportunities to reach out to others with the love of Jesus. We may not feel like doing a good work of love; but as we begin to act in love, regardless of our feelings, we find our feelings changing. All of a sudden, we experience the love of Jesus in our hearts for others.

Check your heart today. Are you loving as you know you should? Have you been reaching out to others with good works of love? If you have not, enter into the presence of the Lord, and let Him refresh you with His love. Then pour out His love to others as the Lord brings opportunities to put your love in action.

Love Fervently with a Pure Heart

"Since you have purified your souls in obeying the truth through the Spirit in sincere love of the brethren, love one another fervently with a pure heart" (1 Pet. 1:22).

The scripture for today encourages us to not only love, but to love fervently with a pure heart. That means that our love is not to be a half-hearted attempt, but we are to love with zeal. We are to express love to each other in such a way that the recipient of that love will know without a doubt that he or she has experienced the love of God through us. They will be so strengthened and encouraged by our expression of fervent love that they will share the love of Jesus with others fervently also. What a glorious place this earth would be if all Christians loved fervently with the love of Jesus! There would be a mushroom effect that would be life-changing to the whole world.

Are you ready and willing to love your brothers and sisters in Christ with the pure and fervent love of Jesus? Are you willing to sacrifice some of your own wants and desires to meet the needs of others? As you walk in His fervent love, you will find that the lives of others will be changed. You will also find that your own life will be changed as you receive abundant blessings that come with giving of yourself to others.

Ask the Lord today to give you an opportunity to fervently express His love to someone in your family, neighborhood, at work, or someone who will cross your path today. Watch in joy and amazement as this person's life is blessed and changed by the wondrous and glorious love of Jesus flowing through you!

313

Be Tenderhearted, Be Courteous

"Finally, all of you be of one mind, having compassion for one another; love as brothers, be tenderhearted, be courteous" (1 Pet. 3:8).

In the scripture for today and the verses that follow, we are told what kind of love brothers should have for one another. We are to be tenderhearted and courteous toward one another. Being tenderhearted means that we are to have the heart of Jesus for each other. Being courteous means that we are to walk in humility toward one another. In other words, we are to consider other persons' needs and desires above our own.

First Peter 3:9 continues by saying, "Not returning evil for evil or reviling for reviling, but on the contrary blessing, knowing that you were called to this, that you may inherit a blessing, for he who would love life and see good days, let him refrain his tongue from evil, and his lips from speaking deceit, let him turn away from evil and do good; let him seek peace and pursue it." Peter shows us, through this scripture, the importance of our speaking only good things and the truth about each other. He also stresses the importance of pursuing peace with each other.

Is there someone to whom you need to express tenderheartedness? Is there someone to whom you have been discourteous recently? Ask the Lord to help you be an expression of His tenderheartedness, and ask Him to show you how to walk in humility toward that person, considering his or her needs above your own. Know the joy of walking in obedience to the Lord as He brings greater and greater love and peace into your life!

Love in Deed and Truth

"My little children, let us not love in word or in tongue, but in deed and in truth" (1 John 3:18).

It is so much easier to tell someone that you love them than to show it. Have you ever been around someone who always says one thing and then does another? We get to the place of not expecting that person to do what he or she says, and we find it difficult to believe him.

Love is an action, and when our actions do not line up with our words, we are not truly loving as Jesus loves. James 2:15–16 says, "If a brother or sister is naked and destitute of daily food, and one of you says to them, 'Depart in peace, be warmed and filled,' but you do not give them the things which are needed for the body, what does it profit?" Actions speak a lot louder than words! We need to be ready to show His love with actions toward meeting needs. We need to care about the homeless on the streets, the abused, the widows and orphans, those who are sick in body or in mind, and those who are in bondage to drugs, alcohol, or overeating. We can demonstrate the love of Jesus "in deed and in truth" in such ways as feeding and clothing the homeless, helping in abused shelters, being a friend to a widow or a child without parents, being available for those that are sick, and supporting rehabilitation programs.

Do you have contact with someone who is desperately in need? Seek the direction of the Lord to find out how you can best express His love to that person. Let His joy rise up within you as you find yourself being a tool in His hand to bring freedom and life to that someone!

Everyone Who Loves Is Born of God

"Beloved, let us love one another, for love is of God; and everyone who loves is born of God and knows God" (1 John 4:7).

We can gauge our closeness with God by the measure of our love for one another. As we draw closer to Him, His love will grow and blossom within us so that we will express His love to others. If we find that we are often irritable, angry, critical, or unforgiving, we know that we need to draw closer to the One who is able to set us free from those ungodly feelings and actions.

As we draw close to the Father, we begin to have a better understanding of His greatness and His everlasting and unconditional love. As we witness and experience His love, we find that our lives are being changed. His love grows in us so that we want to reach out and express His love. This is not something that happens because we will it to happen. It happens because we know Him better and better. I believe we as Christians sometimes try so hard to be like Jesus and then fail so miserably. All we have to do is quit trying and draw close to Him. He is the one who enables us to walk in a manner that is pleasing to Him.

If you are tired of working at trying to walk as you believe Jesus would want you to, draw close into the wonderful presence and rest of Jesus. Let Him wash over you with His love and truth. Receive all that He has for you, and be open to walk in love toward others as He places that desire and opportunity before you.

We Ought to Love One Another

"In this is love, not that we loved God, but that He loved us and sent His Son to be the propitiation for our sins. Beloved, if God so loved us, we also ought to love one another" (1 John 4:10–11).

In the scripture for today, we are admonished to love as God loved us. We are to have the same sacrificial actions for others that Jesus had for us. Can we do this on our own? No, we must depend on Jesus to empower us to walk as He walked. We can receive the power to live sacrificially in the love of Jesus as we take up our cross and follow Him, seeking a closer and deeper relationship with Him.

Just as David, Moses, Elijah, and many others from the Old Testament and Paul, Peter, John, and many others from the New Testament found empowerment to walk in love out of a deep relationship with the Lord, we also can be empowered with His love. We can learn from their experiences. They knew whom to call upon and whom to go to when trouble and problems were all about them. They knew how to overcome in both the circumstances of life and in their relationships. Even though they failed at times, they always turned back to the Lord. He strengthened them and enabled them to be the mighty men of God who are still examples for us today.

When you think of the powerful lives that these men led, do you feel weak in comparison? You do not need to compare yourself with others because God has made each person unique with different gifts to serve Him. Look unto Him who is able to help you overcome and reach out to those around you.

Taught by God to Love One Another

"But concerning brotherly love you have no need that I should write to you, for you yourselves are taught by God to love one another" (1 Thess. 4:9).

*H*ow are we taught by God to love one another? I believe we are taught by Him to love as we study His Word and spend time drawing close to Him in prayer. His Word has instruction for us that comes alive within our spirits as we read and seek to receive from Him through the Bible. Second Timothy 3:16 says, "All scripture is given by inspiration of God, and is profitable for doctrine, for reproof, for correction, for instruction in righteousness." We find reproof and correction, as well as instruction, in the Bible. God's Word has a way of penetrating deep down into the depths of our soul to reveal those things within us that are not pleasing to God.

When we study God's Word and then spend time in His presence, we find that He opens up our understanding and reveals the scope of His love to us. His love is so overpowering that we cannot stay the same when we are enveloped with it. We are changed, and then we become an instrument in the hand of God to bring change into the lives of others. We do not change others, but as we share His overpowering love with them, they are changed by Him.

He wants to use you as His instrument of love today. Are you willing and ready to be molded into His fine-tuned instrument that plays a beautiful love melody? Let Him use you by yielding yourself to Him. Let Him reveal such a glorious love to you that you can do nothing else except submit to Him. Be an instrument in His orchestra, which plays with such beauty that no earthly orchestra could ever begin to compare.

Abides in Love

"And we have known and believed the love that God has for us. God is love, and he who abides in love abides in God, and God in him" (1 John 4:16).

*H*ow wonderful to know that God abides in us! How wonderful to know that we abide in God! How wonderful to know that others receive the love of Jesus because we abide in Him and He in us!

The scripture for today emphasizes the fact that drawing close to the Lord and spending time with Him enables us to love others. Why would we let something keep us from drawing close to Him and spending time with Him? Most often, it is because we are caught up in the busyness of this world and we are not being strengthened by the things of God.

How can we overcome the busyness of this world? We have to decide daily to spend time in the Word of God and to spend time knowing Him through prayer and communion with Him. It is a daily choice that can either draw us close to Him and life abundant or away from Him into the busyness of the world that does not really hold anything of eternal value for us. This world that we know today will one day pass away, but our God and His Word lasts forever. We need to make choices that will affect what really counts—eternity!

Will you enter into the presence of the Lord today by seeking Him through His Word and spending time with Him in prayer? Will you abide in the love of God so that you can be an expression of that love to others? Begin to seek Him now and let Him show you how glorious His love is toward you and how He can use you to spread His love to others!

See the Glory of the Lord

"And in the morning you shall see the glory of the Lord"
(Exod. 16:7).

The children of Israel complained because they thought they would die of hunger. Moses had led them out of Egypt, and now they were in the wilderness. He told them that the glory of the Lord would appear to them in the morning in response to their grumbling.

As the glory of the Lord appeared in the cloud, God spoke to Moses His plan to provide bread from heaven and quail for them to eat. We are told there were approximately three million people that came out of Egypt. How do you think they must have felt when Almighty God appeared to them in answer to their complaints? They must have experienced some fear as they realized that the complaints that they had made to Moses were actually against God Himself.

The glory of the Lord appeared as a cloud. While the Israelites were in the wilderness, the Lord led them during the day by cloud and at night by fire. His glory and His presence were very real to them. They, however, were afraid of the glory and presence of the Lord. They asked Moses to talk to God for them, for they were afraid they would die in His presence.

Can you identify with the Israelites? Have you ever been afraid at the prospect of entering the presence of God and experiencing His glory? God is an awesome God, and the idea of actually experiencing His glory is overwhelming. Once you experience His glory, you will never be afraid again. Ask Him to reveal His presence and His glory to you today.

Glory of the Lord Appeared

"Now it came to pass, as Aaron spoke to the whole congregation of children of Israel, that they looked toward the wilderness, and behold, the glory of the Lord appeared in the cloud" (Exod. 16:10).

God loved His people so much that He was willing to reveal His glory to them. He wanted them to know that He heard their complaints, and He was answering. He actually talked to Moses, but His glory appeared to all the people. What do you think His glory looked like to the people? The scripture says that His glory appeared in the cloud. We see clouds when we look into the sky, but there must have been something different about this cloud that made them realize His glory was present.

We cannot explain or understand the supernatural with our minds. God's power goes beyond anything that we can comprehend with our natural abilities. When He is present, however, there is no doubt. We cannot explain an experience with God—we just know it happened! It is something that no one can take away from us. Any experience that we have with God must be in agreement with God's Word. Experiencing the glory of God should give us a greater love for His Word and bring it even more "alive" within us than ever before.

Seek God with everything that is within you today and present yourself to Him, letting His glory minister to you.

Consuming Fire

The sight of the glory of the Lord was like a consuming fire on the top of the mountain in the eyes of the children of Israel" (Exod. 24:17).

In the scripture for today, the glory of the Lord is described as being like a consuming fire. Fire burns up all that is flammable that comes across its path. A consuming fire from God burns all the dross and impurities out of a person's life. Zechariah 13:9 says, "I will bring the one-third through the fire, will refine them as silver is refined, and test them as gold is tested."

When silver and gold are put in the fire, the impurities float to the top and are skimmed away. The pure metal is left to be used for fine jewelry or other objects of great worth. This pictures for us God's refining fire consuming the impurities and things of darkness from our lives and leaving the things that are pure and holy. We need the fire of God in our lives to set us free from the things that bring bondage and sin into our lives. The fire of God is not something to fear, but it is something that we should welcome in our lives.

Would you like to become an object of great worth in the hands of your heavenly Father? Will you welcome the fire of God into your life today to set you free from those things that keep you from moving forward in the will of God? Pray this prayer: "Father, in the name of Jesus, I ask that You would set me free from the bondage of darkness. Let me shine forth with Your glory so that those around me will come to know Your saving grace. Amen."

The Glory of the Lord Filled the Tabernacle

"Then the cloud covered the tabernacle of meeting, and the glory of the Lord filled the tabernacle. And Moses was not able to enter the tabernacle of meeting, because the cloud rested above it, and the glory of the Lord filled the tabernacle" (Exod. 40:34–35).

When the tabernacle was completed, the glory of the Lord filled the place. His glory was evidence that His presence was with the people in the tabernacle. Exodus tells us over and over that God is in the midst of His people. From the time He led them out of Egypt to the time of the completion of the tabernacle, He made His presence known to them either by cloud, smoke, fire, or by their literally hearing His voice.

The Lord has told us over and over in the Bible that His presence is with us. Hebrews 13:5 says, "For He Himself has said, 'I will never leave you nor forsake you.'" He also says this in Joshua, Deuteronomy, and Genesis. We know through Scripture that His presence is with us, but we do not always "feel" His presence with us. When His glory appears to us, we do literally sense His presence with us.

Would you like to experience the glory of the Lord in your life? Do you believe it is possible for you to sense His presence in your life in a very real way? Look to Him today with the expectation of seeing Him face to face. May His presence be so real that His glory fills you in such a way that you will not doubt His presence again!

Glory of the Lord Will Appear to You

"Then Moses said, 'This is the thing which the Lord commanded you to do, and the glory of the Lord will appear to you.' . . . And fire came out from before the Lord and consumed the burnt offering and the fat on the altar. When all the people saw it, they shouted and fell on their faces" (Levit. 9:6, 24).

*M*oses instructed the people of Israel about sin offering. As they responded in obedience, God's glory appeared in fire to assure them of His presence and His pleasure in their obedience. It must have been an awesome sight to see fire coming down from heaven, consuming the burnt offering. The presence of God, being manifested by His glory, is a wondrous and glorious thing to behold. The people of Israel were so overcome by God's presence that they shouted and fell on their faces.

There are many scriptures that refer to shouting to the Lord. Psalm 47:1 says, "Oh, clap your hands, all you peoples! Shout to God with the voice of triumph!" The people of Israel expressed their emotions of gratitude and excitement that the God of all creation would provide a way of atonement for their sins and that He would make Himself known to them by His glory appearing to them as fire. When they fell on their faces, they worshiped Him as the one true living God and acknowledged that they were placing themselves in total submission to Him. They simply could not stand in the presence and power of Almighty God!

Are you ready to place yourself in total submission to Almighty God today? Choose to walk in obedience to Him and enjoy the beauty and wonder of His presence and glory in your life!

All the Earth Shall Be Filled with the Glory of the Lord

"Then the Lord said: 'I have pardoned, according to your word; but truly, as I live, all the earth shall be filled with the glory of the Lord'" (Num. 14:20–21).

Moses had been interceding to the Lord for the people because of their rebellion. The Lord heard his prayer and responded with pardon. He went on to say that the earth shall be filled with the glory of the Lord. This promise will come to pass. The day is coming when all the earth will truly be filled with the glory of the Lord. This should be our prayer, as it was David's prayer: "And blessed be His glorious name forever! And let the whole earth be filled with His glory. Amen and amen" (Ps. 72:19).

Can we expect to see the glory of the Lord now? Just as there were times in the Old Testament and times in the New Testament that God's people experienced His glory, I believe there are times that we can and will experience His glory today. We do not have to wait until that day when the earth will be filled with His glory, but we can and should look forward to that day prayerfully!

Are you looking forward to the glory of God in your life? Look to Him today and receive His love and His presence with great expectation. Seek His glory that will one day cover the whole earth, and rejoice that you serve the one true living God, who loves you so much that He will reveal Himself to you!

Glory Appeared to All the Congregation

"And Korah gathered all the congregation against them at the door of the tabernacle of meeting. Then the glory of the Lord appeared to all the congregation" (Num. 16:19).

Korah led a rebellion against Moses and Aaron. He was jealous because Moses and Aaron could draw near to the Lord. The glory of the Lord appeared to all the congregation so that all the people could know what God's will was in this conflict between Korah and Moses. The glory of God came into that congregation so that the people would know that God Almighty was the One who had called Moses to lead them. Korah and the other two hundred and fifty leaders of the congregation who had rebelled with Korah lost their lives as a result of their rebellion.

When the congregation saw God's glory and the fire that consumed the two hundred and fifty men, they had a deep respect for the glory of God and His plan. God's glory can be wondrous and comforting in our lives, and it can also be something that reveals the holiness and righteousness of God in such a way that we would never want to go against His known will.

Will you pray this prayer with me today? "Father, in the name of Jesus, I want to thank You for Your gracious love. I thank You that Your glory is awesome and wondrous! Forgive me for the times that I have been selfish and have turned my back on Your way and will. May Your glory be something that I long for and receive in my life in such a way that I will be an instrument in Your hands to reach out to those around me! Amen."

God Has Shown Us His Glory

"And you said: 'Surely the Lord our God has shown us His glory and His greatness, and we have heard His voice from the midst of the fire. We have seen this day that God speaks with man; yet he still lives'" (Deut. 5:24).

It was an amazing revelation to the Israelites that a man could speak with God and live. They had sent Moses to talk with God because they were afraid that in His presence they would die. They saw the glory of the Lord on the mountain when He was giving the Ten Commandments and the Law to Moses. They saw Moses come down from the mountain with the glory of the Lord shining from His face. They themselves had heard God's voice from the midst of the fire.

How could anyone doubt the greatness and power of Almighty God after experiencing what the Israelites experienced at the foot of the mountain?

Do you believe that if you experienced what the Israelites did that you would never doubt again? Well, the Israelites doubted again and again! They muttered and complained against Moses and even against God over and over. The glory of God in your life or in my life will not cause us to never doubt or complain again, but it will help to bring changes within us. We do not become perfect nor does everything fall into place for us, but we come to know Him better.

Will you draw close to Him today and listen to hear Him speak to you? Listen, and be prepared to walk in obedience to His truth found in His Word. Share this wondrous truth with those around you, and you may find that His glory is shining upon your face!

Glory of the Lord Filled the House

"And it came to pass, when the priests came out of the holy place, that the cloud filled the house of the Lord, so that the priests could not continue ministering because of the cloud; for the glory of the Lord filled the house of the Lord" (1 Kings 8:10–11).

When King Solomon had the ark of the covenant brought to the temple, the presence of the Lord came into the place with such power that a cloud of His glory filled the temple. The temple priests could not minister because of the cloud of His glory!

Read the rest of 1 Kings 8, and you will find that Solomon responded to the glory of the Lord filling the temple by leading the assembly of people in prayer. He fell on his knees, and, with his hands outstretched to heaven, He started his prayer with worship to the Lord. Then he confessed his unworthiness to be in the presence of the Lord. (Entering into a place of the glory of the Lord shows us our unworthiness. We find that all we can do is worship and praise our living God!) Then he asked God's forgiveness for the sins of Israel and prayed for victory. He proceeded to bless the people in the assembly, acknowledging that everything that God had promised Moses had been accomplished, and then he asked that the Lord be with them always.

Seek Him with all of your love today, and let Him fill you with His glory that will bring humility and strength into your life so that you can go forth and be a tool in His hands to those around you!

The Glory of the Lord on the Temple

"When all the children of Israel saw how the fire came down, and the glory of the Lord on the temple, they bowed their faces to the ground on the pavement, and worshiped and praised the Lord, saying: 'For He is good, for His mercy endures forever'" (2 Chron. 7:3).

We find the same story of King Solomon dedicating the temple in 2 Chronicles as we looked at in 1 Kings yesterday. In the scripture for today, we find the peoples' response was similar to King Solomon's response. They also fell down before the Lord. King Solomon fell on his knees and raised his hands toward heaven. The people fell with their faces to the pavement. They, as well as King Solomon, uttered words of praise and worship to Him, expressing His goodness and mercy. The Israelites must have been totally overcome with gratitude that Almighty God would reveal Himself to them in such a powerful way!

When the glory of the Lord comes into our presence, we, just as the Israelites in King Solomon's temple, will not be able to stand. His glory is so powerful and awesome that we also will fall on our faces. We will be so aware of our unworthiness and His holiness and goodness that we will not be able to do anything except acknowledge His goodness. Our lips will be filled with praise and worship of Him along with the Israelites of old.

Would you be willing to seek the presence of the Lord today? Let Him fill you with His goodness and His mercy so that you can be an expression of His love to someone close to you that desperately needs to know the love of the Savior.

The Whole Earth Is Full of His Glory!

"And one cried to another and said: 'Holy, holy, holy is the Lord of hosts; the whole earth is full of His glory!'" (Isa. 6:3).

In this chapter, we find Isaiah describing the time he was called to be a prophet. He saw the Lord sitting on His throne. One of the seraphim, an angelic being, cried, "Holy, holy, holy is the Lord of hosts; the whole earth is full of His glory!" As we continue reading in this chapter, the house was filled with smoke, which represents the glory of God. When His glory came into the house, it had a very real and lasting effect on Isaiah.

In verse five, we find Isaiah repenting because the presence and glory of the Lord caused him to be aware of his uncleanness. Once he had repented, he received cleansing as stated in verse seven, "Behold, this has touched your lips; your iniquity is taken away, and your sin purged." The result of the repentance and cleansing was that he was able to hear, understand, and respond to God's call upon his life. When the Lord asked, "Whom shall I send?" Isaiah responded, "Here am I! Send me."

When we experience the glory of God, it leads to repentance and cleansing so that we will have the desire to go forth and fulfill God's call upon our lives. There are so many people waiting for you and for me to answer God's call and share the good news of Jesus Christ with them. Join me as we respond together, "Here we are! Send us."

Crown of Glory

"In that day the Lord of hosts will be for a crown of glory and a diadem of beauty to the remnant of His people" (Isa. 28:5).

"*In* that day" refers to the time in history when God will intervene to fulfill salvation for His people and to bring judgment and punishment to those who are rebellious. The day is coming when those who are truly a part of His church will receive a crown of glory and a diadem of beauty. What is a diadem? It is also a crown or an ornamental headband. This word is used to describe power and dignity. Can you begin to imagine what the Lord's church will look like on that great day when He will fulfill His salvation for His people? They will have crowns of His glory that will rest upon them, and they will be enveloped with His beauty.

In the day in which we live, the church is separated and blemished. In that day, however, His church will have nothing that will hold it back from receiving and reflecting His glory. How does the church go from a place of being separated and blemished to a place of being without spot and blemish? As we in the church draw close to Him and know Him better, we will begin to take on His attributes. We will become more and more a representation of the goodness and mercy of our Lord.

Do you want to reflect the glory of God in your life? Draw close to Him today in such a way that you will find yourself changing before Him. Let those changes be a witness to those around you, and be used to bring glory to His kingdom!

Seeing the Glory of the Lord

"It shall blossom abundantly and rejoice, even with joy and singing. The glory of Lebanon shall be given to it, the excellence of Carmel and Sharon. They shall see the glory of the Lord, the excellency of our God" (Isa. 35:2).

*I*saiah 35 is a promise about the wilderness or the desert blossoming abundantly. The glory and the excellency of the Lord will be revealed to those who have felt as if they were in a desert. The glory and excellency of the Lord will be poured out in such a way that the "eyes of the blind shall be opened, the ears of the deaf shall be unstopped, the lame shall leap like a deer, and the tongue of the dumb will sing" (Isa. 35:5–6). Such a wondrous glory will come upon the earth that those signs and wonders will be performed in order to meet the needs of God's people and to further His kingdom.

Do you want to be a part of the glory of God that is at work in the earth today? Do you want to see blind eyes opened, deaf ears opened, the lame walking, and those who cannot talk being able to speak and sing? Seek the Lord with all that is within you. Let Him draw you so close that His living waters begin to wash over you, and you are filled to overflowing. Let Him pour out His glory upon your life in such a way that those in need around you will find that they can receive the things of the Lord because you are being an instrument in His hand. Pray this prayer today: "Father, I want to be used by You to make a difference in the world around me. I want to draw so close to You that it is no longer me that lives, but it is Jesus Christ alive within me. I want Jesus to increase and me to decrease so that others will see Your glory being reflected from my life. Amen and amen."

Glory of the Lord Revealed

"The glory of the Lord shall be revealed, and all flesh shall see it together; for the mouth of the Lord has spoken" (Isa. 40:5).

One day when Jesus returns as the Triumphant King, all people will see the glory of the Lord. When He came to earth the first time as a baby born in a manger, He gave up His glory to live as a human being. Philippians 2:7–8 says, "But made Himself of no reputation, taking the form of a bondservant, and coming in the likeness of men. And being found in appearance as a man, He humbled Himself and became obedient to the point of death, even the death of the cross." When He comes back, however, He will return in all His glory, and all the earth will see and be amazed. Philippians 2:10–11 goes on to say, "That at the name of Jesus every knee should bow, of those in heaven, and of those on earth, and of those under the earth, and that every tongue should confess that Jesus Christ is Lord, to the glory of God the Father."

Are you prepared to look upon the glory of the soon-coming King? Are your loved ones ready to receive Him? This is the time for all of God's people, including you and me, to share the good news of Jesus Christ with everyone so no one will be excluded from being a part of the family of God. Will you reach out to your family and friends with the love of Jesus? May your life and may my life be used by our Father who is in heaven to minister His grace, love, and mercy to all who are hurting and in need. Join me today in committing to love Him, serve Him, and be an instrument in His hands to win the lost unto Himself!

Glory Shall Be Your Rear Guard

"Then your light shall break forth like the morning, your healing shall spring forth speedily, and your righteousness shall go before you; the glory of the Lord shall be your rear guard" (Isa. 58:8).

The Israelites were fasting as a religious form, but their heart was not close to God because they were not responding to the needs of the people around them. In Isaiah 58, the Lord admonished them to feed the hungry, give them shelter, and clothe those who are cold rather than oppressing the poor. He told them that if they meet the needs of the people around them, His glory will be their rear guard. What does it mean to have the glory of the Lord as a rear guard? It means that His power and His protection would be behind them protecting them from their enemies. His presence would surround them and envelop them in such a way that no enemy could get near them.

Would you like the glory of the Lord to be your rear guard? Would you like to know that His presence is so real in your life that His glory actually protects you? All you have to do is bask in His presence and receive His truth into your life. You will begin to respond to the needs around you because your love for Him will be so great that His love will flow forth from you in greater measure than ever before. Let Jesus reveal the greatness of His nature to you today, and then begin to walk in His love by reaching out to the lonely, brokenhearted, hungry, and destitute.

Glory of the Lord Is Risen Upon You

"Arise, shine, for your light has come! And the glory of the Lord is risen upon you. For behold, the darkness shall cover the earth, and deep darkness the people; but the Lord will arise over you, and His glory will be seen upon you" (Isa. 60:1–2).

When we enter the presence of the Lord in an intimate way, His glory shines upon us. His presence will be so evident in our lives that those around us will actually see His glory upon us. I believe that our faces will glow with His presence. Our countenance will no longer be worried, fearful, upset, or resentful because those things have to flee in the presence of the Lord. Our countenance will shine forth with the love, joy, and peace of the Lord Himself.

Since the world is hungry for the peace that comes only from God, those who see the difference in our lives will probably seek answers from us. People who have not turned their lives over to the Lord do not know what they are hungering for or what seems to be missing in their lives. That void, which is common to every human being, can only be filled by the presence of the Lord Himself. We can share with them that upon accepting Jesus Christ as our Lord and Savior, He comes to dwell within and gives peace. As they open themselves to receive more and more of the Lord, they will find that His glory will be reflected very brightly from within.

Is His glory being reflected in your life? Is your countenance expressing the love, joy, and peace of the Lord Jesus Christ? Let Him reflect in greater measure from your life by entering into a deeper and stronger relationship with Him today.

Glorify the House of My Glory

"All the flocks of Kedar shall be gathered together to you, the rams of Nebaioth shall minister to you; they shall ascend with acceptance on My altar, and I will glorify the house of My glory" (Isa. 60:7).

Where is the dwelling place of God today? Is it in church buildings or somewhere in the heavenlies? I believe Scripture confirms to us that we are the temple or the house of God. First Corinthians 6:19 says, "Or do you not know that your body is the temple of the Holy Spirit who is in you, whom you have from God." Colossians 1:27 says, "Christ in you, the hope of glory." We are the dwelling place of the Lord, and He has promised that He will glorify the house of His glory. In other words, as we allow Him place in our lives, He will bring His glory upon us and within us in such a way that others' lives will be touched and changed. As we become a greater reflection of His glory, His love will spread and mushroom until His glory is being reflected in many "houses" or many people. His house of glory will be glorified in greater and greater measure until we see revival coming!

Are you looking for revival? Do you want to be a part of God's revival? Seek Him and let His glory rise within you in such a way that those around you will know that you have been in the presence of the Lord. They will want what you have. Witnessing will not be difficult because many will begin to ask about the difference they see in your life. All that you will need to do is to answer their questions. Be used by the Lord in these last days as He gets ready to pour out His Spirit in floods of His living water!

337

Glory in Knowing God

"'But let him who glories glory in this, that he understands and knows Me, that I am the Lord, exercising lovingkindness, judgment, and righteousness in the earth. For in these I delight,' says the Lord" (Jer. 9:24).

The greatest thing that can happen to us, the thing that can bring God's glory into our lives, is to know and understand Him! How do we know and understand the God of the universe? It is so simple that we often overlook the answer. The way to know and understand God is to read, study, and obey His Word. We need to spend time daily in the Bible, and we need to spend time daily in prayer and close communication with our Lord.

We need to open our hearts to Him, and we need to listen for His response to us. He speaks to us today through many avenues. First and most important, He speaks to us through His Word. He also speaks to us through sermons, Bible teachers, friends, loved ones, and mentors. He also speaks directly to our spirit in a still, small voice (1 Kings 19:12). When we hear God speaking to us through others or through a still, small voice deep within our spirit, we always need to confirm what is said through His Word. The Bible is always our source for understanding the nature and truth of God.

Do you want to have greater understanding of His nature and His ways? Seek Him through His Word and through listening for His voice and direction. Be aware and listen for His voice today!

The Appearance of the Glory of the Lord

"Like the appearance of a rainbow in a cloud on a rainy day, so was the appearance of the brightness all around it. This was the appearance of the likeness of the glory of the Lord" (Ezek. 1:28).

Ezekiel had a vision of God. If you read all of chapter one of Ezekiel, you will find that in his vision he saw an appearance of the throne with a likeness of a man above it. He was surrounded with fire and brightness. We are told that this was the appearance of the likeness of the glory of the Lord.

Ezekiel 2:1 tells us that Ezekiel fell on his face! He could not stand in the presence of the glory of God. He was totally overwhelmed by the magnitude of the power and majesty of Almighty God!

God appeared to Ezekiel in a vision because He had a message for the people of Israel, who had been rebellious. In the Old Testament days, only a few men and women of God had the Spirit of God come upon them. Only a few saw visions, received prophecies from God, and entered into His presence. When Jesus went to the cross for you and for me, He opened up the way for us to enter into the holy of holies. Just as Ezekiel, we can be surrounded with the glory of God in such a way that our lives and the lives of those around us will be changed.

Come into the presence of the Lord today, expecting to bask in His glory! Receive all that He has for you so that you can go forth with His strength and His power to share His life with a lost and dying world!

339

Blessed Is the Glory of the Lord

"Then the Spirit lifted me up, and I heard behind me a great thunderous voice: 'Blessed is the glory of the Lord from His place!'" (Ezek. 3:12).

Ezekiel continued with his assignment from the Lord to go to the rebellious people of Israel with God's message. He was sent as a watchman. That means that he watched and heard from God so that he could warn the people of impending danger. There can be danger from without (other nations), and there can be danger from within (their own rebellion). The Lord encouraged Ezekiel for the task ahead by making His presence known to him in a powerful way. A thunderous voice acknowledged the wonder of the glory of the Lord.

How would you like to be sent to the rebellious people of this nation today with a message from God? Do you think that they would believe you? Do you believe they would even listen? Probably not! Ezekiel had a momentous task before him. His responsibility was to be obedient to God. He went with the glory of God surrounding him to relay God's message to the people.

You are probably not being called to be a spokesman as Ezekiel was, but you and I are called today to be watchmen for our nation by praying and interceding for our country. Will you answer that call today by spending time in prayer for our leaders, schools, and churches? Will you pray for wisdom, peace, and unity within our cities and nation? Will you pray for victory over violence, death, and destruction? May His glory surround us as we pray with fervor for our nation!

The Glory of the Lord Stood There

"So I arose and went out into the plain, and behold, the glory of the Lord stood there, like the glory which I saw by the River Chebar; and I fell on my face" (Ezek. 3:23).

The Lord had told Ezekiel to go out to the plain because the Lord would talk with him there. When he went to the plain, the glory of the Lord was waiting for him. When we enter into the presence of the Lord, we will experience His glory. Where He is, His glory is also. If He dwells within us, then His glory is in us also. We simply are not aware of it because we are so caught up with the world around us and all that we have to do that we are not seeking the presence of the Lord. When we do seek Him, we will find that He is with us! His glory is with us! He has told us, "I will never leave you nor forsake you" (Heb. 13:5). The apostle Paul wrote, "Christ in you, the hope of glory" (Col. 1:27). If we can let the knowledge of His indwelling presence come alive within us, we will be reflecting His glory more and more to those around us.

Are you willing to respond to the Lord with the obedience that Ezekiel exhibited? He heard from the Lord, and then he did what the Lord told him to do. All you have to do is simply listen for God's direction and instruction to you. When you hear and respond in obedience, you will find that there will be such joy and excitement in your life that you will wonder why you did not listen for God's direction sooner. There is nothing boring about the Christian walk if you follow God's direction for your life.

Being obedient to the Lord will bring about an aliveness within you that only comes from serving Him. Begin to move in that aliveness today as you seek Him with all that is within you!

341

Brightness of the Lord's Glory

"Then the glory of the Lord went up from the cherub, and paused over the threshold of the temple; and the house was filled with the cloud, and the court was full of the brightness of the Lord's glory" (Ezek. 10:4).

What would it be like for our churches to be full of the brightness of the glory of the Lord? I believe that we would be so overcome by His presence that we could do nothing but worship and glorify Him. I believe that our lives would be so changed that we would be expressions of His love everywhere that we would go. I believe that we would begin to reach out to the lonely, bring comfort to the brokenhearted, feed the hungry, clothe those without clothes, pray for the sick and see them healed by God's hand, and so much more. I believe that we would begin to see people saved by the multitudes, and I believe that we would see revival breaking forth in our churches.

The brightness of the glory of God shines forth His nature and character for us to see clearly. As we see Him in all His goodness and mercy as well as His strength and power, we know and understand His plan and purpose for our lives.

Let the brightness of the glory of God minister His very nature and character to you today. Begin to move out in response to Him by reaching out to those around you. Let the brightness of His glory shine forth to you in the great strength and power of the Holy Spirit!

Glory of the Lord Filled the Temple

"The Spirit lifted me up and brought me into the inner court; and behold, the glory of the Lord filled the temple" (Ezek. 43:5).

God gave Ezekiel a vision of a new temple. This temple is not an earthly temple but a spiritual temple. It emphasizes holiness and spiritual growth and reveals what worship should really be like. This temple parallels the New Jerusalem in Revelation 21:1 and is an ideal for God's people. God has a plan for His church, and He wants His people to enter a worship of Him that totally changes their lives. He knows that if we will only seek Him and enter His presence so that we can see Him for who He truly is, our lives will be turned around so that we will be a glorious example to those around us. They will see the love and peace of Jesus residing within us. They will see the strength and power that only comes from Him to overcome the adversities of this world. The Lord God Almighty wants to use us to further His kingdom on this earth.

Will you be one of God's people who will say yes to Him? Are you willing to be an instrument of His glory in this world? If your answer is yes, pray this prayer with me: "Father, in the name of Jesus, I commit myself to You. Pour forth Your glory upon me in such a way that I will be an example of the brightness of Your glory everywhere I go. Use me to further Your kingdom on this earth as I bask in the greatness and goodness of Your presence. Amen."

Glory of the Lord Filled the House

"Also He brought me by way of the north gate to the front of the temple; so I looked, and behold, the glory of the Lord filled the house of the Lord; and I fell on my face" (Ezek. 44:4).

Several times Ezekiel tells about falling on his face when the glory of the Lord was present. The glory of the Lord is so marvelous and overwhelming that it is difficult to stand in the presence of His great power. There are many recordings in Scripture of God's presence and glory bringing this same response. The apostle John told of his experience in Revelations 1:17: "And when I saw Him, I fell at His feet as dead. But He laid His right hand on me, saying to me, 'Do not be afraid; I am the First and the Last.'"

These accounts by Ezekiel and John give us an idea of the power of our Lord. If His presence were manifested in our midst, I wonder what our response would be? We sometimes worship quietly in our churches, but do we really understand what it means to enter the presence of God with His glory coming down in our midst? If that happens (and I believe it certainly can and in some cases has), I believe we will find ourselves on our faces before Him for we serve a mighty God who is full of majesty and power.

Would you like to see your worship of the Lord God Almighty move into a deeper realm? Seek Him with expectancy and faith. You will be amazed as He manifests Himself to you in order to strengthen your walk with Him and to enable you to fulfill His purposes for your life.

Knowledge of the Glory of the Lord

"For the earth will be filled with the knowledge of the glory of the Lord, as the waters cover the sea" (Hab. 2:14).

A day is coming when this verse will be fulfilled. When Jesus returns, the earth will truly be filled with the knowledge of the glory of the Lord. Does that mean that we must wait for that day to experience the glory of God in our lives? No! We can enter His presence in deep humility and know His glory in our lives. He is a generous and loving God who wants to share Himself with us daily. He wants to share Himself with us moment by moment. He is not a God who allows us to know Him only one day a week, or just one hour a day: He is a God who is always available to us.

As we spend more time knowing and loving God, we will be so filled with His presence that we will desire to share His love and goodness with others. God's purpose for all of us is that we share Him with those that are in need and hurting. He also wants us to share Him with those who do not look or act as if they have a need in the world, for they may be among the most needy. We live in a world where people are afraid to express what they are feeling. As we draw close to the Lord, He enables us to be sensitive to those who hide their hurts.

Do you long to know the living God better? Do you want to walk so closely with Him that you are aware with His sensitivity of the needs of those around you? He waits to share Himself with you in such a precious way today that your life will be totally changed by your encounter with Him. Draw close to Him today and bask in His glorious presence!

345

Christ in You, the Hope of Glory

"To them God willed to make known what are the riches of the glory of this mystery among the Gentiles: which is Christ in you, the hope of glory" (Col. 1:27).

I believe that the scripture for today is one of the most important in the Bible. It reveals a mystery that is more precious than silver and gold. It reveals the fact that Jesus Christ dwells within us, and the knowledge and understanding of what that means is truly the hope of glory. There is nothing within God's will that the church cannot accomplish when we walk in the knowledge that Jesus, and all that He reflects, dwells within us. He waits for us to allow Him freedom to live and move through us.

Jesus said, "Most assuredly, I say to you, he who believes in Me, the works that I do he will do also; and greater works than these he will do, because I go to My Father" (John 14:12). Because Jesus dwells within us, we can, through His strength and power, do the works that He did when He walked on this earth. This world can be turned upside down and completely around by the church if we take hold of this truth and begin to walk in it. A great move of God is stirring all around us, and the Lord wants us to be a part of this great revival!

Are you ready to let Jesus live through you? Are you excited about being a part of bringing change to the world through revival? Get ready because the Lord of the whole universe wants to use you as He brings revival into your life and the life of your church. Revival is already on the move in other countries of the world, and this nation is ripe and ready to be a part of what God is doing. Be prepared to be involved in the mighty move of God that is stirring in the earth today!

Wall of Fire All Around Her

"'For I,' says the Lord, 'will be a wall of fire all around her, and I will be the glory in her midst'" (Zech. 2:5).

In the scripture for today, the Lord tells us that He will be a wall of fire around Jerusalem and the glory in her midst. The Lord lets us know that His glory, which is in our midst, will be a wall of protection around us. Do we experience His glory in our midst? Some may answer yes; others may answer no. That "no" can be turned into a "yes" because God waits upon us to be open to receive His glory in our lives.

God has such love for His church that He wants to protect her from harm. He sends His glory to be like a wall of fire around her so that nothing can destroy her. His glory is powerful and holy. There are many aspects to the glory of God. His glory is all that is found in the attributes and character of God Himself. When He tells us that His glory will be around us like a wall of fire, we can know that He protects us with His great power. Can anything match or defeat the power of God? No! We truly are safe in His hands.

Do you feel safe in the hands of God? Let Him reassure you that His presence and His glory surround you like a wall of fire. Rest in the knowledge that there is nothing that can come against you that He cannot handle.

He Shall Bear the Glory

"Yes, He shall build the temple of the Lord. He shall bear the glory, and shall sit and rule on His throne; so He shall be a priest on His throne, and the counsel of peace shall be between them both" (Zech. 6:13).

The scripture for today prophesies the coming Messiah. Jesus, the Messiah, will build the temple (or the church) of the Lord. "He shall bear the glory" means that glory will rest upon Him. If He builds the church of God and the glory of God rests upon Him, then His glory will be available to the church. The glory of God can bring the life of God into the church, causing it to become what God created it to be on this earth: the church of God is called to set this world on fire with the good news of Jesus Christ!

Can you imagine what the world would be like if God's people lived as Jesus lived? If we preached as He preached, taught as He taught, healed as He healed, and set the captives free as He did, there would not be any room in any church because multitudes would come through the doors. A lot of church programs would be past history because the presence and glory of God Almighty would render them totally unnecessary. Zechariah 4:6 says, " 'Not by might nor by power, but by My Spirit,' says the Lord." All of our plans that are based on man's wisdom and not brought about by the Spirit of God are to no avail.

"Lord, we ask for Your glory to come down on the church and bring revival to Your people. Let Your glory come in such strength and power that we are totally changed. Use us to change the world that we live in by Your Spirit. Amen."

May God Be Glorified

"'Go up to the mountains and bring wood and build the temple that I may take pleasure in it and be glorified,' says the Lord" (Hag. 1:8).

*I*s God calling us today to build a literal temple made of wood and brick? In most cases, He is not. He is, however, calling us to build His church by reaching out to the people around us with the good news of Jesus Christ. He calls us to be so filled with His presence and His glory that others will be drawn to Him. He knows that as we draw closer to Him, we become more like Him. We begin to take on His attributes and character so that those around us will be amazed at the life that we live.

We have a tremendous treasure dwelling within our spirits. That treasure is the Lord Jesus Christ Himself residing within us with all His goodness, strength, power, love, and mercy. If we allow Him first place in our lives and let Him live through us, we will see a tremendous revival within His church. He will certainly take pleasure in His church and be glorified.

Are you willing to allow the Lord of life first place in your life? Are you willing to let Him live through you today? Ask Him to take over and be Lord of your life, and watch and see the glorious things that occur as you yield yourself to Him! Watch and see how He uses you to bring others into the saving knowledge of the Lord Jesus Christ as you become a part of the revival springing up in His church!

349

Beholding the Glory of the Lord

"But we all, with unveiled face, beholding as in a mirror the glory of the Lord, are being transformed into the same image from glory to glory, just as by the Spirit of the Lord" (2 Cor. 3:18).

What a glorious scripture to encourage us today! As we look into the face of the Lord, His glory transforms us into His image! When we spend time with Him day by day, we are being changed from one level of His glory to greater degrees of His glory. We cannot be in His presence without change occurring in our lives. The more time we spend with Him, the greater the transformation that occurs and the greater the measure of His glory that comes upon us. He is a transforming God!

Do you want to be transformed by the glory of God? Draw close to Him and look into His face. Behold Him in all His beauty and glory! Bask in His wondrous presence as you find yourself being changed from glory to glory! Begin to move out among your family and friends, and expect God to use you to minister His grace and goodness to them. Do not plan how you will approach them, but trust the Lord to open opportunities for you to share with them. Be sensitive to His Holy Spirit that dwells within you as He leads and guides you day by day. He will give you the words that you need to speak to those around you. He will show you where to go, what to say, and how to say it. Be encouraged as you find yourself being a powerful witness for the Lord Jesus Christ! Know the joy of leading someone to the Lord. Be a part of the great revival that is beginning to come upon the earth by leading many into His kingdom and letting His glory radiate through you!

DECEMBER 1

Take the Anointing Oil

"And you shall take the anointing oil, pour it on his head, and anoint him" (Exod. 29:7).

In the scripture for today, the Lord gave Moses instructions about anointing Aaron for the office of priest. Anointing oil is symbolic of the anointing of God. When the anointing oil was poured on his head, the anointing of God came upon him for the office and calling that God had planned for him.

God has told us that He will equip us to do what He has called us to do. He has said that we "can do all things through Christ who strengthens [us]" (Phil. 4:13). His anointing is His presence and power at work upon and within us to accomplish His will and purposes. Whatever God does, He does right! When He is at work within us through the power of His Holy Spirit, what comes forth is good and right. Those things that do not turn out well are things that we do on our own. When God's anointing is there, we sense and feel His presence. We find life and excitement in whatever we are doing for the Lord. We are so overjoyed at His presence in our lives that we want to continue to follow His ways.

Have you ever experienced His anointing in your life? Think about a time that you were doing something for the Lord, and you thought, "I never dreamed I could do anything like this!" You were not doing it on your own. The Spirit of God dwelling within you brought the anointing of God in your life to enable you to do it. Nothing can bring more joy to your life than walking in obedience to Him and experiencing His anointing!

You Shall Anoint Them

"You shall anoint them, as you anointed their father, that they may minister to Me as priests; for their anointing shall surely be an everlasting priesthood throughout their generations" (Exod. 40:15).

Aaron's sons were to be anointed as priests also. The priests were the ones who could minister in the tabernacle where the presence of the Lord dwelled. God anointed a priesthood, who went through certain cleansing rituals, so that they could minister unto the Lord on behalf of the people.

First Peter 2:5 says, "You also, as living stones, are being built up a spiritual house, a holy priesthood, to offer up spiritual sacrifices acceptable to God through Jesus Christ." We no longer need priests to go into the presence of God to make sacrifices for us because Jesus became the ultimate sacrifice on the cross for us. When we accept Him as our Lord and Savior, we are able to enter the holy of holies, the most sacred part of the temple which was separated by a veil. Only the high priest could encounter God's presence there and live. We are able to experience the priestly anointing to come into His presence, for our high priest, Jesus Christ, has torn apart the veil of separation.

Enter into the presence of the Lord today, and know the joy of experiencing His anointing. Be open to His direction to you to step out in faith and share His goodness with those around you. The anointing that rests upon and within you will draw them to His goodness!

DECEMBER 3

Anointing the Tabernacle

"Also Moses took the anointing oil, and anointed the tabernacle and all that was in it, and consecrated them" (Levit. 8:10).

*W*hat was the purpose of anointing the tabernacle and all that was in it with anointing oil? Since anointing oil symbolizes the anointing and presence of the Lord, Moses' application of the oil symbolized the presence of the Lord being there. It represented the holiness of God in the place.

Consecration means to be set apart for the worship or service of the Lord. The anointing procedure that took place in the tabernacle was for setting it apart for the work of the Lord. It was to be a holy place where the presence of the Lord would be evident. When God's presence was made manifest, the priests and the people were overcome with the glory of God that accompanied His anointing.

Do you believe that God's anointing is only for the clergy? Is it difficult for you to believe that God's anointing could be for you? Seek the Lord today and let Him show you about His anointing. Let Him show you that His anointing is just as much for you as for anyone. Draw near to Him as He reveals His presence and His glory in your life. Receive all that He has for you by consecrating yourself to Him. Tell Him of your willingness to be obedient to Him in all that He would ask you to do, and know that He will supply all that you need through His anointing that resides within you for the fulfillment of His plan!

Yoke Will Be Destroyed

"It shall come to pass in that day that his burden will be taken away from your shoulder, and his yoke from your neck, and the yoke will be destroyed because of the anointing oil" (Isa. 10:27).

The anointing oil here is symbolic of the work of the Holy Spirit within us. The scripture for today helps us to understand that those things that are so heavy and burdensome to us will be destroyed because of the anointing of God in our lives. The anointing of God is the Holy Spirit at work within us to help us become free. It is important to recognize that the Spirit of God works within us to help us be free of fear that would keep us from being powerful witnesses to the wonderful news of Jesus Christ. We need to submit ourselves to Him in order that the yokes of envy, pride, resentment, and everything that besets us and keeps us from being used by Him will be removed from our lives.

God's anointing makes such an overwhelming change in our lives that we can actually do those things that we never dreamed we could do. We find that He is at work within us, molding and making us into His image so that those around us will also be changed into His image. He wants to draw all men unto Himself, and we are the instruments that He wants to use. What a powerful and wondrous God that we have!

Are there yokes of bondage in your life from which you want to be free? All you have to do is trust the God of the whole universe to set you free. He has placed His anointing upon and within you to bring freedom into your life.

DECEMBER 5

Call the Elders

"Is anyone among you sick? Let him call for the elders of the church, and let them pray over him, anointing him with oil in the name of the Lord" (James 5:14).

The anointing of God represents the presence of the Holy Spirit. In the scripture for today the anointing of the Holy Spirit is present to bring healing. Many scriptures throughout the Bible show us that God's perfect plan for us as His children is that we be whole people. He provided healing as a part of the atonement, according to Isaiah 53:4–5 and also Matthew 8:17, which says, "He Himself took our infirmities and bore our sickness."

There are times when we pray for ourselves or others, and healing does not seem to occur. This fact does not change the message of the Bible. Exodus 15:26 says, "For I am the Lord who heals you." When healing does not seem to occur, we can keep trusting God. Healing comes in many ways— through His sovereign hand, through doctors and medicine, and also the ultimate healing of going home to be with Him.

Do you need the healing touch of the Lord in your life? Read the above scriptures about healing to help seal within your mind the fact that God does want to heal you. Use the concordance in your Bible to find other verses to build your faith. Call the elders of your church, who should be people of faith and prayer; ask them to pray for your healing, anointing you with oil. Then reach out to Him, expecting to receive from Him. Continue to trust Him daily as you begin to thank Him for His provision of healing in your life.

The Anointing Abides in You

"But the anointing which you have received from Him abides in you, and you do not need that anyone teach you; but as the same anointing teaches you concerning all things, and is true, and is not a lie, and just as it has taught you, you will abide in Him" (1 John 2:27).

Is it not amazing that the anointing of God abides in us? The apostle John tells us in his letter to the churches that His anointing enables us to know His truth in ways that cannot come from human wisdom or teaching. The scripture for today does not say that there is no need for teachers. It simply tells us that we can and will receive understanding from the Holy Spirit who will guide us into all truth.

Teachers, no matter how mature or spiritually strong, can and will be guided by their flesh from time to time. No teacher is perfect, and we should not expect them to be perfect. What we hear from a teacher should be filtered through the anointing of God that abides within us. We should receive what is good and acceptable according to the Word of God and put anything that is questionable on a shelf. We should, in other words, pray about that which is questionable, asking the Lord to reveal His truth to us.

Are you open to the anointing of God within you teaching you and bringing you into all truth? When there seems to be some question in your mind, do not be swayed by the thinking and teaching of others. Study Scripture to bring light and revelation into your life. Seek the Lord today, and let Him reveal His love and anointing to you as you surrender yourself to His truth!

Heed the Words of the Lord

"Samuel also said to Saul, 'The Lord sent me to anoint you king over His people, over Israel. Now therefore, heed the voice of the words of the Lord'" (1 Sam. 15:1).

In the days that the Israelites asked God for a king, He sent Samuel, who was a prophet, to anoint Saul as king over the Israelites. We find that Samuel admonished Saul to listen to the voice of God. Samuel gave Saul directions from the Lord concerning a battle with Amalek. When Saul did not heed the voice of the Lord, the Lord regretted that He had set up Saul as king.

God's anointing abides within us as Christians, but we have the responsibility to be obedient to Him. When we are continually disobedient to Him, we find that His anointing lifts from us. He tells us in John 15:5–6, "I am the vine, you are the branches. He who abides in Me, and I in him, bears much fruit; for without Me you can do nothing. If anyone does not abide in Me, he is cast out as a branch and is withered; and they gather them and throw them into the fire, and they are burned." The anointing of God is the presence of the Holy Spirit at work within us. When we are disobedient to the Lord, we quench the Spirit of God and the anointing cannot flow from us.

Is the anointing of God flowing freely within and through you? If you believe that you have been quenching the Spirit of God at work within you, ask the Lord's forgiveness today. Begin to move in the joy and freedom that comes from His forgiveness. Let His anointing reach out to those you know who are in deep need.

357

Arise, Anoint Him

"So he sent and brought him in. Now he was ruddy, with bright eyes, and good-looking. And the Lord said, 'Arise, anoint him; for this is the one!'" (1 Sam. 16:12).

When the Lord rejected Saul as king because of his disobedience, Samuel was sent to anoint David as king. Samuel did not know which of the sons of Jesse was to be anointed king when he arrived at their home. He looked at all the older brothers, but the Lord said, "I have not chosen one of these." When Samuel asked Jesse if he had any more sons, he told him that his youngest was keeping the sheep. When David came from the field, the Lord immediately told Samuel that he was the one. When Samuel anointed David with oil before his brothers, the Spirit of the Lord came on David from that day forward.

Did David become king immediately when he was anointed? No! In fact, for many years he had to flee from Saul's presence because he feared for his life. David was not crowned king for approximately fifteen years. When he did become king, he was the kind of king that followed after God's heart. Even when he sinned, he knew where to turn to receive forgiveness. The anointing of God upon him was powerful and mighty because David sought to follow after the ways of God.

Do you want to be a person who follows after the ways of God with the fervor of David? Ask the Lord to fill you with a hungering and thirsting after Him that cannot be quenched. Ask Him to give you a holy zeal that will enable you to reach out to others with a commitment that will bring about results. Let His holy presence minister His anointing in your life today.

DECEMBER 9

Long Live King Solomon

"There let Zadok the priest and Nathan the prophet anoint him king over Israel; and blow the horn, and say, 'Long live King Solomon!'" (1 Kings 1:34).

When David neared the end of His life, he proclaimed his son Solomon to be king. Zadok, the priest, and Nathan, the prophet, anointed Solomon with oil to be the new king of Judah and Israel. Then they blew the horn, announcing the new king to the people; and all the people shouted, "Long live King Solomon!"

The anointing of God was strong on Solomon. He walked in a tremendous anointing of wisdom. In great humility, he had prayed and asked God to give him wisdom because he realized that as king of a great multitude of people he needed an understanding heart to judge the people. It pleased the Lord that Solomon had asked for wisdom rather than long life or riches. As long as Solomon walked in the ways of the Lord, there was great anointing and wisdom upon him.

Would you like an anointing of wisdom in your life? Pray the following prayer: "Father, in the name of Jesus, anoint me with wisdom that I may follow after Your ways in all things. Let me be an example of Your grace and wisdom in my everyday life. Let me shine forth with such an expression of Your light and understanding that those around me will want to have what I have. May Your kingdom grow and prosper because I follow in obedience to Your Word and truth. I know that Your Word is an expression of Your wisdom, and I ask that You open the pages of the Bible with fresh revelation so that I can understand and walk in Your wisdom. May You be glorified greatly through my life. Amen and amen."

Shows Mercy to His Anointed

"Great deliverance He gives to His king, and shows mercy to His anointed, to David and his descendants forever-more" (Ps. 18:50).

*D*avid was aware of the mercy that the Lord bestowed upon Him as His anointed king. David needed the mercy of God because he fell into sin. The difference between David and Saul, who both fell into sin, was the fact that David had a heart that followed after God. He sought the Lord with every-thing that was within him. He did not live in continual sin. When he did sin, his heart was filled with true repentance. He could not stand to be separated from the Lord. David had ex-perienced the presence of the Lord in such powerful ways on so many occasions that he could not bear to think about los-ing that close relationship. He was willing to do whatever it took to restore his relationship with the living Lord.

We need to know the Lord as David knew the Lord. We need to draw so close to Him that we would let nothing in-terfere with our relationship with Him. We need to have the zeal and fervor for Him that David had. We need to be will-ing to be considered "peculiar" because of our love for Him. First Peter 2:9 says, "But ye are a chosen generation, a royal priesthood, an holy nation, a peculiar people that ye should show forth the praises of him who hath called you out of darkness into his marvelous light" (KJV). The term "peculiar" used in this scripture does not mean weird, but it does mean special. We need to be known as God's special people. When others look at us, they should see something that shows that we belong to Almighty God!

The Lord Saves His Anointed

"Now I know that the Lord saves His anointed; He will answer him from His holy heaven with the saving strength of His right hand" (Ps. 20:6).

The Twentieth Psalm was probably a prayer that was lifted up before going into battle. In this context, it seems that the psalmist says that the Lord saves and protects the life of His anointed. Another translation for anointed in this context is commissioned one. He will extend His powerful right hand to bring about what is needed to the one whom He has called in battle. His anointed one relies completely upon the Lord for victory.

When we rely completely on the Lord, He supplies what we need. He is always there for His people, who are called by His name and put their trust in Him. Hebrews 11:6 says, "But without faith it is impossible to please Him, for he who comes to God must believe that He is, and that He is a rewarder of those who diligently seek Him." When we put our trust in Him and rely completely upon Him, we walk in faith. Since He rewards those who diligently seek Him and walk in faith, He will respond to our trust and reliance upon Him with great and glorious victory.

Are you facing some type of trouble or problem today? Place your trust in the One who has every answer. Draw into His presence and be aware of the greatness of His power and mercy. Let Him reassure you that there is not one thing in your life that He cannot handle or change. He will bring victory to you!

Saving Refuge of His Anointed

"The Lord is their strength, and He is the saving refuge of His anointed" (Ps. 28:8).

David wrote Psalm 28 in gratitude to answered prayer. He expressed that the Lord waits to extend His hand of protection to His anointed. He is ready and willing to be a place of refuge when there are problems and difficulties. David helps us realize that the Lord waits for us to bring needs and supplications to Him in prayer.

He wants us to come into His presence and talk to Him about what we are going through. When we are in His presence, we find such reassurance of His love and mercy that we will know that Jeremiah was correct when he said, "Ah, Lord God! Behold, You have made the heavens and the earth by Your great power and outstretched arm. There is nothing too hard for You." No matter how difficult the circumstances, we can know that the one true living God is able and willing to meet our needs and bring victory into our lives.

Do you need the Lord to be a strong refuge in your life today? Begin to worship Him with all that is within you. Thank Him for His great goodness and mercy, and express your gratitude for all the wondrous things that He has done in your life in the past. Seek His direction for what you are going through at this time, and you will find that He will bring wisdom and guidance into your life. He will bring victory and strength as you seek Him and draw closer to Him.

Oil of Gladness

"You love righteousness and hate wickedness; therefore God, Your God, has anointed You with the oil of gladness more than Your companions" (Ps. 45:7).

Psalm 45 is written about the Messiah and His bride. God will anoint Him with the oil of gladness more than His companions. Does that mean that we will not be anointed with the oil of gladness? No! We also will be anointed with the oil of gladness when we seek His presence in our lives and desire to walk in obedience to Him. Psalm 45:15 says, "With gladness and rejoicing they shall be brought; they shall enter the King's palace."

What is the oil of gladness? We know that oil represents the anointing of the Lord, and gladness means that He will fill us with His exceeding joy and mirth. If joy and gladness were ever needed, they are needed in our lives today. So much in this world brings sorrow and grief that only the joy of the Lord can continually lift us up. We need to be lifted into the very presence of the Lord where He will fill us to overflowing with the oil of gladness.

Do you need the joy of the Lord in your life today? Pray this prayer in the name of Jesus: "Father, I need to receive Your joy in my life. I need to have that sweet contentment that comes with Your joy and gladness. I give You everything in my life that burdens me. I give You everything that brings sorrow and grief in my life. Help me to place these at the foot of Your throne and reach out and receive Your glorious freedom that comes through Your oil of gladness. In Jesus' precious name. Amen."

Look Upon the Face of Your Anointed

"O God, behold our shield, and look upon the face of your anointed" (Ps. 84:9).

Some excerpts from Psalm 84 are as follows: "How lovely is Your tabernacle," "My heart and my flesh cry out for the living God," and "Blessed are those who dwell in Your house." The psalmist knew the Lord in such intimacy that he wanted to be in the dwelling place of the Lord. His heart and flesh cried out for God. He recognized that those who dwelled in the house of God were tremendously blessed. He placed himself in a position of being where he could make himself available to the Lord. He wanted the Lord to look upon his face.

What happens when the Lord looks upon our face? His face shines upon our uplifted face. We receive His countenance upon us, and we are changed into His likeness and image. When we spend time in such intimacy with Him that He looks upon our face, we see Him in all His fullness and glory. We receive those wondrous and glorious attributes of His into our lives. What a magnificent Lord that we serve! He loves us so much that He will actually look upon our face. We are not worthy to receive such goodness, but He has made us worthy through the blood of His Son.

Enter into His presence today and let Him look upon your face. Know Him in such intimacy and nearness that you can gaze into His eyes as He looks upon you. Receive the character and strength that dwells within Him into your life. Walk in a newness and freshness that come only from knowing your wondrous Lord and receiving the anointing that He holds out to you!

Anointed Him with My Holy Oil

"I have found My servant David; with My holy oil I have anointed him" (Ps. 89:20).

The Lord anointed David with holy oil through His servant Samuel. When the oil of God was poured upon David's head, he received an anointing that came from God Almighty to fulfill His plan. How did the anointing of God affect David?

David was not perfect, but he followed after the Lord with such obedience and exuberance that David is still remembered and talked about approximately 3,000 years later. Many sermons and teachings are based upon David and his extraordinary life.

A good definition of anointing could possibly be extraordinary. When the anointing of God is released within believers, their lives change from ordinary to extraordinary. There is new life and vibrancy in the way that they respond to those around them. If the anointing of God is released in a preacher, he begins to preach with such life that those listening hardly know any time has passed. If the anointing is released in a singer, she sings with such freshness and vibrancy that her listeners are often moved to tears of joy.

Would you like for the anointing of God within you to be released so that you can serve Him with new boldness, courage, and exuberance? Draw so close to Him that He will look into your face and you will look into His face. Begin to move out in obedience to what He shows you in such special times of nearness with Him, and watch as He moves and works through you with great anointing!

Footsteps of Your Anointed

"With which Your enemies have reproached, O Lord, with which they have reproached the footsteps of Your anointed" (Ps. 89:51).

Why were the enemies of God reproaching the foot steps of David? Where were David's footsteps going? What were they doing? In most cases, David followed the Lord's way for his life. His footsteps followed after God! God's enemies reproached David because they wanted to thwart the plan of God. David probably referred to literal people in this psalm, but who is behind all evil? Satan is out to cause havoc and to try to steal, kill, and destroy, according to John 10:10.

We need to walk in the footsteps of the Lord with confidence in His ability to protect us and keep us from evil. When we seek Him and His ways, we can know that He will reveal Himself to us. We can be assured that He will respond to us with such closeness that we will truly know that we are in His presence. When we walk in His presence, we certainly will walk in His footsteps. His anointing will be released with such power in us that we will see many saved, healed, and set free. His words will be the words that come out of our mouth, and His love will flow from us to those around us.

Be ready to walk in the footsteps of the Lord today. Let Him reveal Himself to you in a powerful way as you prepare to move out in response to His anointing that is within you. Let Him show you someone who needs a special touch from the Master and reach out in faith as He fills your mind and mouth with His holy words. Be His instrument to help bring revival in the life of someone in need today!

Anointed with Fresh Oil

"But my horn You have exalted like a wild ox; I have been anointed with fresh oil" (Ps. 92:10).

In the scripture for today, the term horn could also be translated "strength," which gives us better understanding of what the psalmist said. When the anointing of the Lord is released within us, our strength is as great as a wild ox! The anointing of the Lord brings us everything that we need to fulfill God's plan for our lives. We do not have to lack anything! We, along with the psalmist, can praise the Lord for His greatness and lovingkindness!

Walking in the anointing of the Lord brings such joy and gladness into our lives that we want to share with all those we know about the greatness of His glory! We find that we are people filled to overflowing with praises for Him, and others see and are aware of how our close walk with Him has changed us. They see the life of God at work within us and know that something very special has happened to us. Often they will come to us and ask what has made the difference. What a wonderful opportunity to be a witness for our Lord!

Do you want to be anointed with fresh oil from the Lord so that you can be a powerful witness for Him? He waits with His special anointing that He has reserved just for you! He wants to enable you to go forth and be the man or woman of God that He created you to be. He wants to see you reaching out in your community to those who are in desperate need of a Savior. He wants to work through you to let these people know of His love. His anointing is for a very special reason—to share the good news of Jesus Christ with those that are hurting and in need.

Do Not Touch My Anointed Ones

"He permitted no one to do them wrong; yes, He rebuked kings for their sakes, saying, 'Do not touch My anointed ones, and do My prophets no harm'" (Ps. 105:14–15).

As the anointed children of God, we can be assured that He does not want anyone to treat us in a wrong way. He also does not want us to treat another anointed child of His in a wrong way. The scripture for today can truly bring change in our lives if we have been guilty of grumbling against or criticizing someone who is in the service of the Lord. Most of us have been guilty of this at some time or another. It is much easier to see the negative and be critical than to look for the good and be positive.

Our pastors and those in leadership need our prayers daily. God has called them to carry a tremendous responsibility, and He has enabled them to do the job to which He has called them. They are not perfect people (as we are not), and they will not always do everything according to God's will. Most of them, however, have hearts that seek to serve God to the best of their knowledge and understanding. We need to support them, care for them, and pray for them. The Lord takes very seriously the treatment that His anointed receive. Let us walk in lovingkindness and humility toward one another.

"Father, in the name of Jesus, we ask for Your forgiveness for the times that we have spoken critical words or have been judgmental against one of Your anointed. We ask that You would fill us with compassion, understanding, and acceptance for them. Anoint them in a greater way to serve You, and bless them mightily. May You receive glory from their lives and from our lives as well. Amen and amen."

Do Not Turn Away the Face of Your Anointed

"For Your servant David's sake, do not turn away the face of Your anointed" (Ps. 132:10).

In Psalm 132, David wrote about the dwelling place of the Lord. In verse 7, he said, "Let us go into His tabernacle; let us worship at His footstool." David implored the Lord not to turn away from his face when he came into the dwelling place of the Lord. David recognized and acknowledged the anointing of God upon his life. He was not being boastful to call himself "anointed." He yielded himself to the calling that God had upon him.

David also acknowledged that even though he was anointed of God, he was not perfect, and God could have reason to turn from his face. He wrote in verse 11, "The Lord has sworn in truth to David; He will not turn from it." David recognized that his salvation and the anointing that was upon him did not come because of his works but because he believed and trusted in the one true living God. He believed in the promise of the coming Messiah and yielded his life to Him.

Do you ever feel that God is turning away from your face? If you are a born-again Christian, God does not turn away from your face. You may disappoint Him at times, but He always waits for you and holds out His arms to you. Draw near to Him today and let Him reveal His love to you. Do not hold back from Him because you may feel guilty about something that you have done or said. Simply ask His forgiveness, and then move into His arms as He looks down upon your trusting face!

369

A Lamp for My Anointed

"There I will make the horn of David grow; I will prepare a lamp for My anointed" (Ps. 132:17).

The Lord spoke to David in the scripture for today. He indicated to David that He will light his way and show him the plans that He has for him. He assured David that He will give him revelation to understand and accomplish whatever He calls him to do. God told David that his horn or kingdom will grow. David was assured that the Lord will provide all that was needed for David's kingdom to grow. All that David had to do was to listen to the Lord and obey His instructions.

God does not anoint us, His people, and then leave us to figure things out for ourselves. His provision and revelation are available to all His children. His anointing is upon and within each of us, and all that we have to do is yield ourselves to Him. He will reveal His plan and direction in such a way that we will know and understand each step that we are to take to fulfill His purposes. He will show us through His Word, through His still, small voice, and through sermons, Bible teachers, and friends. He will confirm to us in several ways what His direction is for our lives. Second Corinthians 13:1 says, "By the mouth of two or three witnesses every word shall be established."

Let the lamp of God reveal to you all that you need to know in order to fulfill His call upon your life. Walk in the anointing that is within you as you help bring the good news of Jesus Christ to those around you.

370

The Lord Has Anointed Me

"The Spirit of the Lord God is upon Me, because the Lord has anointed Me to preach good tidings to the poor; He has sent Me to heal the brokenhearted, to proclaim liberty to the captives, and the opening of the prison to those who are bound" (Isa. 61:1).

Isaiah 61 is prophetic of the coming Messiah, Jesus Christ. When Jesus was in the temple, He read today's scripture to the people and told them that this scripture had been fulfilled that day. In John 14:12, Jesus said, "Most assuredly, I say to you, he who believes in Me, the works that I do he will do also; and greater works than these he will do, because I go to My Father." Isaiah 61:1 is basically the ministry of Jesus Christ, but it also is the ministry that He has passed on to all true believers in Him.

The anointing of God is upon us to preach good news to the poor, to be an instrument of the healing of God to the brokenhearted, and to proclaim the liberty and freedom of Jesus Christ to those who are in bondage and in prison. How can we accomplish this call upon our lives? We need to allow the Holy Spirit full reign in our lives so that He can show us day by day what to say and what to do in each situation that comes up. His anointing is upon and within us. All we need to do is to be sensitive to His direction for us.

Do you believe that the Lord can use you to bring Isaiah 61:1 to pass? Put your trust in Him who is able to do all things well. Allow Him first place in your life, and seek to listen and hear from Him as He directs you into a place of anointing and service that will bring more joy and excitement to you than you can ever imagine!

Salvation with Your Anointed

"You went forth for the salvation of Your people, for salvation with Your Anointed. You struck the head from the house of the wicked, by laying bare from foundation to neck" (Hab. 3:13).

Jesus Christ is the Anointed One who brings salvation to His people. He has placed His anointing within us so that we can be used by Him to bring the good news of salvation through the blood of Jesus to the world. His anointing brings courage, boldness, and wisdom to handle any and every opportunity that comes our way to be a witness for Him and His saving grace.

If we are afraid to be a witness for Jesus Christ, then we are not releasing the anointing that He has placed within us. We need to read His Word so that we can be encouraged and built up in the knowledge and understanding of His plan. We need to spend time in close communication with Him through praise and prayer so that we can receive from Him the encouragement and boldness that we need to go forth. We also need to spend time with other believers so that we can be encouraged and challenged by one another. The anointing is definitely with us: we simply need to stir up that which already abides within us. We find that boldness, courage, and strength will come forth strongly as we seek to put Him first in our lives.

Does the message of salvation burn deeply within your soul? Be an instrument of the Lord to share that message with a lost and dying world.

Anointed Ones

"So he said, 'These are the two anointed ones, who stand beside the Lord of the whole earth'" (Zech. 4:14).

God's anointing is on His people to stand beside Him and to carry out His plans. In Zechariah 4, the two anointed ones are Joshua, the high priest, representing the religious authority, and Zerubbabel, the political leader of Judah. They were called to rebuild the temple. Zechariah 4:6 says, "'Not by might nor by power, but by My Spirit,' says the Lord." They were told by God and found out through experience that the only way that the temple could be rebuilt was by the power of the Holy Spirit.

Joshua and Zerubbabel encourage us as believers that we can fulfill everything that the Lord has anointed us to do. We know that we cannot do it in our own strength or our own power, but we can do anything that God calls us to do through the power of the Holy Spirit who is at work within us. When we learn to quit trying to make things happen or to make plans in our own strength, we find great freedom in trusting the Lord to reveal His plan. As we lean on Him and His strength, we find that we have greater aptitude to go forth and accomplish His will.

Are you struggling with knowing what God's will is and what it is not? Are you finding yourself trying to make plans without that special unction that comes from the Lord? Place everything in the hands of the Lord and trust Him to show you how to move out and accomplish those things that He has ordained for you to do!

His Anointed

"Thus says the Lord to His anointed, to Cyrus, whose right hand I have held—to subdue nations before him and loose the armor of kings, to open before him the double doors, so that the gates will not be shut" (Isa. 45:1).

God had a special calling on Cyrus, who was king of Persia and ruler of Babylon. He set him apart and anointed him to release Israel to return to Jerusalem to rebuild the temple under the leadership of Zerubbabel. The amazing thing about Isaiah 45 is the fact that Isaiah prophetically wrote this, calling Cyrus by name, one hundred years before the event happened. According to Josephus, Cyrus released the Jews to return after he was read this scripture from the Book of Isaiah. This is an example of how God can take an unbelieving ruler and use him. The term anointed, however, used in the scripture for today, means that he was anointed in the sense that he was chosen by God for a specific purpose. According to Ezra 1:1, the Lord stirred up the spirit of Cyrus so that he made a proclamation in writing to his entire kingdom, saying, "Thus says Cyrus king of Persia: All the kingdoms of the earth the Lord God of heaven has given me. And he has commanded me to build Him a house at Jerusalem which is in Judah." Cyrus certainly recognized that God had given him his success, and he also recognized the call of God upon him to build a house for the Lord in Jerusalem.

Will you accept the anointing and calling of God upon your life? Will you, as a believer, trust Him with all your heart and begin to move out as He gives you direction to be a shining example of the love and grace of the Lord Jesus Christ?

God Anointed Jesus of Nazareth

"How God anointed Jesus of Nazareth with the Holy Spirit and with power, who went about doing good and healing all who were oppressed by the devil, for God was with Him" (Acts 10:38).

Jesus was anointed by God with the Holy Spirit and with power. Because He was anointed, He went about doing good and healing all who were oppressed by the devil.

Jesus was God in the flesh, but He gave up His heavenly position and power to come to this earth as a human. He lived a perfect life as a human, yet died the death of a rank sinner to pay the price for the sins of humanity. God's anointing enabled Jesus to live and function on this earth as a human and to fulfill God's plan for the redemption of mankind.

God's anointing on us enables us to function on this earth according to God's plan. Jesus went to the cross for us, ascended to the right hand of the Father in heaven, and sent His Spirit to dwell within us so that we can continue His ministry on this earth. The only way we can continue His ministry is to trust completely in the Spirit of God that dwells within us. It is by His strength and power that we can accomplish the works of God.

On this Christmas day, submit yourself to the living Lord, and let Him reveal His plan for your life. Trust in Him to bring about all that is necessary to fulfill His plans and purposes. Bask in His presence on this special holy day and acknowledge His Lordship in your life.

Anointed with Oil

"And they cast out many demons, and anointed with oil many who were sick, and healed them" (Mark 6:13).

Jesus sent the twelve disciples out two by two and empowered them to preach repentance and heal the sick. These disciples anointed the sick with oil and they were healed. Anointing with oil symbolizes the work of the Holy Spirit in our lives. The anointing of God is powerful and strong; it is able to bring about healing, deliverance, freedom from bondage, and life from God.

Just as the anointing of God was available to the disciples, it is available to us today. As born-again Christians, the anointing of God already resides within us. Even though we may not be aware of the anointing of God in our lives, it is there. His anointing needs to be released within us so that we can be the powerful people of God that He created us to be. How is His anointing released within us? As we draw close to Him, worshiping Him and communicating with Him, and as we are steeped in His Word, we find that His anointing will begin to come forth more and more in our lives. We will have the courage and boldness to be powerful witnesses for Him. We will lay hands on the sick, anointing them with oil, and they will recover. We will find that as we share life-giving words with those in bondage, they will be set free.

Do you want to be used as God's tool to see people set free? Bask in His presence and allow Him to release and bring forth His anointing within you that you may be the powerful man or woman of God that He created you to be!

Anointed Jesus' Feet with Fragrant Oil

"And stood at His feet behind Him weeping; and she began to wash His feet with her tears, and wiped them with the hair of her head; and she kissed His feet and anointed them with the fragrant oil" (Luke 7:38).

The woman who anointed the feet of Jesus was a sinner. When she came into the presence of Jesus, she was very aware of who she was and also who Jesus was. Her tears represented the repentance that was going on within her heart. She was so very grateful that the Lord of lords and King of kings was there with her, holding out forgiveness for her sins. She anointed His feet as an act of love because she recognized the greatness of His mercy.

The washing of feet was an act of hospitality in the days that Jesus lived because the people walked everywhere they went. They wore sandals, and their feet became dusty and dirty. Jesus was at the house of Simon when the woman anointed His feet. Simon, as His host, should have washed His feet but failed to do so. Not only did the woman wash His feet with her tears, she also anointed them with fragrant oil. Fragrant oil was expensive, and the woman gave the Lord the very best that she knew to give.

"Father, help us to give the very best that we have to the Lord Jesus Christ. Help us to be so full of gratitude for all that He has done for us that we will want to move out in the anointing that You have placed upon and within us and share His goodness and grace with others. Use us mightily for Your kingdom, Lord, and fill us anew and afresh with the wonders of Your glorious presence in our lives!"

Anointed the Eyes of the Blind Man

"When He had said these things, He spat on the ground and made clay with the saliva; and He anointed the eyes of the blind man with the clay" (John 9:6).

When Jesus saw a need, He knew how to take care of it. When He saw the blind man, He anointed his eyes with clay. The result was healing and sight for the blind man. Many times throughout Scripture we find the anointing of Jesus bringing about healing, deliverance, and freedom.

His anointing resides within us, and He wants to use us to reach out to those around us with His same sensitivity and compassion. He wants to release His anointing within us to lay hands on the sick so that they will recover. He wants to use us to bring freedom to those in bondage, and He wants us to move out in His compassion to bring comfort to those who are brokenhearted. He wants us to be sensitive to the needs around us and then to reach out in faith, trusting Him to provide the anointing that is needed to bring about restoration, healing, and deliverance.

Would you like to be used by the Lord to pray for someone to be healed either physically, spiritually, or emotionally? Begin to read every scripture that you can find in the Bible related to healing. You will find that your faith will grow as you read about the Lord's will to bring healing into the lives of His people. As God brings the opportunity across your path, step out in faith and pray for someone who is in great need. Know the joy of being used by the Lord to bring peace and healing into the life of a dear soul!

You Anoint My Head with Oil

"You prepare a table before me in the presence of my enemies; You anoint my head with oil; my cup runs over" (Ps. 23:5).

Just as the Lord sent Samuel to anoint David's head with oil, He has anointed us as born-again Christians to fulfill His plan for our lives. Each one of us is unique and different, and His anointing may seem different in each of our lives. David had an anointing to serve as king and lead the people of Israel. He also had an anointing to write and sing psalms or songs. Elijah, on the other hand, had an anointing as a strong prophet who spoke with power. The Lord used him to perform mighty miracles in the lives of many people. Deborah was anointed as a prophetess and as a judge. She was the spiritual and governmental leader of the people of Israel.

Romans 12 tells us that there are many members of the body of Christ with many giftings and anointings. We should not try to compare ourselves with others nor try to be like someone else. The Lord has different callings on our lives. When we act in obedience to Him and His call on our lives, we will see many peoples' lives being changed by His power and anointing working in and through us in different ways.

Will you begin to seek the Lord about His giftings and anointing that dwell within you? Begin to move out as the unique and individual person that He created you to be. Let His Spirit move in your midst, bringing about great and glorious works that will bring glory and honor to Him!

He Who Has Anointed Us Is God

"Now He who establishes us with you in Christ and has anointed us is God" (2 Cor. 1:21).

*P*aul told the Corinthians that God had anointed them. If the Lord anointed the Corinthians, He has surely anointed us as well. Any believer in Jesus Christ is anointed of God to carry out His will on this earth. He waits for us to receive His direction and move out in His anointing to bring about His kingdom on earth.

When Jesus was praying what the church calls "The Lord's Prayer," He said, "Thy kingdom come, Thy will be done on this earth as it is done in heaven." How is His kingdom going to come on this earth? How is His will going to be done on this earth?

Although His kingdom will not fully come until Jesus returns, today wherever God is welcome to reign, His kingdom comes. More and more His kingdom will come and His will will be done on this earth as we, His believers, move in obedience to Him in the anointing that He has placed upon us. When we do this, we will see this world turned upside down and all around. We will see the power of God at work in this world, and we will see many people saved, set free, and moving out in the anointing that He places within them. We will truly see revival break forth on this earth!

Would you like to be a part of the revival that is about to break forth on this earth? Do not be left behind during the most exciting time that the world has ever known. Be a part of a great move of God that will usher in the Second Coming of the Lord Jesus Christ!

You Have an Anointing from the Holy One

"But you have an anointing from the Holy One, and you know all things" (1 John 2:20).

The Holy One, God Almighty, has anointed us to serve Him. He reveals and gives us wisdom in every situation that comes up so that we can fulfill His purpose. His purpose for our lives is great and glorious! Nothing that we can imagine on our own would be more glorious than His holy plan and purpose for our lives.

When we think about the fact that the anointing of God rests upon us, it is more than we are able to comprehend. His anointing is powerful and strong. His anointing is full of compassion and mercy. No matter what we may encounter, or no matter what someone we know may encounter, His anointing has every answer. He has placed within us the power to hear Him, to respond to His instruction, and to participate in the changing of people's lives. What a glorious plan our God has! He allows us to be a part of the wondrous events that are occurring to change the world and bring multitudes into His kingdom.

Be a part of the excitement that comes with serving your wondrous King! Let Him use you to bring the good news of Jesus Christ to someone today. May His anointing be released in you in such a way that others will know that you belong to God Almighty, and they will want to have what you have. Be a shining light to the world around you, and let His glory flow through you to a hurt and dying world. Jesus is the only answer! Share Him with many!

For speaking engagements, please contact:

Touching Hearts Ministries
Mary R. Bolton
P.O. Box 5333
Knoxville, Tennessee 37928

Phone: 865-687-5266
Fax: 865-689-2162
Email: mrbolton@touchinghearts.org

To order additional copies of

BEHOLD
YOUR
GOD

Have your credit card ready and call

(877) 421-READ (7323)

or send $12.99 each plus $4.95* S&H to

**WinePress Publishing
PO Box 428
Enumclaw, WA 98022**

* Add $1.00 S&H for each additional book ordered.